Managing Legacy and Change

De Gruyter Studies in Organizational and Management History

Series Editors
Sonia Coman and Andrea Casey

Volume 2

Managing Legacy and Change

New Frontiers for Theory and Practice

Edited by
Hamid Foroughi, Andrea Casey and Sonia Coman

DE GRUYTER

ISBN 978-3-11-163133-2
e-ISBN (PDF) 978-3-11-163146-2
e-ISBN (EPUB) 978-3-11-163160-8
ISSN 2701-8873

Library of Congress Control Number: 2025935653

Bibliographic information published by the Deutsche Nationalbibliothek
The Deutsche Nationalbibliothek lists this publication in the Deutsche Nationalbibliografie;
detailed bibliographic data are available on the internet at http://dnb.dnb.de.

© 2025 Walter de Gruyter GmbH, Berlin/Boston, Genthiner Straße 13, 10785 Berlin
Cover image: clu/iStock/Getty Images Plus
Typesetting: Integra Software Services Pvt. Ltd.
Printing and binding: CPI books GmbH, Leck

www.degruyter.com
Questions about General Product Safety Regulation:
productsafety@degruyterbrill.com

Contents

About the authors — VII

Hamid Foroughi, Andrea Casey, and Sonia Coman
Preface — 1

Hamid Foroughi, Andrea Casey, and Sonia Coman
Chapter 1
Perspectives on organizational legacy and change — 9

Part I: Legacy transmission between memory and identity

Matthew C. B. Lyle
Chapter 2
Distilling memories—a redefinition of organizational identity — 23

Trevor Israelsen and Roy Suddaby
Chapter 3
Inheritance as an organizational purpose — 47

Micki Eisenman and Andrea Casey
Chapter 4
Constructing legacy: Managing legacy in discursive and embodied ways — 67

Part II: Organizational legacy in the broader ecology

Peter Trümmel, Vittoria Magrelli, Paola Rovelli, Alfredo De Massis, and Christof Rissbacher
Chapter 5
Embedded legacy and the role of entrepreneurial family firms in business ecosystems: The Aspiag case — 87

Hanna Aschhoff and Matthias Waldkirch
Chapter 6
Acquiring history? Foreign imprint management during postmerger integration — 107

Peter K. Spink, Mary Jane P. Spink, José Hercílio P. de Oliveira, and Roberth M. Tavanti
**Chapter 7
Legacy and collective action: Learning from faith-based communities and parishes —— 129**

Part III: The role of legacy in organizational change and imagined futures

Viviane Sergi, Joëlle Basque, Ann Langley, and Nora Meziani
**Chapter 8
The power of the mundane: Small stories as ambivalent carriers of legacy —— 149**

Ian G. Jones
**Chapter 9
Rhetorical history as history: Legacies of a rhetorical history strategy —— 173**

Pamela A. Popielarz
**Chapter 10
Obstacles to change in racialized organizations: Imprinting, memory, and legacy —— 189**

Hamid Foroughi, Andrea Casey, and Sonia Coman
**Chapter 11
Conclusion: Legacy—New frontier in research and practice —— 207**

List of figures —— 223

List of tables —— 225

Index —— 227

About the authors

Hanna Aschhoff is a Ph.D. student at the Entrepreneurship & Family Firm Institute at EBS University, Germany. Her research focuses on identity transformation during organizational change, and her doctoral work explores organizational identity change during mergers and acquisitions. In her professional career, she advises and supports organizations in how to successfully manage cultural transformations.

Joëlle Basque is professor of communication and methodology at Université TELUQ, Montréal, Canada. Her research focuses on discursive approaches to organizational communication, identity issues in organizations, and practice theories of strategy and organizational change. She is the initiator and coeditor of the *Routledge Handbook of the Communicative Constitution of Organization*. Her work has appeared in *Organization Studies, M@n@gement*, and several edited books.

Andrea Casey is associate professor emerita of human and organizational learning at The George Washington University (GW) where she taught doctoral courses in organizational culture, organizational dynamics, and research. Her research interests include organizational memory and history and identity-related theories such as organizational and professional identity. Her recent books include *Organizational Identity and Memory: A Multidisciplinary Approach* (Routledge) and *New Directions in Organizational and Management History* (De Gruyter). She has served on the Board of Governors of the Academy of Management and as division chair for the Managerial and Organizational Cognition Division. Before joining the GW faculty, Dr. Casey was a consultant focusing on organizational change, strategic planning, and leadership development.

Sonia Coman is Vice President of Elm Street Consulting Group and Treasurer of the Board of AIBA International, a DC-based global trade association for the AI industry. She also serves as Senior Advisor to the Dean for Digital Strategy at Washington National Cathedral, where she has led the institution's digital transformation. Previously, she led Marketing and Communications at the Smithsonian's National Museum of Asian Art as Audience Engagement Strategist. Additionally, she serves on the core team of The World Innovation Network, a network of networks for Fortune 500 CEOs, entrepreneurs, and innovators. She has a PhD from Columbia University, where she brought social network analysis to bear on a transcultural art study. Dr. Coman is the co-author of the book *New Directions in Organizational and Management History*. Her research focuses on the intersection of art, business, and technology. She has published extensively on creativity and distinctiveness and on legacy and organizational history.

Alfredo De Massis is a professor of entrepreneurship and family business who serves as an advisor to family enterprises and policymakers. Ranked as a Family Capital Top 100 Family Business Influencer, he has been inducted into The Family Business Hall of Fame. He is an editor of *Entrepreneurship Theory & Practice*, associate editor of *Family Business Review*, serves on the boards of international public and private organizations, and collaborates with the IMD Business School as a scientific advisor and the Wild Group Chair in Family Business. His research has been published in leading academic and practitioner journals.

José Hercilio P. de Oliveira is a social psychologist and research fellow at the Center for Public Administration and Government Studies, Getulio Vargas Foundation, São Paulo, Brazil.

Micki Eisenman is head of the Strategy and Entrepreneurship Department at the Hebrew University Business School. She earned her Ph.D. in management from Columbia University, her M.B.A. from Tulane University, and her B.A. in English and communications from Hebrew University. Her most recent research projects focus on examining organizational memory and how shared interpretations of the past affect the emergence of a new field. Her earlier research dealt with the intersection between the aesthetic qualities of materials and their social interpretations and explored how the materiality of organizational artifacts impacts organizational processes such as identity construction, innovation, and collective memory.

https://doi.org/10.1515/9783111631462-203

About the authors

Hamid Foroughi is Associate Professor of Responsible Management at Warwick Business School, University of Warwick (UK). He is an Associate Editor of *Management & Organizational History* and serves on the Editorial Review Board of *Organization Studies (FT50 Management Journal)*. He is best known for his research on collective memory and organizational amnesia, with a particular focus on how institutional memory and legacy shape power dynamics, inequality, and strategic action in organizations. His work critically examines the politics of memory, exploring its links to authenticity, inclusivity, and ethics. In addition to his academic career, he has over a decade of experience as a consultant, advising organizations in the IT sector as well as in philanthropy and the non-profit sector on managing organizational legacy and heritage.

Trevor Israelsen is an assistant professor of organization theory at the Smeal College of Business at Penn State University. He studies the historical situatedness of entrepreneurship and organizations and has particular interests in the role of legacies, traditions, and values in the processes of institution building and the creation of enduring value in organizations and society.

Ian G. Jones is a lecturer in strategy at the University of Sheffield, and his research focuses on corporate strategy, the British banking industry, uses of the past, corporate ethics, organizational memory, and the history of the wrestling industry. He has previously published in journals such as *Business History* and the *Journal of Management Inquiry*. He has also coauthored the book *Business History: A Research Overview* (2022; Routledge) and coedited six volumes of Routledge's *Focus on Industrial History* series.

Ann Langley is emerita professor of management at HEC Montréal and distinguished research environment professor at the University of Warwick. Her research deals with strategic processes and practices in complex organizations, with an emphasis on qualitative research methods. She is coeditor of the book series *Perspectives on Process Organization Studies* and was deputy editor of the *Academy of Management Journal* from 2022 to 2025.

Matthew C. B. Lyle is an assistant professor of strategic management at Binghamton University's School of Management. He primarily researches organizational memory, attending specifically to the processes through which actors attempt to shape it through the strategic deployment of history. His work in this area has appeared in outlets including *Organization Studies*, *Strategic Organization*, and the *Journal of Management Studies*. He retains a broader interest in studying social cognitive processes in organizations.

Vittoria Magrelli has been an assistant professor at the Centre for Family Business Management, part of the Free University of Bozen-Bolzano (Italy), since January 2020. Her research interests include intergenerational dynamics, innovation, and temporality in family boundary organizations. She conducts qualitative research, including single and multiple case studies, adopting ethnographic methods and other data-gathering techniques. In 2019, Vittoria obtained her Ph.D. in management from the Lancaster University Management School in the UK. Her work has been published in leading academic journals.

Nora Meziani is an assistant professor in organization studies at ESCP Business School. Her research focuses on the role of embodiment in teamwork, exploring its various forms and implications. She has a genuine passion for communicational dynamics and is empirically interested in artistic organizations, extreme contexts, and entrepreneurs.

Pamela A. Popielarz is an associate professor of sociology at the University of Illinois at Chicago. Her research focuses on organizations and race and gender inequality. She is completing a book called *Order of Business: The Golden Age of Fraternity and Its Legacy of Inequality* (University of North Carolina Press). She has published in the *American Sociological Review*, *American Journal of Sociology*, *Gender & Society*, *Annual Review of Sociology*, *Research in the Sociology of Organizations*, *Business History*, and *Social Networks*. Her research has been supported by the National Science Foundation and American Sociological Association Fund for the Advancement of the Discipline.

Christof Rissbacher is currently the CEO of Aspiag Service srl. He studied economics in Innsbruck and Strasbourg and has been working in the food retail and real estate sectors in Italy, Austria, and Slovenia for more than 20 years.

Paola Rovelli is an assistant professor at the Faculty of Economics and Management of the Free University of Bozen-Bolzano, working at the Centre for Family Business Management and the Competence Centre for Mountain Innovation Ecosystems. She conducts research on the organizational design of firms and their top management teams, with particular attention to family firms, innovation, delegation of decision authority, narcissism, and gender. Her research articles have been published in leading academic journals.

Viviane Sergi is a professor of management in the Department of Management at ESG UQAM in Montréal, Canada. She explores how communication is, in various settings, constitutive of organizational phenomena such as leadership and strategy. She also has a keen interest in methodological issues related to qualitative research. Her work has been published in journals such as *Academy of Management Annals, Human Relations, Organization Studies, Strategic Organization, Long-Range Planning, Qualitative Research in Organizations and Management, M@n@gement*, and *ephemera*.

Mary Jane P. Spink is a professor of social psychology at the Pontifical Catholic University of São Paulo, Brazil.

Peter K. Spink is an emeritus professor of public administration and government at the Getulio Vargas Foundation, São Paulo, Brazil.

Roy Suddaby is the Winspear Chair of Management at the Peter B. Gustavson School of Business, University of Victoria, Canada, and a professor of management at the Carson School of Business, Washington State University, USA. His research focuses on the role of social value judgments (legitimacy, authenticity, identity) and their mechanisms (rhetoric, history) in organizations.

Roberth M. Tavanti is an associate professor of social and institutional psychology at the State University of Londrina, Paraná, Brazil.

Peter Trümmel is a postdoctoral researcher at Jönköping International Business School, working at the Centre for Family Enterprise and Ownership. He received his Ph.D. in Management and Economics from the Free University of Bozen-Bolzano, studying the emergence, transmission, and endurance of entrepreneurial families' legacies. He conducts qualitative research and is particularly interested in the aesthetics and intergenerational dynamics of family firms and their entrepreneurial families.

Matthias Waldkirch is the EBS Alumni Endowed Professor in Family Business and director of the Entrepreneurship & Family Firm Institute at EBS University, Germany. His research focuses on innovation and professionalization processes in family firms, dynamics around ownership and change, and how organizational phenomena unfold in digital spaces. He is an associate researcher at the Centre for Family Entrepreneurship and Ownership at Jönköping International Business School, Sweden, and has been a visiting researcher at Stanford University and the University of British Columbia, among others. His research has been published in leading journals, such as *Journal of Business Venturing, Human Resource Management Review,* and *Organization,* and he is an associate editor of the *Family Business Review*.

Hamid Foroughi, Andrea Casey, and Sonia Coman
Preface

Legacy is defined as "something transmitted by or received from an ancestor or predecessor or from the past" (Merriam-Webster, n.d.). At its core, legacy entails a double ontological connection to the past and to the present; it cannot exist without its roots in the past, and yet its visibility in the present is what ensures its survival and relevance. The thread of transmission from past to present is central to the concept of legacy, which makes it a dynamic and processual phenomenon. The dynamic aspect of transmission also dictates the complex relationship that legacy has with history. By its nature, legacy is recorded, narrated, and remembered, often with iterations that change over time and respond to various factors, both internal and external. In organizations, legacy is therefore vital to understanding organizational identity and change; it provides a lens through which to understand how the organization remembers its past, how it defines itself (and is externally defined) in relation to narratives of its founding and history, and how it utilizes such narratives to influence change and imagine its future.

The past decade has seen an important field crystallize and mature in organizational studies, zeroing in on the role of history in organizations and best known as 'historical organization studies' or 'organizational and management history' (Godfrey et al., 2016; Maclean et al., 2016). These advances pushed for the rediscovery and development of different avenues for integrating history and organization studies, such as organizational memory studies (Foroughi et al., 2020), rhetorical history (Suddaby et al., 2023), and historiographical reflexivity (Decker et al., 2021). Influential articles such as "History and Organizational Change" (Suddaby & Foster, 2016), one of whose authors also contributed to this volume, not only opened multiple channels of scholarly inquiry but also solidly placed the interest in history in relation to the study of change in organizations and management. The present volume contributes to this important body of scholarship by focusing on the notion of legacy in organizations and exploring how the interrelationships between legacy and change help organizations move between histories—recorded, (mis)remembered, (re)imagined—and futures—feared, anticipated, maneuvered.

Our interest in this topic was also fueled by its prominence outside of academia, from political commentary on preserving or erasing complex legacies to the practical benefit of knowing how to navigate legacy in the face of change, especially for long-lived organizations. Legacy has become a prominent topic of debate in the public square around questions of organizations' historical responsibility vis-à-vis civic issues on a local, national, and global scale. Executives whose names resonate beyond their organizations carry legacies whose public reception changes with the fluctuations of value of the public discourse; what was once celebrated is now blamed and vice versa. For younger companies, including startups, building a legacy may not

https://doi.org/10.1515/9783111631462-001

seem like a priority, but the example of more mature companies and the prominence of the benefit or burden of legacies in both specialized literature and the broader public realm encourage more intentional focus on how founding stories and legacies are narrated and how founding executives are perceived. Business magazine articles, trade conferences, workbooks for practitioners, and consultancies provide an increasing volume of practical approaches to organizations seeking to understand their legacies as they strive for successful change management, whether in the context of survival or longevity, rebranding or continuity. While written by scholars for students and peers, this volume has direct applications in practice, and it is our hope that it will reach and help organizations as they navigate legacy and change.

As editors, each of us has dedicated our scholarly research to history and organizations in different ways. A couple of years ago, after several publications in the field (e.g., Coman & Casey, 2022; Foroughi, 2020; Foroughi et al., 2020), the three of us decided to join forces and convene a scholarly symposium on the topic of organizational history, with a focus on legacy, collective memory, and change. Our symposium became one of the subthemes of the 2023 annual conferences of the European Group for Organization Studies (EGOS) and the fulcrum for the present volume.

In the subtheme "Organizational History for the Good Life: Legacy, Collective Memory, and Change," we aimed to bring together scholars to explore different ways that past legacies both enable and restrict opportunities for organizational renewal, social change, and the emergence of new forms of organizing. We sought papers that shed light on the ways in which organizations can imagine constructive models for navigating this fundamental tension. Out of many high-quality submissions, we selected 22 papers, which were grouped into six thematic sessions on the following subtopics: imprinting, organizational identity, oral histories, forgetting, remembering difficult pasts, and politics and temporal orientations. Soon after the conference, we crystallized the idea of the present volume and circulated our call for chapters. The volume includes some of the papers from the EGOS subtheme, plus others submitted to the volume independently of the conference by invited scholars. We are grateful to those who contributed to the conference and to all of our volume contributors for inspiring this project.

We invited chapters encompassing both theoretical and empirical contributions that delve into the intricate interplay between legacy and change, examining this dynamic from a diverse array of theoretical vantage points. Our call extended a special invitation to submissions that not only usher in fresh concepts to enrich the existing literature but also embark on the task of critically examining and redefining established theories. We welcomed a wide spectrum of inquiries, and as a result, the volume reflects a diversity of theoretical, methodological, and empirical approaches to legacy in organizations.

By bringing together varied perspectives, this volume aims to contribute to a deeper understanding of the interplay of legacies and imagined futures as it pertains to organizational identity and change. On the one hand, tangible and intangible legacies can be a source of authentication, legitimation, and strategy restoration; on the other hand, past legacies can restrict our imagination by enforcing path dependency. Managing legacy can be a challenge for both old and new organizations. Older organizations often find that their legacy is at odds with present realities or future directions. In contrast, newly formed organizations often feel they have a deficit in legacy compared with long-established organizations and seek to boost credibility by engaging in activities that can be retrospectively claimed as their legacy. In either case, when aspects of an organization's raison d'être change, the organizational identity is threatened, and legacy can become an obstacle to change. The volume's 11 chapters investigate this core topic from different theoretical viewpoints, multidisciplinary methodologies, and a rich range of case studies, from family firms and wine industry mergers to fraternal orders and faith-based communities.

Framed by introductory and concluding chapters authored by the editors, the contributions to the volume are structured in three parts, as detailed below. In the introductory chapter, we present our understanding of legacy as a multifaceted construct that can be understood from various theoretical perspectives. We explain these perspectives and discuss how they are addressed throughout the book, especially unpacking the concepts of imprinting, tradition, collective memory, storytelling, and identity.

Part I focuses on legacy transmission between memory and identity. The chapters in this first part—"Distilling memories: A redefinition of organizational identity" by Matthew C. B. Lyle, "Inheritance as an organizational purpose" by Trevor Israelsen and Roy Suddaby, and "Constructing legacy: Managing legacy in discursive and embodied ways" by Micki Eisenman and Andrea Casey—focus on the transmission aspect of legacy within the frameworks of memory and identity. They explore how the transmission occurs and how it affects both the understanding of the legacy and the impact of the legacy thus perceived on future leaders and managers, as well as on organizational identity more generally over time.

In "Distilling memories: A redefinition of organizational identity," Lyle proposes that memories coalescing into legacy are intrinsic to organizational identity and discusses how building organizational identity can be understood as a process of distilling memories. He argues that much of the discussion surrounding 'who we really are' as an organization involves the past, particularly legacy. In particular, the chapter explores how legacy weighs heavily on the identities of organizations founded by former employees, similarly to how institutional legacies showcase the influence of past organizations on the form—and even identities—of those who follow within a given community.

In "Inheritance as an organizational purpose," Israelsen and Suddaby theorize the processes of intergenerational transmission and inheritance in organizations as part of the core organizational purpose and as ends in themselves. These processes are key to organizational survival. This chapter explores the factors that influence these critical processes and offers implications of these ideas for research and practice.

In "Constructing legacy: Managing legacy in discursive and embodied ways," Eisenman and Casey theorize legacy as a collective understanding of a past significant event or individual that creates affinities among those who understand its significance in similar ways; it also explains such collective understanding as both cognitive and embodied. The chapter theorizes how legacy is sustained, highlighting that sustained legacy happens through both discursive and material mechanisms that allow the collective understanding to be transmitted over time. The chapter concludes with suggestions for how firms can maximize the strategic potential of their legacies.

Part II, on organizational legacy in the broader ecology, focuses on the interrelationships between legacy in organizations and influences that can be considered external, for example in response to sociopolitical conditions ("Embedded legacy and the role of entrepreneurial family firms in business ecosystems: The Aspiag case" by Peter Trümmel et al.), in the case of a merger ("Acquiring history? Foreign imprint management during postmerger integration" by Hanna Aschhoff and Matthias Waldkirch), and in organizations that are heterogeneous or inherently in dialogue with the larger societal context ("Legacy and collective action: Learning from faith-based communities and parishes" by Peter K. Spink et al.).

In "Embedded legacy and the role of entrepreneurial family firms in business ecosystems: The Aspiag case," Trümmel and his co-authors (Vittoria Magrelli, Paola Rovelli, Alfredo De Massis, and Christof Rissbacher) explore the interconnections of multiple actors and legacies in a shared geographic, historic, and socioeconomic context. As relevant contributors to a local economy, entrepreneurial family firms present legacies that forge organizational identity and bind them to a territory. Yet, despite multifaceted connections with their environment, legacies have mostly been investigated in isolation, i.e., at the individual, familial, or organizational level. If the focus shifts from the actors to their relationships, we shift our attention from isolated cases of legacies to multiple locally embedded, socially and economically interconnected systems of legacies. To understand how interconnected legacies that are locally embedded develop entrepreneurial relevance for their respective stakeholders and the territory at large, the chapter explores these relationships within an established business ecosystem.

In "Acquiring history? Foreign imprint management during postmerger integration," Aschhoff and Waldkirch apply an imprinting lens in a study of the merger of two traditional wine companies to explore how acquiring organizations and their actors can manage imprints that are not their own ("foreign imprints"). This inductive case study based on ethnographic field research reveals a two-step process of how organizations manage and ultimately transform foreign imprints into integrated imprints. The chapter provides new insights on imprint renewal and postmerger integration.

In "Legacy and collective action: Learning from faith-based communities and parishes," Spink and his coauthors (Mary Jane P. Spink, José Hercílio P. de Oliveira, and Roberth M. Tavanti) focus on everyday organizations, which have not been thoroughly studied. The chapter explores how legacy presents different characteristics for such organizations, adopting the perspective that legacy, in its relation to history, influences and in turn is being influenced by ongoing events. The chapter applies its theoretical lens to a case study of faith-based parishes and their communities in Brazil.

Part III, on the role of legacy in organizational change and imagined futures, explores how legacies are seen and utilized in the present and how their reception in the present will shape the organization's future. The chapters it includes ("The power of the mundane: Small stories as ambivalent carriers of legacy" by Viviane Sergi et al., "Rhetorical history as history: Legacies of a rhetorical history strategy" by Ian G. Jones, and "Obstacles to change in racialized organizations: Imprinting, memory, and legacy" by Pamela A. Popielarz) present diverse theoretical and methodological approaches to the tension between legacy and change in organizations as they look toward the future.

In "The power of the mundane: Small stories as ambivalent carriers of legacy," Sergi, Basque, Langley, and Meziani argue that modest elements, such as small stories about an organization's founder, can become powerful in a variety of contexts. Small stories can anchor elements from the past in present times, transmitting the organization's raison d'être, culture, and values while presenting a more human side of the person who has passed away. These small stories may also serve as vectors of continuity in times of change. Yet, the messages they carry are subject to multiple and shifting interpretations. As time passes, stories that once seemed to reflect the deepest values of the organization can appear quaint or even ridiculous. Elements once signaling positive traits can take on a darker meaning. Finally, some small stories may carry forward elements of legacy that can inhibit rather than inspire future leaders and employees. This chapter explores some of these implications, drawing on three empirical vignettes.

In "Rhetorical history as history: Legacies of a rhetorical history strategy," Jones examines how the legacy of using the past as a strategy can affect future managers of the organization, focusing on Barclays Bank PLC. While many studies have looked at the agency of managers in using history as a resource, relatively few have explored the constraints that this decision creates for future managers.

In "Obstacles to change in racialized organizations: Imprinting, memory, and legacy," Popielarz illustrates the path-dependent nature of legacy by looking at the Fraternal Order of Police in the US. The chapter reviews and applies new theory about how race operates in organizations. It also extends this theory by putting it in conversation with literature on organizational imprinting, identity, and memory.

In the final chapter, "Legacy: New frontier in research and practice," as editors, we discuss the implications of all the chapters in the volume for both practice and future research. We return to each of the theoretical approaches brought to bear on the central topic of legacy and change, discussing major findings, directions for new research, and applications for organizations. The final chapter includes a robust section on how leaders and managers can adopt an active approach to understanding and leveraging legacy in their organizations. It is structured to address three themes: first, the retrospective creation and awareness of legacy assets; second, legacy in the interrelationships of organizations, their larger fields, and society more broadly; and third, the merits and limits of storytelling in legacy narratives. The attention dedicated to practice, not only in this concluding section but also throughout the chapters, recommends the volume as a fruitful exploration of organizational legacy for both researchers and managers.

References

Aschhoff, H., & Waldkirch, M. (2025). Acquiring history? Foreign imprint management during postmerger integration. In H. Foroughi, A. Casey, & S. Coman (Eds.), *Managing legacy and change: New frontiers for theory and practice* (Chapter 5). DeGruyter.

Coman, S., & Casey, A. (2022). *New directions in organizational and management history*. De Gruyter. https://doi.org/10.1515/9783110693539

Decker, S., Hassard, J., & Rowlinson, M. (2021). Rethinking history and memory in organization studies: The case for historiographical reflexivity. *Human Relations*, *74*(8), 1123–1155. https://doi.org/10.1177/0018726720927443

Eisenman, M., & Casey, A. (2025). Constructing legacy: Managing legacy in discursive and embodied ways. In H. Foroughi, A. Casey, & S. Coman (Eds.), *Managing legacy and change: New frontiers for theory and practice* (Chapter 4). DeGruyter.

Foroughi, H. (2020). Collective memories as a vehicle of fantasy and identification: Founding stories retold. *Organization Studies*, *41*(10), 1347–1367. https://doi.org/10.1177/0170840619844286

Foroughi, H., Casey, A., & Coman, S. (2025). Legacy: New frontier in research and practice. In H. Foroughi, A. Casey, & S. Coman (Eds.), *Managing legacy and change: New frontiers for theory and practice* (Chapter 10). DeGruyter.

Foroughi, H., Coraiola, D. M., Rintamäki, J., Mena, S., & Foster, W. M. (2020). Organizational memory studies. *Organization Studies*, *41*(12), 1725–1748. https://doi.org/10.1177/0170840620974338

Godfrey, P., Hassard, J., O'Connor, E., Rowlinson, M., & Ruef, M. (2016). What is organizational history? Towards a creative synthesis of history and organization studies. *Academy of Management Review*, *41*(4), 590–608. https://doi.org/10.5465/amr.2016.0040

Israelsen, T., & Suddaby, R. (2025). Inheritance as an organizational purpose. In H. Foroughi, A. Casey, & S. Coman (Eds.), *Managing legacy and change: New frontiers for theory and practice* (Chapter 3). DeGruyter.

Jones, I. G. (2025). Rhetorical history as history: Legacies of a rhetorical history strategy. In H. Foroughi, A. Casey, & S. Coman (Eds.), *Managing legacy and change: New frontiers for theory and practice* (Chapter 9). DeGruyter.

Lyle, M. C. B. (2025). Distilling memories—a redefinition of organizational identity. In H. Foroughi, A. Casey, & S. Coman (Eds.), *Managing legacy and change: New frontiers for theory and practice* (Chapter 2). DeGruyter.

Maclean, M., Harvey, C., & Clegg, S. (2016). Conceptualizing historical organization studies. *Academy of Management Review*, *41*(4), 609–632. https://doi.org/10.5465/amr.2014.0133

Merriam-Webster. (n.d.). Legacy. In *Merriam-Webster.com dictionary*. Retrieved March 5, 2025, from https://www.merriam-webster.com/dictionary/legacy

Popielarz, P. A. (2025). Obstacles to change in racialized organizations: Imprinting, memory, and legacy. In H. Foroughi, A. Casey, & S. Coman (Eds.), *Managing legacy and change: New frontiers for theory and practice* (Chapter 9). DeGruyter.

Sergi, V., Basque, J., Langley, A., & Meziani, N. (2025). The power of the mundane: Small stories as ambivalent carriers of legacy. In H. Foroughi, A. Casey, & S. Coman (Eds.), *Managing legacy and change: New frontiers for theory and practice* (Chapter 8. DeGruyter.

Spink, P. K., Spink, M. J. P., Hercílio P. de Oliveira, J., & Tavanti, R. M. (2025). Legacy and collective action: Learning from faith-based communities and parishes. In H. Foroughi, A. Casey, & S. Coman (Eds.), *Managing legacy and change: New frontiers for theory and practice* (Chapter 6). DeGruyter.

Suddaby, R., & Foster, W. M. (2016). History and organizational change. *Journal of Management*, *43*(1), 19–38. https://doi.org/10.1177/0149206316675031

Suddaby, R., Israelsen, T., Bastien, F., Saylors, R., & Coraiola, D. (2023). Rhetorical history as institutional work. *Journal of Management Studies*, *60*(1), 242–278. https://doi.org/10.1111/joms.12860

Trümmel, P., Magrelli, V., Rovelli, P., De Massis, A., & Rissbacher, C. (2025). Embedded legacy and the role of entrepreneurial family firms in business ecosystems:The Aspiag case. In H. Foroughi, A. Casey, & S. Coman (Eds.), *Managing legacy and change: New frontiers for theory and practice* (Chapter 4). DeGruyter.

Hamid Foroughi, Andrea Casey, and Sonia Coman

Chapter 1
Perspectives on organizational legacy and change

Legacy is of significant interest to both management researchers and practitioners, particularly those who navigate its complexities in their daily work. For managers and policymakers, legacy is not just a theoretical construct—it is a lived reality that influences decision-making, organizational identity, and long-term strategy. Whether in family businesses, multinational corporations, or government institutions, leaders must balance the weight of the past with the demands of the future. Yet, what makes legacy particularly puzzling is its dual nature—it can be both a powerful asset and a potential constraint.

On the one hand, legacy can be a source of inspiration and motivation, shaping corporate values, reinforcing purpose, and guiding future strategy. For instance, in family businesses, legacy often serves as a unifying force that strengthens continuity and fosters long-term commitment. It motivates the next generation of leaders by providing them with a sense of purpose and entrepreneurial direction (Jaskiewicz et al., 2015). Many organizations capitalize on their legacy to build trust and credibility, using it as a foundation for branding, employee engagement, and stakeholder relations.

On the other hand, legacy is not always a positive inheritance; it can become a burden that restricts innovation and locks organizations into outdated practices. A strong legacy can create resistance to change, as employees and stakeholders may feel obligated to uphold traditions even when they no longer serve the firm's best interests. In some cases, legacy manifests as a heavy responsibility passed down through generations, making it difficult for successors to redefine strategic priorities (Wade-Benzoni & Tost, 2009). Managing legacy, therefore, requires a delicate balance—honoring the past while ensuring it does not hinder adaptation and future growth.

In this chapter, we seek to advance a perspective that views legacy not as a static burden or asset, but as a semi-fluid yet sticky entity that can be enriched and molded by different actors and developed and transformed over time by generations, demonstrating enduring yet malleable traits (Barbera et al., 2018) that can serve both internal and external stakeholders (Manelli et al., 2023). Therefore, for organizations, the key challenge is not merely preserving legacy but actively shaping it. This means recognizing when legacy should be leveraged for competitive advantage and when it needs to be reinterpreted or even challenged. Organizations that skillfully navigate their legacy can use it as a springboard for innovation, ensuring that the past remains a source of strength rather than stagnation.

Legacy and its multiple facets in organizations

Legacy is a multifaceted and multilayered construct, encompassing a diverse range of meanings across management disciplines. At its core, the concept of legacy refers to how the past continues to shape the present and future, influencing individuals, organizations, and societies in profound ways. Scholars have conceptualized legacy as the ongoing presence of past actors, sometimes referred to as "legators," "legacy senders," or "organizational ghosts," who leave enduring imprints that are carried forward by "legatees" or "legacy receivers" (Bednar & Brown, 2023; Colquitt et al., 2023; Israelsen & Suddaby, 2025; Radu-Lefebvre et al., 2024). These imprints manifest in various forms, including traditions, material artifacts, narratives, and institutional practices. Building on this idea, Taraday (2013) defines legacy as "the sum of valued accomplishments, traditions, assets, histories, experiences, lives, places, and memories that flow from the past through the present into the future" (p. 200). This definition highlights the continuity of legacy—how it operates as a bridge across time, ensuring that historical values, achievements, and identities persist.

This definition demands clarification. The continuity of legacy is always intertwined with its appropriation. Legacy is not simply about preservation but also about interpretation and adaptation. The way organizations and societies choose to engage with their legacies determines whether they reinforce continuity, challenge existing structures, or repurpose inherited meanings for new contexts. This active and evolving nature of legacy is often overlooked by management and leadership gurus who place more emphasis on the genesis and stability of legacy.

In contrast, seeing legacy as a practice and a performance allows us to understand how legacy functions as an ongoing process that both enables and constrains how organizations and societies operate, shaping present-day decision-making, cultural norms, and institutional structures. In this way, legacy creates 'affordances'—opportunities and constraints that emerge from historical imprints, influencing the trajectories of individuals and organizations. Whether legacy serves as a source of inspiration, legitimacy, or limitation depends on how it is enacted, contested, or reinterpreted over time.

In what follows, we present four perspectives that provide alternative explanations for understanding and managing legacy in organizations. Our view is that these four perspectives are not competing explanations but complementary, and each provides a unique and useful lens to understand the complexities of managing legacy in organizations.

Legacy as imprints from the past

One approach to conceptualizing legacy is through the lens of imprinting theory. Imprinting refers to the process by which "organizations in any historical conjuncture take on elements of their founding contexts [or other sensitive periods], elements that may be an important consequence for their later trajectories" (Johnson, 2008, pp. 113–114; information in brackets added for clarity). This theory is particularly well suited for understanding the legacy of certain historical periods, such as colonization, within organizational settings. Imprinting allows us to comprehend how particular conditions made a lasting impact on individuals or organizations undergoing key developmental stages at the time.

For instance, Popielarz (2025, in this volume) uses this perspective to explain how the founding history of the Fraternal Order of Police in the United States imprinted a racial identity in the association, which it found difficult to shed. Other examples can be seen in studies that trace current partnership practices in the International Aid Industry as residues of colonization history (Foroughi, 2019; Ziai, 2016). Research has shown that the historical periods and conditions under which organizations are founded leave a long-lasting mark. Albu et al. (2021) discussed how social and environmental reporting in post-communist countries has been shaped by the imprints (legacy) of communist governance that persist today.

Research on imprints highlights that they reflect forces present during relatively short, susceptible periods in an organization's history (Johnson, 2007; Marquis, 2003). While scholars have long sought to understand their "stickiness" in the face of internal and external changes (de Cuyper et al., 2020; Stinchcombe, 1965), there is no consensus on the exact mechanisms of imprinting. Factors range from traditions, interests, and ideologies to routines, inertia, and institutionalization (Simsek et al., 2015). In their review article, Simsek et al. (2015) identified two broad explanations: (a) the adoption or development of structures, routines, and capabilities in response to environmental conditions, opportunities, and constraints, and (b) the creative selection and synthesis of environmental elements within the context of situational constraints. More recently, this theory has been used to explain how the meaning of legacy changes over time, which has led to concepts such as imprint reforming, targeted activities to change original imprints, and imprint coupling, when actors use original imprints as a resource to legitimate imprint changes (de Cuyper et al., 2020). Similarly, Aschhoff and Waldkirch (2025, in this volume) discuss the process through which during an organizational merger a foreign imprint (from the acquirer firm) can be embedded in the acquired firm. This literature also recognizes that certain imprints (manifested in norms, routines, etc.), if they persist beyond their period of technical utility, become more challenging to alter than other cultural features that are more susceptible to external and internal influences (Hatch & Schultz, 2002).

While useful, imprinting theory has some limitations too. As a whole, it pays less attention to the actual processes by which imprints form and often takes imprinting processes as "givens." Except for a few recent exceptions (e.g., Lyle et al., 2024; Marquis & Huang, 2010), imprinting theory does not engage with how individuals interpret and negotiate imprints. Despite such limitations, imprinting theory is useful for understanding legacy, particularly in capturing legacy forms that may not be immediately visible and tangible. Imprinting often shapes organizational attributes, such as identities, ideologies, mental models, and schemas, in a way that has a lasting effect on organizational practices and routines (Lamertz et al., 2016). This can be invisible in the sense that the link between these practices and the past in which they originated is not readily apparent.

Legacy as traditions/heritage

Another perspective to understand organizational legacy is traditions and heritage. The common understanding is that heritage is a tangible remnant of the past (physical artifacts, monuments, buildings, and landscapes), while traditions are a form of intangible heritage and often are performative in nature. This distinction helps clarify tradition and heritage as the two main ways legacy is passed down through generations.

Traditions and heritage are both building blocks of legacy. If legacy is understood as the lasting impact someone or some event leaves behind, traditions and heritage act as the vehicles to carry that legacy forward through generations, connecting people to their past by actively passing down values, customs, and stories from one generation to the next.

Traditions uphold legacy by continuously reproducing and reenacting elements of legacy. (Tangible) heritage passes legacy through a material anchor that provides a stable, enduring reference point connecting the past with the present. This anchoring function operates by providing symbolic weight, embedded meanings that reinforce identity, authority, and belonging, as well as emotional and sensory resonance that reinforces legacy through sensory engagement and authentication.

Importantly, unlike imprints that are often invisible, the link between the past, legacy, and traditions/heritage is visible and is a manifested aspect of legacy. An accessible organizational example is an administrative ritual, such as the presidential farewell address in the United States. In this tradition dating back to George Washington, U.S. presidents deliver a farewell speech at the end of their term, reflecting on their time in office and offering guidance for the future. Such rituals and traditions are designed to reinforce a democratic legacy and the stability of institutions—albeit not always a desirable one. For instance, the legacy of educational elitism rooted in the history of higher education institutions, such as Cambridge, is carried forward by scripted and ritualized dining practices that habituate the participants to their privileged status and reinforce a sense of exclusivity, hierarchy, and continuity with the institution's historical traditions (Dacin et al., 2010). Dacin and colleagues showed how formalized gatherings, such as High Table dinners, cultivate an embodied understanding of elite social norms, strengthening networks of influence and maintaining the prestige associated with Cambridge's institutional legacy.

This literature also highlights the importance of 'custodianship' work in how legacy is carried forward (e.g., Dacin et al., 2019; Shils, 1981; Suddaby & Jaskiewicz, 2020). Traditions can be both (a) constraints for organizations, whose members are obliged to participate, and in so doing become transformed by their experiences, and (b) an actively managed resource that is (re)'invented.' Legacy as traditions and heritage requires the 'conscious articulation' by custodians—"the process of naming, defining, and making coherent—which distinguishes tradition from custom or habit, which are similar in that they all deal with recurrence" (Eyerman & Jamison, 1998, p. 27). Custodians here are not only those with curatorial roles (organizer or carrier) but also those who engage in traditions and heritage as an audience, either in performing or regulating capacity (Dacin et al., 2019).

This framework is particularly useful when examining legacy as a form of inheritance that is associated with a specific individual or collective actor from the past (see Israelsen & Suddaby, 2025, in this volume). The legacy of Steve Jobs echoes in Apple's product launch events, which follow a scripted presentation style reminiscent of Jobs' famous keynotes, keeping his showmanship and storytelling alive. As Bell and Taylor (2016) showed, different custodian roles play their part in giving meaning to such a legacy.

Heritage and traditions can also carry the legacy of a specific era (less so of a specific event). For instance, the legacy of an industrial past in a city can be manifested in the industrial heritage of a place. Understanding legacy as heritage draws our attention to the material testimony of the past, a remnant of the past that generates significant emotions, often through evoking sensory and aesthetic experiences. These remnants—whether historic buildings, artifacts, or even archival documents—serve as tangible links to a shared past, evoking nostalgia, reverence, or even critique. The way they are preserved, displayed, or ritualized shapes how legacy is interpreted and sustained across generations.

Legacy as rhetorical history

Legacy can also be understood as rhetorical history. With its highly agentic and strategic approach to managing legacy in organizations, rhetorical history is increasingly used by corporations (e.g., "our story" page on corporate websites, advertisements, product launch) and refers to the use of 'historical narratives' as a persuasive strategy to manage key stakeholders (Anteby & Molnar, 2012; Foster et al., 2011; Suddaby et al., 2010; Wadhwani et al., 2018). In this perspective, organizational legacy is a rich source of storytelling that current actors may use to legitimize the status quo or to design actions and garner support for change (Sasaki et al., 2020; Suddaby et al., 2020). For instance, Foster et al. (2011, p. 102) showed how Tim Horton draws upon its founding legacy in an attempt to legitimize a corporate narrative that the fast food chain is an authentic Canadian household brand. Similarly, Hatch and Schultz (2017) discussed how Carlsberg drew on the legacy of its founder as a pioneer in the industry to authenticate the launch of a new microbrewery on the Carlsberg premises. In this way, Carlsberg used its founding legacy rhetorically to respond to the microbrewery movement that overtook the industry by surprise. Not all organizations are adept at using history. In fact, Smith and Simeone (2017) argued that organizations should learn how to use their historical legacy strategically over time. They showed how Hudson's Bay Company's use of history was inspired and in line with its contemporary organization at the end of World War I, when it began making substantial investments in heritage infrastructure.

Importantly, companies might also attempt through rhetorical history to forget or eliminate certain unpleasant legacies, such as those pertaining to a major failure or an episode of corporate wrongdoing. Anteby and Molnar (2012) discussed how a French aeronautical engineering firm used rhetorical history in its internal bulletin to leave out part of its history—its dependence on German expertise—in an attempt to strengthen the national underpinning of its identity. Such selective use of history and legacy, however, can backfire when firms are accused of overlooking the legitimate concerns of some stakeholders (see Jones, 2025, in this volume), as shown in the case of Lloyds and Barclays, which largely ignored the legacy of slavery in their founding history until it was unearthed by social activists (Foroughi & Smith, 2024).

Overall, rhetorical history provides an interesting angle to study organizational legacy, one that promotes strategic and intentional use and appropriation of legacy. This requires heavy engagement with organizational history and investment in archives, but more importantly a readiness and agility to reflect on how the past can propel the organization forward. This is best captured by a mantra adopted by the founder of History Factory, Bruce Weindruch: "Start with the future and work back."

Legacy as collective memory

The final approach that we introduce for the study of legacy is collective memory. Legacy from collective memory can be understood as a salient collective understanding of a past event or individual. For instance, when we talk about the legacy of Steve Jobs, we can think of how Steve Jobs is remembered. Jobs' legacy is marked by his innovative products and ideas that changed the way people use technology and interact with businesses. His legacy is particularly intertwined with the company Apple and its products, even though he was involved in other ventures too.

A collective remembering approach to organizational legacy focuses on the 're-constructive' quality of legacy (see, in this volume, Eisenman & Casey, 2025; Lyle, 2025; Sergi et al., 2025; Spink et al., 2025); legacy is seen not as fixed and fully shaped by the past and the agency of past actors, but by the 'mnemonic work' (Coraiola et al., 2023) of individuals or groups who have certain affinities toward said past or past actors. In this sense, we cannot talk about the legacy of Steve Jobs separate from the mnemonic work of diverse actors. Importantly, this also means that legacy cannot be fully regulated by corporate actors or others. Bell and Taylor (2016), for instance, showed how Apple attempted to control the legacy of Steve Jobs by regulating memorialization to sway customers, employees, and admirers of Jobs to restore trust in Apple as a company. Yet, they also showed that that effort was only a partial success.

Another aspect that collective memory brings to the discussion of legacy is an understanding that legacy is socially constructed and can be contested and changed over time. A collective memory approach to legacy also begs the question of whose perspectives on the past we are interested in.

A key concept in memory studies is the idea that memories are shaped and nourished in different 'mnemonic communities,' communities in which the past is constitutive of the ethos of the community (Coraiola et al., 2023; Foroughi et al., 2020), or more specifically, a group of people who coalesce around a definite understanding of a past event (Mena et al., 2016). Mnemonic communities are sustained by collective memories, which are distilled into the labels that form the group identity (Lyle, 2025, in this volume).

In the same vein, the legacy of historical events or characters can be contentious and seen differently in various mnemonic communities and at different epochs. For instance, some groups might celebrate strong financial institutions in the UK as the legacy of Margaret Thatcher, while others may remember the loss of the UK industrial sector as Thatcher's legacy. Similarly, while Jack Welch is hailed as a corporate hero in business circles and among executives who helped mainstream his business practices, such as Six Sigma and business restructuring (Khurana, 2011), his (positive) legacy has recently been questioned by many, including *New York Times* reporter David Gelles, who argued that Jack Welch's focus on shareholder value maximization has contributed to a fractured capitalist system. This has fostered societal issues such as growing income inequality, eroded job security, and a short-term profit mindset that undermines long-term social and environmental responsibility.

Finally, a collective memory perspective also sheds light on organizational responsibilities for legacy/historical wrongdoing, such as transatlantic slavery. Recent scholarly work has proposed different approaches to historic corporate social responsibility (Schrempf-Stirling et al., 2016), ranging from active engagement to distancing from the past. Research is just beginning to understand the implications of such approaches for businesses and organizations (Foroughi & Smith, 2024; Vives-Gabriel et al., 2024; see also Jones, 2025, in this volume).

In summary, collective memory provides an interesting lens to understand and manage legacy, one that brings attention to 'stakeholder mnemonic communities' both inside and outside an organization. This lens is particularly useful for understanding contentious aspects of legacy for organizations. It also invites managers to pay attention to their responsibilities toward stakeholder communities that wish to engage in remembering such legacies and may demand corporate corrective or reparatory actions.

Conclusion

In this chapter, we propose that legacy should be understood as a semi-fluid yet 'sticky' phenomenon—one that can be enriched and molded by different actors and developed and transformed over time by successive generations. To explore this multifaceted nature of legacy, we present four distinct perspectives, each offering valuable insights into how legacy operates, transforms, and influences organizations (Table 1.1). While each perspective comes with its own biases and limitations, in combination they provide a toolkit for both management researchers and practitioners, enabling them to navigate legacy-related challenges in various organizational contexts.

Table 1.1: Four Perspectives on Legacy and Change in Organizations.

Perspectives on legacy	Trace to the past	Key constructs	Source of legacy	Chapters in the book
Imprinting	Invisible	- Imprints - Imprint reforming - Imprint coupling	A certain historical period	6, 10
Tradition/ heritage	Visible	- Custodianship	A historical period or a historical character	3
Rhetorical history	Mostly visible	- Selective forgetting - Strategic re-presentation	A historical character	9
Collective memory	Visible and invisible	- Mnemonic communities - Mnemonic work	A historical event or a historical character	2, 4, 8, 10

These four perspectives are not meant to be exhaustive but rather to serve as a foundation for the discussions in the book in the following chapters. Most chapters in the book have built on the above perspectives, but not exclusively. For instance, Sergi, Basque, Langley, and Meziani (2025, in this volume) build on a specific aspect of collective memory which they labeled 'small stories' as a carrier of legacy (e.g., anecdotes from the founders). They further develop their analysis of the legacy of deceased founders in organizations, building on narrative theory. Similarly, other chapters offer a unique and in-depth exploration of the intricate relationship between legacy and change, illustrating how organizations engage with their past to shape their future.

References

Albu, N., Albu, C. N., Apostol, O., & Cho, C. H. (2021). The past is never dead: The role of imprints in shaping social and environmental reporting in a post-communist context. *Accounting, Auditing & Accountability Journal*, 34(5), 1109–1136.

Anteby, M., & Molnar, V. (2012). Collective memory meets organizational identity: Remembering to forget in a firm's rhetorical history. *Academy of Management Journal*, 55(3), 515–540. https://doi.org/10.5465/amj.2010.0245

Aschhoff, H., & Waldkirch, M. (2025). Acquiring history? Foreign imprint management during postmerger integration. In H. Foroughi, A. Casey, & S. Coman (Eds.), *Managing legacy and change: New frontiers for theory and practice* (Chapter 5). DeGruyter.

Barbera, F., Stamm, I., & DeWitt, R.-L. (2018). The development of an entrepreneurial legacy: Exploring the role of anticipated futures in transgenerational entrepreneurship. *Family Business Review*, 31(3), 352–378. https://doi.org/10.1177/0894486518780795

Bednar, J. S., & Brown, J. A. (2023). Organizational ghosts: How "ghostly encounters" enable former leaders to influence current organizational members. *Academy of Management Journal*, 67(3), 737–766. https://doi.org/10.5465/amj.2022.0622

Bell, E., & Taylor, S. (2016). Vernacular mourning and corporate memorialization in framing the death of Steve Jobs. *Organization*, 23(1), 114–132.

Colquitt, J. A., Sabey, T. B., Pfarrer, M. D., Rodell, J. B., & Hill, E. T. (2023). Continue the story or turn the page? Coworker reactions to inheriting a legacy. *Academy of Management Review*, 48(1), 11–31.

Coraiola, D. M., Foster, W. M., Mena, S., Foroughi, H., & Rintamaki, J. (2023). Ecologies of memories: Memory work within and between organizations and communities. *The Academy of Management Annals*, 17(1), 373–404. https://doi.org/10.5465/annals.2021.0088

Dacin, M. T., Dacin, P. A., & Kent, D. (2019). Tradition in organizations: A custodianship framework. *The Academy of Management Annals*, 13(1), 342–373. https://doi.org/10.5465/annals.2016.0122

Dacin, M. T., Munir, K., & Tracey, P. (2010). Formal dining at Cambridge colleges: Linking ritual performance and institutional maintenance. *Academy of Management Journal*, 53(6), 1393–1418. https://doi.org/10.5465/amj.2010.57318388

de Cuyper, L., Clarysse, B., & Phillips, N. (2020). Imprinting beyond the founding phase: How sedimented imprints develop over time. *Organization Science*, 31(6), 1579–1600. https://doi.org/10.1287/orsc.2020.1372

Eisenman, M., & Casey, A. (2025). Constructing legacy: Managing legacy in discursive and embodied ways. In H. Foroughi, A. Casey, & S. Coman (Eds.), *Managing legacy and change: New frontiers for theory and practice* (Chapter 3). DeGruyter.

Eyerman, R., & Jamison, A. (1998). *Music and social movements: Mobilizing traditions in the twentieth century*. Cambridge University Press.

Foroughi, H. (2019). Global North and Global South: Frameworks of power in an international development project. In J. Mahadevan, H. Primecz, & L. Romani (Eds.), *Cases in critical cross-cultural management* (pp. 174–185). Routledge.

Foroughi, H., Coraiola, D. M., Rintamaki, J., Mena, S., & Foster, W. M. (2020). Organizational memory studies. *Organization Studies, 41*(12), 1725–1748.

Foroughi, H., & Smith, A. (2024). Media review: Slavery and the bank—A commentary on historic corporate social responsibility. *Organization Studies, 45*(6), 913–917. https://doi.org/10.1177/01708406231209854

Foster, W. M., Suddaby, R., Minkus, A., & Wiebe, E. (2011). History as social memory assets: The example of Tim Hortons. *Management & Organizational History, 6*(1), 101–120. https://doi.org/10.1177/1744935910387027

Hatch, M. J., & Schultz, M. (2017). Toward a theory of using history authentically: Historicizing in the Carlsberg Group. *Administrative Science Quarterly, 62*(4), 657–697.

Hatch, M. J., & Schultz, M. (2002). The dynamics of organizational identity. *Human Relations, 55*(8), 989–1018. https://doi.org/10.1177/0018726702055008181

Israelsen, T., & Suddaby, R. (2025). Inheritance as an organizational purpose. In H. Foroughi, A. Casey, & S. Coman (Eds.), *Managing legacy and change: New frontiers for theory and practice* (Chapter 3). DeGruyter.

Jaskiewicz, P., Combs, J. G., & Rau, S. B. (2015). Entrepreneurial legacy: Toward a theory of how some family firms nurture transgenerational entrepreneurship. *Journal of Business Venturing, 30*(1), 29–49. https://doi.org/10.1016/j.jbusvent.2014.07.001

Johnson, V. (2007). What is organizational imprinting? Cultural entrepreneurship in the founding of the Paris opera. *American Journal of Sociology, 113*(1), 97–127. https://doi.org/10.1086/517899

Johnson, V. (2008). *Backstage at the revolution: How the Royal Paris Opera survived the end of the Old Regime*. University of Chicago Press.

Jones, I. G. (2025). Rhetorical history as history: Legacies of a rhetorical history strategy. In H. Foroughi, A. Casey, & S. Coman (Eds.), *Managing legacy and change: New frontiers for theory and practice* (Chapter 8). DeGruyter.

Khurana, R. (2011). *Searching for a corporate savior: The irrational quest for charismatic CEOs*. Princeton University Press

Lamertz, K., Foster, W. M., Coraiola, D. M., & Kroezen, J. (2016). New identities from remnants of the past: An examination of the history of beer brewing in Ontario and the recent emergence of craft breweries. *Business History, 58*(5), 796–828. https://doi.org/10.1080/00076791.2015.1065819

Lyle, M. C. B. (2025). Distilling memories—a redefinition of organizational identity. In H. Foroughi, A. Casey, & S. Coman (Eds.), *Managing legacy and change: New frontiers for theory and practice* (Chapter 2). DeGruyter.

Lyle, M. C. B., Hockensmith, A. S., & Walsh, I. J. (2024). Up in smoke? The lingering influence of history on community identity dynamics. *Strategic Organization, 22*(4), 825–851. https://doi.org/10.1177/14761270231169103

Manelli, L., Magrelli, V., Kotlar, J., Messeni Petruzzelli, A., & Frattini, F. (2023). Building an outward-oriented social family legacy: Rhetorical history in family business foundations. *Family Business Review, 36*(1), 143–168. https://doi.org/10.1177/08944865231157195

Marquis, C. (2003). The pressure of the past: Network imprinting in intercorporate communities. *Administrative Science Quarterly, 48*(4), 655–689. https://doi.org/10.2307/3556640

Marquis, C., & Huang, Z. (2010). Acquisitions as exaptation: The legacy of founding institutions in the U.S. commercial banking industry. *Academy of Management Journal, 53*(6), 1441–1473. https://doi.org/10.5465/amj.2010.57318393

Mena, S., Rintamäki, J., Fleming, P., & Spicer, A. (2016). On the forgetting of corporate irresponsibility. *Academy of Management Review, 41*(4), 720–738. https://doi.org/10.5465/amr.2014.0208

Popielarz, P. A. (2025). Obstacles to change in racialized organizations: Imprinting, memory, and legacy. In H. Foroughi, A. Casey, & S. Coman (Eds.), *Managing legacy and change: New frontiers for theory and practice* (Chapter 10). DeGruyter.

Radu-Lefebvre, M., Davis, J. H., & Gartner, W. B. (2024). Legacy in family business: A systematic literature review and future research agenda. *Family Business Review, 37*(1), 18–59. https://doi.org/10.1177/08944865231224506

Sasaki, I., Kotlar, J., Ravasi, D., & Vaara, E. (2020). Dealing with revered past: Historical identity statements and strategic change in Japanese family firms. *Strategic Management Journal, 41*(3), 590–623. https://doi.org/10.1002/smj.3065

Schrempf-Stirling, J., Palazzo, G., & Phillips, R. A. (2016). Historic corporate social responsibility. *Academy of Management Review, 41*(4), 700–719.

Sergi, V., Basque, J., Langley, A., & Meziani, N. (2025). The power of the mundane: Small stories as ambivalent carriers of legacy. In H. Foroughi, A. Casey, & S. Coman (Eds.), *Managing legacy and change: New frontiers for theory and practice* (Chapter 8). DeGruyter.

Shils, E. (1981). *Tradition*. University of Chicago Press.

Simsek, Z., Fox, B. C., & Heavey, C. (2015). "What's past is prologue": A framework, review, and future directions for organizational research on imprinting. *Journal of Management, 41*(1), 288–317. https://doi.org/10.1177/0149206314553276

Smith, A., & Simeone, D. (2017). Learning to use the past: The development of a rhetorical history strategy by the London headquarters of the Hudson's Bay Company. *Management & Organizational History, 12*(4), 334–356. https://doi.org/10.1080/17449359.2017.1394199

Spink, P. K., Spink, M. J. P., Hercílio P. de Oliveira, J., & Tavanti, R. M. (2025). Legacy and collective action: Learning from faith-based communities and parishes. In H. Foroughi, A. Casey, & S. Coman (Eds.), *Managing legacy and change: New frontiers for theory and practice* (Chapter 7). DeGruyter.

Stinchcombe, A. (1965). Social structure and organizations. In J. G. March (Ed.), *Handbook of organizations* (pp. 142–193). Rand McNally.

Suddaby, R., Coraiola, D., Harvey, C., & Foster, W. (2020). History and the micro-foundations of dynamic capabilities. *Strategic Management Journal, 41*(3), 530–556. https://doi.org/10.1002/smj.3058

Suddaby, R., Foster, W. M., & Quinn Trank, C. (2010). Rhetorical history as a source of competitive advantage. In J. A. C. Baum & J. Lampel (Eds.), *The globalization of strategy research* (pp. 147–173). Emerald.

Suddaby, R., & Jaskiewicz, P. (2020). Managing traditions: A critical capability for family business success. *Family Business Review, 33*(3), 234–243. https://doi.org/10.1177/0894486520942611

Taraday, H. (2013). Book review: Family Legacy and Leadership: Preserving True Family Wealth in Challenging Times. *Family Business Review, 26*(2), 200–202. https://doi.org/10.1177/0894486512474163

Vives-Gabriel, J., Schrempf-Stirling, J., & Coraiola, D. M. (2024). Dealing with organizational legacies of irresponsibility. *Academy of Management Perspectives, 38*(3), 286–303.

Wade-Benzoni, K. A., & Tost, L. P. (2009). The egoism and altruism of intergenerational behavior. *Personality and Social Psychology Review, 13*(3), 165–193. https://doi.org/10.1177/1088868309339317

Wadhwani, R. D., Suddaby, R., Mordhorst, M., & Popp, A. (2018). History as organizing: Uses of the past in organization studies. *Organization Studies, 39*(12), 1663–1683. https://doi.org/10.1177/0170840618814867

Ziai, A. (2016). *Development discourse and global history: From colonialism to the sustainable development goals* (p. 252). Taylor & Francis.

Part I: **Legacy transmission between memory and identity**

Matthew C. B. Lyle
Chapter 2
Distilling memories—a redefinition of organizational identity

Organizational identity has, since its inception as a construct, been framed as a key factor underlying strategic outcomes. Defined by social constructionists as the collective answer to the question "'is this who we really are as an organization?', or, more provocatively, 'is this who we are becoming as an organization?'" (Gioia et al., 2000, p. 76), organizational identity reifies the collection of thoughts regarding an organization's variably central, distinctive, and (possibly) enduring features (Ravasi et al., 2019) as labels (i.e., language used to describe an identity, such as 'fixer doers' or 'conservative lobby') and sets of ascribed meanings (i.e., values and/or actions ascribed to those labels, such as relying on craftsman-like principles or soliciting donations from wealthy individuals—Lyle et al., 2022; Ravasi & Schultz, 2006). These self-definitions, once constructed, serve as critical inputs into strategic decision-making (Gioia et al., 2013). For instance, decisions to enter new markets (Cannon & Kreutzer, 2018), pursue global expansion (Hatch & Schultz, 2017), set a direction as a spinoff organization (Corley & Gioia, 2004) or set of organizations (Patvardhan et al., 2015), achieve political goals (Alvesson et al., 2008), establish stakeholder relationships (Brickson, 2005; Lyle et al., 2022), and/or craft an image for the public (Anteby & Molnar, 2012; Foster et al., 2011) have been theoretically rooted in the construction of a coherent, relatively unambiguous identity on which key decision-makers can lean in claiming that plans are based not on whims but rather rooted in a sense of "who we [really] are as an organization" (Ashforth et al., 2020, p. 34).

What cannot be avoided, however, is the realization that much of the discussion surrounding 'who we really are' as an organization involves the past. Perhaps the most illustrative example of this influence concerns legacy, as legacy organizational identities (i.e., mutual understandings of 'who we were' as an organization—Walsh & Bartunek, 2011; Walsh & Glynn, 2008) weigh heavily on the identities of organizations founded by a particular organization's former employees, similarly to how institutional legacies (i.e., "institutions that persist and affect the community over long periods of time"—Greve & Rao, 2014, p. 27) showcase the influence of past organizations on the form—and even identities—of those that follow within a given community (Chiles et al., 2004).

While this work showcases the influence of historic, extraorganizational identities, an organization's own past also serves as a vital input into its central and distinctive features. Indeed, all reflection on 'who we are' involves recollection of "who have we been" (Parker, 2002, p. 614), including the discussions, artifacts, and other mnemonic traces (i.e., "a reminder . . . that helps members of a community remember what the shared narrative of their past is"—Mena et al., 2016, p. 723) from the distant and more recent past brought to bear on defining one's organization in the current moment. Indeed, Gioia and colleagues (2000) noted, "Whenever the question comes up about 'who we are' or, especially, 'who we want to be,' not only do organization members revise their current perceptions of their organization . . . they also engage in a process of revising their current perceptions of the past" (p. 71). More recent work has showcased the importance of the remembered past to identity, as in Patvardhan and colleagues' (2015) work highlighting the importance of past identities in forming a coherent self-definition for an emerging academic field and Ravasi and colleagues' (2019) framing of the past as containing the material needed to construct organizational identity. Much like collective memories (i.e., shared recollections—Olick, 1999; Rowlinson et al., 2010), organizational identities are, thus, for organization members, "formed in the past but continually present to them" (Halbwachs, 1950, p. 6).

This natural reliance on the past in organizational identity construction thus raises an important question: How, precisely, does the construction of organizational identity differ from that of organizational memory? Viewed through the lens of organizational memory studies (OMS), a field concerned with the work through which individuals and collectives remember, forget, and/or represent (i.e., reconstruct) the past—a process deemed *memory work* (Coraiola et al., 2023; Foroughi et al., 2020; Rowlinson et al., 2010)—organizational identity construction or work (Kreiner et al., 2015) may be seen as simply relabeling memory work. For instance, Lyle and colleagues' (2022, p. 1993) attestation that "the persistence of meanings ascribed to [identity] labels entails ongoing negotiation with members and revised understandings of organizational history" could be credibly reconstrued as 'ongoing memory work can, under certain circumstances, produce similar memories over time' (cf. Coraiola et al., 2023). Especially as similar evidence is drawn upon to illustrate the change and/or stasis of memory and identity alike, including statues (Eury et al., 2018; Lyle, Hockensmith, & Walsh, 2024), rites and ceremonies (Connerton, 1989; Do & Lyle, 2022), and artifacts housed in corporate museums (Ravasi et al., 2019; Suddaby et al.,2016), there arises a need to reconsider organizational identity's uniqueness and theoretical importance.

Therefore, in this chapter I argue for a redefinition of organizational identity as the distillation, following memory work, of organizational memory into labels and meanings capturing an organization's currently central, distinctive, and (possibly) enduring features. This definition positions organizational identity as extant scholarship, if not explicitly, already has: as the reification of collective attempts to understand an organization through reliance on narratives and materials based in the past (Hatch & Schultz, 2017; Lyle, Hockensmith, & Walsh, 2024; Ravasi et al., 2019).

For purposes of establishing both construct clarity and the theoretical utility of this redefinition, I structure this chapter around a processual framework linking an organization's past (i.e., the collection of largely unknowable events predating the present—Suddaby et al., 2016) to its strategy (i.e., the language deployed to describe organizational plans—Mantere, 2013) through organizational memory, identity, and desired future image. I argue that, by drawing upon the past to construct and coauthor organizational memories, our natural inclination to apply labels and meanings to our memories (Souza et al., 2021) gives rise to the organizational self-definitions that, to date, have been referred to as organizational identity. By comparing scholarship on the social construction of organizational identity to work in the field of OMS, I offer evidence that organizational identity indeed fits this definition of a distilled, simplified organizational memory that organizational decision-makers can compare to a postalgic or antidystopian vision (i.e., desired future image—Gioia & Thomas, 1996) to construct organizational strategy (Figure 2.1).

Despite its potential appearance, this line of argumentation is not meant to discredit work on organizational identity nor the efforts of those engaged in it. I firmly agree with the community of organizational identity scholars, amongst whom (at least based upon publication record) I consider myself a member, that such identities can influence, and in turn be influenced by, a host of constructs (Foroughi, 2020; Gioia et al., 2013; Hatch & Schultz, 2002). Rather, by augmenting its definition to meaningfully consider the mnemonic processes through which I see the construct as built, I aim to extol a processual connection between memory and identity (e.g., Casey, 2019; Ravasi et al., 2019). Furthermore, as scholars operating under the social symbolic work perspective (i.e., those who view our socially constructed realities as necessitating continuous effort to maintain or change—Lawrence & Phillips, 2019) continue identifying and refining various forms of 'work,' I argue for a natural overlap between *memory work* and *identity work* that positions them as one and the same, thus reducing scholarly redundancy.

From past to future: The role of memory and identity

Linking past to memory: A review

Given our focus on memory and identity as socially constructed rather than objective realities, I find it theoretically consistent to discuss the links between an organization's past and memory through an interpretive lens, wherein "remembering and forgetting are ... about the collectively shared reinterpretation, re-enactment and reframing of the past through social interactions" (Foroughi et al., 2020, p. 1729). This view, one long established by social memory studies and OMS scholars alike, holds that the past is largely unknowable, as specific events, intentions, and outcomes are largely lost to time (Halbwachs, 1950; Suddaby & Foster, 2017). Organizational memory thus becomes a product of exploring this 'foreign country' (Lowenthal, 1985), as organization members variably remember, forget, and/or represent this landscape. This process—labeled memory work—involves a host of mnemonic practices (i.e., storying,

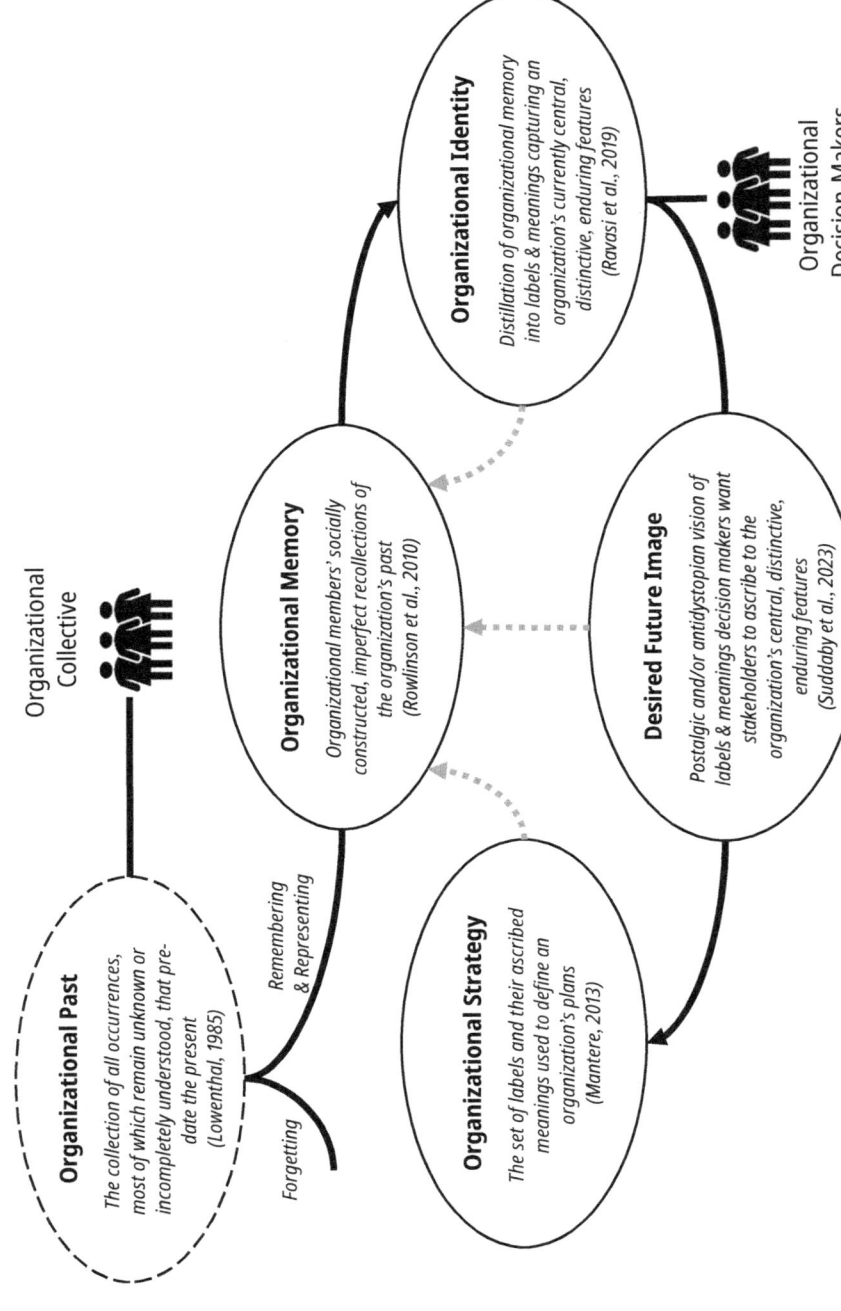

Figure 2.1: Theoretical Relationships Among Organizational Memory, Identity, and Strategy.

curating, suppressing, etc.) through which members become coauthors of a narrative leading to the present day (Coraiola et al., 2023).

Key to collective memory construction in organizational scholarship is the agent of memory (Suddaby & Foster, 2017; Vinitzky-Seroussi, 2002), considered here as the individual or group of individuals attempting to instill in organization members a particular memory (Do & Lyle, 2022). Scholarship addressing rhetorical history, or the strategic use of the past (Suddaby et al., 2010, 2016), positions such agents as critical to the construction of organizational memory as they—to put it generously—'massage' the past to spur collective remembering, forgetting, or representing through what they do (and do not—Anteby & Molnar, 2012) present as history (i.e., elements of the past brought to bear on the present—Wadhwani et al., 2018).

Regarding *remembering*, Crawford and colleagues (2022) recounted how the founder of Grand Canyon Dories drew stakeholders' attention to the historic destruction of the region through practices such as naming their dories after now-destroyed natural wonders, while Ravasi and colleagues (2019) and Suddaby and colleagues (2016) pointed to the importance of corporate museums in providing agents with a wealth of mnemonic traces from which to draw in commemorating the past (see also Do et al., 2019). Studies of remembering thus explore "the set of practices used to preserve the integrity of the past" (Coraiola et al., 2023, p. 379).

Regarding *forgetting*, Anteby and Molnar's (2012) seminal work shows leaders of a French aeronautical firm promoting *selective forgetting*, concealing their history of international collaboration by removing traces of it to bolster a collective memory of having relied solely upon French engineering and expertise. Such ideas have been extended by Mena and colleagues (2016) and, more recently, Coraiola and Derry (2020) in their conceptualizations of how corporations conceal histories of irresponsibility and public harm (see also Foroughi & Al-Amoudi, 2020). Each of these studies draws further attention to the importance of materiality in processes of remembering, as additions to (Wagner-Pacifici & Schwartz, 1991) or subtractions from (Connerton, 2009) the physical environment, in tandem with the stories told about what remains visible within it, influence what collectives remember through what they forget (Cutcher et al., 2019; Jones et al., 2019; Lyle, Hockensmith, & Walsh, 2024).

Perhaps most common is *representing*, wherein agents curate a particular version of the past, drawing attention to—or perhaps inventing—particular elements. Hatch and Schultz (2017) beautifully captured this practice by unpacking how Carlsberg's leadership, having identified the carving of *Semper Ardens* ("always burning") above their historic brewhouse, gave different meanings to this phrase at different points in time to support the launching of a craft brew line in the 1990s and the pursuit of global expansion in the 2010s. This and other work capturing processes of representing (e.g., Basque & Langley, 2018; Booth et al., 2007; Dacin et al., 2010) supports a view of history as partly truth and partly fiction (Foster et al., 2011; Lyle et al., 2022; Suddaby & Foster, 2017) and translated into collective memory through materiality and rhetoric (Foroughi et al., 2020; Lyle, Hockensmith, & Walsh, 2024; Suddaby et al., 2016).

While these practices belie different desires, each supports a conceptualization of the past as a largely unknown territory (Lowenthal, 1985) containing an innumerable sum of elements (i.e., events, intentions, cognitions, actions, affective states, etc.). This fundamental difference between the totality of the past and what agents present as history underscores the necessity of scholarly work on collective memory construction (e.g., Foroughi et al., 2020; Rowlinson et al., 2010), as members alternatively embrace (Foster et al., 2011) or reject (Booth et al., 2007) what they are proffered through discourse and action, notably collective discussions and actions taken towards the material environment (e.g., Do et al., 2019). These collective processes create a collective memory, one that—owing to these agentic influences and collective processes—might differ substantially from the past, could it be accurately comprehended (Lyle et al., 2022).

Linking memory to identity: A redefinition

OMS scholars have similarly identified links between the organizational memory that results from memory work and an organization's self-definition, or identity. Prominent organizational identity scholars, perhaps most notably Ravasi and colleagues (2019) and Suddaby and colleagues (2016), have gone so far as to incorporate memory directly into their investigations of organizational identity construction, holding that an organization's past contains the material used to build it. Indeed, what many regard as a foundational text for the social constructionist view of organizational identity—Gioia and colleagues' (2000) *Academy of Management Review* piece on the construct's adaptive instability—draws a similar connection.

However, what these and other investigations of organizational identity overlook is the overlap between constructing memory and identity, or between memory and identity work. Indeed, any discussion of 'who we are' naturally relies upon a discussion of 'who we have been,' both in the distant and recent past (Basque & Langley, 2018; Cannon & Kreutzer, 2018; Corley & Gioia, 2004; Patvardhan et al., 2015). Still, while some have framed organizational identity as relying, at least in part, on organizational memory (Gioia et al., 2013), I view the work underlying them (i.e., memory and identity work) as more closely related (Casey, 2019) and, perhaps, one and the same (Table 2.1).

Consider Lyle and colleagues' (2022) case study of the cannabis reform group NORML. Through their work, the authors found evidence of the identity label 'grassroots lobby'—one meant to reflect a current understanding of the organization as valuing support from everyday cannabis users above wealthy, politically connected donors—appearing for the first time in the 1980s, nearly a decade after its founding. In discussing this shift, the authors focused on the agents (i.e., NORML's national director and board of directors) who proffered this label and meaning and the collective of organization members (i.e., donors and volunteers) who 'authenticated' it through discussion and the creation of artifacts that supported it, including promotional materi-

Table 2.1: Key Construct Definitions.

Construct	Definition	Scholarly example	Notes
Organizational past	The collection of all occurrences, most of which remain unknown or incompletely understood, that predate the present	An aeronautical firm, despite its focus on nationalism, having previously worked with and, per company archives, relied upon international partners (Anteby & Molnar, 2012)	Is in line with SMS and OMS scholarship theorizing the past's largely unknowable nature (Lowenthal, 1985; Suddaby & Foster, 2017)
Organizational memory	Organizational members' socially constructed, imperfect recollections of the organization's past	Technology firms remembering a local, now-defunct manufacturer as a technological forebearer while forgetting the pain caused by its closure (Do, Lyle & Walsh, 2019)	Is in line with SMS and OMS scholarship on outcomes of 'memory work' (Coraiola et al., 2023)
Organizational identity	Distillation of organizational memory into labels and meanings capturing an organization's currently central, distinctive, enduring features	Members of a nonprofit referring to their organization as a 'peace-builder' following reflections on the success of their recent initiative (Cannon & Kreutzer, 2018)	Defines organizational identity as a reflection of organizational memory rather than a potential outcome of mnemonic processes (cf. Ravasi et al., 2019)
Desired future image	Postalgic and/or antidystopian vision of labels and meanings decision-makers want stakeholders to ascribe to the organization's central, distinctive, enduring features	Board members of a social justice organization publishing pamphlets appealing to grassroots—rather than wealthy—supporters in hopes of altering their identity from 'conservative lobby' to 'grassroots lobby' (Lyle, Walsh, & Coraiola, 2022)	Roots desired future image in organizational decision-makers "longing for a heavenly future" (Ybema, 2004, p. 832)
Organizational strategy	The set of labels and meanings used to define an organization's plans	Decision-makers at a statewide transit authority extolling a commitment to build homeless shelters to reflect their newfound identity label as 'fixer-doers' (Dutton & Dukerich, 1991)	Ties strategy to considerations of identity and image reflected in recent scholarship (Mantere, 2013)

Note: OMS, organizational memory studies; SMS, social memory studies.

als (Hatch & Schultz, 2017; Lyle, Hockensmith, & Walsh, 2024). The framing of this process as capturing identity work (e.g., Kreiner et al., 2015) appears consistent with Gioia and colleagues' (2000) discussion of identity labels and meanings, as well as the processes through which they shift over time depending upon current realities (Dutton & Dukerich, 1991).

However, this label and its associated meaning also appear to reflect collective attempts—spurred by leaders—to influence memory by shaping history. Notably, this process involved both selectively forgetting NORML's overwhelming denunciation of grassroots supporters in the 1970s and the creation of new memories that positioned a grassroots focus as dating back to their inception. Referencing recent memory work scholarship (Coraiola et al., 2023; Foroughi et al., 2020), such actions bear a striking resemblance to the mnemonic practice of *remembrance*, or historical "reconstruction . . . against a background of preexisting texts" (Coraiola et al., 2023, p. 381) to use the past in creating a desired narrative of historical continuity (Suddaby et al., 2016). Viewed this way, 'grassroots lobby' appears as the label used to encompass the outcome of a wider web of mnemonic practices (i.e., memory work) aimed at creating a coherent sense of the past in the present, foregrounding bits of historical record that support this memory while selectively forgetting the wider tome of evidence that would position it as a turn away from historic precedent (cf. Ybema, 2014). In other words, NORML's leaders argued to its members that they had always been a grassroots organization dependent upon everyday cannabis users, thus positioning their current strategy as a continuation of the past (Do & Lyle, 2022; Suddaby & Foster, 2017). In this case, identity work does not appear distinct from memory work. Rather, memory work seems to have resulted in a collective memory that could be distilled into the label 'grassroots lobby' alongside its ascribed meaning.

Focusing on the three broader forms of memory work (i.e., remembering, forgetting, and representing—Coraiola et al., 2023), we can see how this overlap between memory work and identity work—where practices enacted to construct organizational memory appear indistinguishable from those enacted to construct organizational identity—occurs with regularity. Indeed, the overlap between methods and evidence deployed to illustrate organizational memory and identity would seem to support this argument (Table 2.2), as quotations showcasing individual stances on organizational identity can be credibly interpreted as evidence of various mnemonic practices deployed in remembering, forgetting, and representing.

Regarding remembering, those investigating the initial formation of collective identities often present evidence of agents' attempts to retain continuity with a past that predates the collective's founding. Such efforts have been framed as intended to lessen the experience of ambiguity that often accompanies new venture formation (e.g., Do et al., 2019; Walsh & Bartunek, 2011). For instance, Corley and Gioia (2004) show members of Bozkinetic, a corporate spin-off, struggling to understand their place in an as-yet-undefined venture historically rooted in a parent company. With understanding company history a focus of their interviews, the authors uncovered se-

Table 2.2: Examples of Organizational Identity/Memory Overlap in Extant Scholarship.

Article	Primary data sources/ purpose	Illustrative quote	OMS overlap
Dutton & Dukerich (1991, AMJ)	Open-ended interviews supplemented with archival data and observations from organizational training sessions for the purpose of "construction of the issue's [identity threat's] history as depicted in interpretations, actions, and events from 1982 into 1989" (p. 522) from which to explain organizational identity change	"It wasn't until homeless people started to show up at the World Trade Center . . . that people started to say 'Wait, geez, this is a problem. . . . ' It [homelessness] started to show up finally in corporate documents as an issue. It never did before. . . . Then it began to touch upon the heart and soul of the organization" (Informant, p. 531).	**Invented transitions** Retrospective accounts linking past to present wherein informants explain current arrangements (i.e., identity-related concerns) as rooted in a key historical event (Do & Lyle, 2022; Ybema, 2014)
Corley & Gioia (2004, ASQ)	Semi-structured interviews asking "questions about company experience, involvement in work at Bozkinetic, thoughts about the company's historical evolution and perceptions of the impending, current, or recent spin-off, the business and strategic context of the spin-off, plans for the spin-off, and early indicators and understandings of organizational identity and image" (p. 181), supplemented with archival documents and observation, to explain organizational identity formation	"Suddenly some people have to remember what it's like to be an independent company. Even for some of the people who are still here, they weren't in senior enough positions then to really know what it means and others are just not sure what it means to begin with" (Informant, p. 188).	**Storying** Presenting a narrative of the past to those more or less familiar with it to "[provide] order, logic and meaning to incidents and events from the past" (Coraiola et al., 2023, p. 379; Crawford et al., 2022).

Table 2.2 (continued)

Article	Primary data sources/purpose	Illustrative quote	OMS overlap
Patvardhan, Gioia, & Hamilton (2015, AMJ)	Semi-structured interviews that, "when concepts with potential for theoretical insight emerged (e.g., those surrounding the important identity crisis), we 'zoomed in' and focused in greater depth on the processes involved in experiencing and resolving them" (p. 410), alongside archival documents and years of observing key events as both organizational outsiders and insiders, to explain the difficulties of constructing a cross-organizational, 'consensual' identity	"Whereas most senior faculty perpetuated their legacy identities by continuing to maintain strong ties with their 'home' disciplines, attending conferences, publishing in their journals, and collaborating with former colleagues, junior faculty members did not" (Interpretation, p. 425).	**Protecting** Contests between those with different memories of prior events that can form—or keep separate—distinct mnemonic communities (Coraiola et al., 2023; Foroughi, 2020)
Ravasi, Rindova & Stigliani (2019, AMJ)	Semi-structured interviews, archival collection, and visits to corporate museums to "[create] historical accounts about how and why each museum was established, who was involved in the founding, and where the collection came from" (p. 1526) to explain individuals' understanding of organizational identity through engagement with the past	"We do not consider the museum . . . a room full of motorcycles. It is a sort of time machine, where different generations of fans and non-fans can interact. . . . My job is like opening a casket full of family memories" (Informant, p. 1535).	**Memory workers** Individuals who see their role as necessitating the telling of history to sustain a particular memory of it (Bodnar, 1989; Suddaby et al., 2016)

Note: AMJ, *Academy of Management Journal;* ASQ, *Administrative Science Quarterly;* OMS, organizational memory studies.

nior members telling stories about what life was like within the parent company in its early years, a tactic that gave newcomers a template for cognition and behavior. Such practices reflect *storying,* wherein agents of memory present past-oriented narratives to give order to the present (Coraiola et al., 2023; Crawford et al., 2022). While such actions resulted in the formation of a novel identity, that identity appeared rooted in the stories told of another organization's founding, thus positioning it as an outcome of memory work.

Similarly, Patvardhan and colleagues' (2015) work on identity construction in an emerging academic field shows senior faculty acting in accordance with legacy identities (Walsh & Glynn, 2008), choosing to work within pre-established coauthor arrangements rather than create novel ties with junior faculty. These efforts showcase *protecting* (Foroughi, 2020; Lyle, Hockensmith, & Walsh, 2024), wherein a group harboring distinct memories (i.e., mnemonic communities—Zerubavel, 2003) resists integration by continuing to evangelize and act in accordance with them. The resulting, highly ambiguous identity captured by Patvardhan and colleagues (2015) thus serves as the simplest language organization members could use to capture this plurality of memories. Other foundational examples of actors constructing identities reflective of and honoring their past (e.g., Chreim, 2005; Howard-Grenville et al., 2013; Pratt, 2000; Ravasi & Schultz, 2006) suggest that remembering serves as a core tenet of identity construction.

Regarding forgetting, a host of studies addressing organizational identity construction include in the identity work process reference to the importance of disregarding the past, perhaps most prominently through *suppression* (Coraiola et al., 2023; Hernes, 2007). Paramount here are Anteby and Molnar (2012), who framed the deliberate removal of reference to foreign partnerships by an organization's bulletin board editors as a cornerstone of their nationalistic identity (see also Foster et al., 2011). Removing all reference to these collaborations within their walls—while simultaneously bolstering those honoring their national heritage—naturally led to a memory, and eventually identity, of the company as distinctly French. Other examples include Schultz and Hernes' (2013) work on LEGO, particularly how "the joint use of oral and material memory forms . . . enhanced the depth of identity reconstruction, enabling both a deliberate 'forgetting' of past identity claims and a fundamental renewal of claims intended to be brought forward into the future" (p. 16; see also Hernes, 2007), and Cutcher and colleagues (2019) in exploring how historical figures deemed less central to identity claims, even when materially commemorated, are 'othered' insofar as their commemorations lack the grandiosity of those viewed as more central. This work thus offers a kind of 'middle ground,' wherein memories of a historical touchstone might fail to emerge even when subjected to the relative light of day. The active suppression of memories appears central to these studies, as these actions ensure that they cannot be integrated into identity labels and meanings, thus again raising the question of what about this identity work remains distinct to this form of social symbolic work and what instead captures memory work undertaken in the construction of organizational identity.

Finally, regarding representing, one need look no further than Dutton and Dukerich's (1991) foundational paper. With a keen eye towards understanding the historical unfolding of identity threats to the Port Authority of New York and New Jersey (p. 522), the authors found Authority representatives engaging in *historicizing* (Lyle et al., 2022; Suddaby et al., 2023), wherein actors selectively—and strategically—construct a historical narrative (Assmann, 2011; Suddaby et al., 2023). For Dutton and

Dukerich (1991), this narrative treated the influx of homeless persons to the World Trade Center in the mid-1980s as marking a historic turning point that demarcated the 'old' and 'new' Port Authority, one that cared genuinely for this population. This narrative device specifically embodies a subcategory of historicizing—*invented transitions*—through which actors create discontinuity with the past by presenting what came before a certain moment as not reflective of the better organization that followed in its wake (Suddaby & Foster, 2017; Ybema, 2014). Again, we can see mnemonic practices—specific forms of memory work—playing a critical role in the identity that organization members construct.

One could, however, rightly claim that the Port Authority—and indeed the wider range of organizations engaged in identity-based discussions—enacted more than one practice in their construction of organizational identity. For instance, Dutton and Dukerich (1991) theorized both how looking into 'the mirror' unveiled a history in need of change (historicizing through invented transition—Suddaby & Foster, 2017; Ybema, 2014) and a focus on what they would become following this historic transition. In this manner, my focus on one past-oriented manner in which the Port Authority constructed its novel identity would seem to cherry-pick a mnemonic practice that, alone, did not produce it. However, memory work often involves a multitude of actions aimed at "reinsert[ing] the past in the present" (Coraiola et al., 2023, p. 380). Organizational memory, then, does not result purely from one mnemonic practice but from multiple means of remembering, forgetting, and/or representing.

Viewed through the language of memory work, Dutton and Dukerich (1991) appear to have uncovered both the aforementioned historicizing, as members periodized their shameful past as existing before their own invented transition, alongside a selective forgetting tied to "the launching of a $5.8 billion capital plan for the organization, aimed at updating facilities and improving the image of regional services to enhance the area's international competitiveness" (p. 536). While the authors did not refer to these actions as such, memory scholars have described such material action as likely to draw focus towards a desired goal (i.e., an organizational identity that includes helping the homeless as a central and distinctive feature) while focusing it away from an undesired past, as when civic leaders demolished remnants of the defunct Studebaker Factory while highlighting the construction of South Bend's novel ventures (Do et al., 2019). Echoing Cutcher and colleagues (2019), remembering and forgetting coexist such that new construction enabled the remembering of the Port Authority's newfound focus through the forgetting of what it had been, effectively creating an organizational identity reflective of the recent—as opposed to distant—past (Hernes & Schultz, 2020). This action restricted what memories remained available to be distilled into the organization's identity label and meanings.

This evidence suggests to me that organizations do not construct identities through processes separate from those used to coauthor organizational memory. Rather, the authoring of organizational identity involves practices associated with memory work. Once this authoring occurs, organizational identity serves as a linguistic simplification of the memories that remain foregrounded (Souza et al., 2021).

Linking identity to strategy: A mnemonic twist

This language, per prior scholarship (Gioia & Chittipeddi, 1991; Gioia et al., 2013), can then be imputed into (and influenced by—Mantere et al., 2012) strategic decision-making. Specifically, those responsible for organizational strategy can now compare the labels and meanings that capture what organizational memories remain salient following processes of memory work with a vision of where they want the organization to go. This vision has been conceptualized as a *desired future image* (Gioia & Thomas, 1996), or a view of the organization that decision-makers wish for stakeholders to adopt. For instance, law firm partners—having reviewed their current state and decided to pursue a new specialty area (desired future image)—might then pursue a strategy of hiring star employees known for their expertise in that area to help their organization pursue this image (Lyle et al., 2023). Strategic decisions, before crafted and enacted, thus involve consideration of organizational identity and desired future image.

However, returning again to OMS, the desired future image relied upon in making strategic decisions appears identical to Ybema's (2004) concept of *postalgia* (i.e., the 'heavenly' vision of where an entity could go) or Suddaby and colleagues' (2023) unpacking of *dystopia* (i.e., the apocalyptic vision that an entity should strive to avoid). Integral to both constructs is the growing recognition within memory studies that "future thought is . . . dependent on the past" (Szpunar & Szpunar, 2016, p. 376), which highlights our difficulty imagining what is to come without drifting towards thoughts of what came before (Sasaki & Ravasi, 2024).

Resolving this seeming paradox, Ybema (2004) considered how strategic planning involves individuals first acting as if they, in the future, are looking back upon what they have achieved. Consider Suddaby and colleagues' (2023) articulation of *historical myths*, pairs of emotionally resonant, societally understood tropes that combine where an entity has been with where it plans to go. The authors theorized how entrepreneurs construct a postalgic view of their proposal, envisioning the present moment as one they and their potential stakeholders will look back upon as either beginning or rekindling a proud history (periodization or continuation—Suddaby & Foster, 2017). Much like an individual decides to go running after imagining the feeling of having completed that run, so too do decision-makers decide upon a strategic turn after viewing themselves in the future looking back upon the wisdom of their decision (Ybema, 2004). Alternatively, decision-makers adopting an antidystopian view would envision investing in their proposal as a decision that will be remembered as having prevented an otherwise bleak future (Zucker, 1988), in essence imagining an *undesired future image* for the organization to avoid. In either case, the past cannot be thoroughly disentangled from the future; deciding upon the direction in which strategists want their organization to go depends upon their inserting themselves into the future to 'remember' the importance of that decision.

I therefore view desired future image as encompassing the mnemonic components of postalgia and/or antidystopia, as decision-makers weigh their organization's identity against what they should—and should not—become. Desired future image, then, becomes redefined through this mnemonic lens as a postalgic and/or antidystopian vision. Critically, the deployment of these tropes acts as the final consideration before a process that began with translating an organization's past into memory materializes as a strategy for its future.

Memory and identity work: Putting the old wine back

My aim in this chapter has been to consider the uniqueness of organizational identity —particularly the work underlying it (identity work)—when compared to organizational memory and memory work. In so doing, I proposed a theory linking several concepts that, per this new definition, involve mnemonic practices (i.e., organizational memory, organizational identity, desired future image). Furthermore, and perhaps most critically, I have deemphasized identity work by framing it as indistinguishable from memory work, a process through which members create and distill memory into labels and meanings. This language, following comparison with postalgic and/or antidystopian views, can then be imputed into organizational strategy.

There is no eluding my diminishing of organizational identity work in this chapter, and I would not insult the reader by claiming otherwise. My reason for proposing such changes, however, comes not from a place of disdain for organizational identity but rather from an (albeit young) career researching the construction of both identity *and* memory, often within the same manuscript (Do et al., 2019; Lyle et al., 2022, 2023; Lyle, Hockensmith, & Walsh, 2024). Having reviewed this and other work addressing both pivotal constructs in organizational scholarship (e.g., Anteby & Molnar, 2012; Casey, 2019; Foster et al., 2011; Hatch & Schultz, 2017; Ravasi et al., 2019; Suddaby et al., 2016), I find theoretical utility in arguing for a reduction—what I see as 'placing the old wine back within its original bottle'—wherein those seeking to understand organizational identity construction turn towards enriching our understanding of organizational memory construction. While one could argue the reverse—that memory work is the theoretically redundant of the two processes—overwhelming mention of the past in studies of identity *and* memory work leads me to view focusing purely on memory work as most appropriate. In other words, by pooling our efforts in the study of memory work and its associated constructs, I hope that we can better understand the nuances associated with our organizational realities.

Turning from *identity work* to *identity,* however, I see great theoretical utility in continued study of this socially constructed entity. Specifically, our field lacks knowledge surrounding how ecologies of memory (Coraiola et al., 2023) become distilled into organizational identity claims and, once constructed, how identity, image, and strategy act as connective tissue between organizational realities and, critically, the memories from which they were formed. I thus propose a series of avenues for future research that reflect these two broad gaps in understanding.

Why study identity?

The filtration of memory

In their recent *Academy of Management Annals* piece on organizational memory, Coraiola and colleagues (2023) drew upon a wealth of prior scholarship (Do et al., 2019; Fleming, 2012; Foroughi, 2020; Foroughi et al., 2020; Lubinski, 2018; Lyle et al., 2022; Suddaby & Jaskiewicz, 2020) to characterize organizations as *ecologies of memory*, or collectives composed of groups who construct and act in accordance with different versions of the past (Hoon et al., 2023). For instance, occupational groups (nurses, doctors, and administrative staff) might—due to the relative strength of occupational boundaries (Farchi et al., 2023)—construct memories primarily amongst themselves, thus resulting in multiple versions of an organization's past (Bartunek et al., 2006; Lyle et al., 2022). Indeed, those adopting an interpretivist view recognize the plurality of voices in processes of memory work (Foroughi et al., 2020) and the ways in which memories proffered by agents of memory might encounter resistance (Booth et al., 2007). While I have focused to this point on the construction of an 'organizational memory' (and 'organizational identity'—more on that later) for purposes of simplicity, the array of memories held by intraorganizational groups cannot be ignored.

What is necessitated, should we define organizational identity as the distillation of organizational memory, is greater attention to the ways in which these different versions of the past—constructed and deemed legitimate within established organizational subgroups (i.e., occupational groups, levels of occupational hierarchy, informal groups, etc.)—become variably represented in organizational identity. The question here goes beyond which memories are silenced or deemed illegitimate *during* memory work (Trouillot, 2015) towards those that exist with relative endorsement up to the point at which actors distill memory into identity.

Important questions regarding this 'filtering' of certain organizational memories arise when potentially complex and incongruent organizational memories become central, peripheral, or absent from the simplified labels and meanings that drive strategic decision-making. For instance, how do the subgroups who view their memories as absent from identity labels and meanings react when decision-makers broadcast those self-definitions? One could see the failure to include a subgroup's important mnemonic touchstones, such as historical figures and events they view as constitutive of their own intraorganizational mnemonic community (cf. Booth et al., 2007; Cutcher et al., 2019), leading to decreased job satisfaction and even mass turnover. Intraorganizational conflict and status differences might also emerge between groups that see their memories as more or less represented in identity claims (cf. Ashforth & Reingen, 2014), thus creating further divides between groups that might have, until recently, coordinated across boundaries with little to no issues (cf. Farchi et al., 2023).

Framing memory as undergirding identity also reveals avenues for scholarship addressing the dynamics between the construction of memories and their distillation into identity. While given fairly scant attention here, this process likely involves multiple actors and might occur over relatively long time horizons as groups appeal to organizational leadership in hopes of 'codifying' their memory as identity. Conversely, decisions by leadership to quickly distill an ecology of memories into identity labels and meanings—or decisions to promote an identity bearing little semblance to organizational memories—might lead a host of subgroups to question the authenticity of this identity (Hatch & Schultz, 2017) and take as-yet-untheorized action. Returning to Dutton and Dukerich (1991), what might happen if one subgroup refused to 'bury' their organization's history of apathy towards homeless persons and view the updating of facilities as nothing more than a public relations stunt? What factors influence the extent to which this group affects the construction, or perhaps efficacy, of a novel identity label?

Scholars investigating the construction of hybrid organizational identities, or those reflecting divergent logics (i.e., 'care' and 'profit'—Battilana & Dorado, 2010; Besharov, 2014), might similarly focus on the period between the construction of divergent organizational memories and their distillation into multiple, competing identities. Such efforts could include the exploration of how and why they are sometimes distilled into multiple, relatively enduring labels (Battilana et al., 2017) and sometimes refined into multiple labels that are variably foregrounded and backgrounded over time (Smith & Besharov, 2019). While these decisions are typically considered an outcome of strategic need, perhaps the relative strength of intraorganizational mnemonic communities plays a role here, as organizations with more powerful mnemonic communities grant their memory a more central place in identity labels or, to avoid conflict while retaining their hybridity, choose to hide or downplay an alternate identity in communications with them. These ideas reflect only a small portion of the potential future work that can result from a greater focus on the interplay between memory construction and distillation.

Identity, image, and strategy: Connective tissue

The other avenue for future scholarship suggested by this work has already been attended to by organizational identity scholars: identity's influence. Scholars have developed important theories surrounding how the individual and/or group perception of organizational identity shapes outcomes ranging from identification (Ashforth et al., 2016; Caprar et al., 2022) and commitment (Pratt & Rosa, 2003) to collective remembering (Foroughi, 2020) and organizational strategy (Gioia & Chittipeddi, 1991; Lyle et al., 2022). This body of work confirms the importance of organizational identity as a cornerstone of affective, cognitive, and behavioral outcomes (Gioia et al., 2013), and exploring the host of constructs influenced by it has been—and rightly remains— a rich and important domain for study.

Within my framework specifically, questions abound regarding recursive relationships between organizational identity (alongside the desired future image and strategy that flow from it) and organizational memory (Figure 2.1, dotted arrows). For instance, given the complexity of organizational memory and the relative simplicity (and broadcasting—Gioia et al., 2000; Lyle et al., 2023) of organizational identity, these labels and meanings likely serve as benchmarks for understanding organizational memory (Foroughi, 2020) for both newcomers and those lacking strong investment in their organization's history (Lyle, Hockensmith, & Cocieru, 2024). Much like the difference between a story (memory) and its headline (identity), such individuals are likely to read the latter while foregoing the former, thus leading them to an inherently oversimplified version of their organization's past. These versions will naturally omit the contributions of some (Cutcher et al., 2019) while bolstering the influence of others (Anteby & Molnar, 2012). While these effects might take place naturally as the desire for simplification erodes some memories from the organizational canon (Coraiola et al., 2023), they can also result from careful strategic decisions to eliminate undesired memories from the record (Coraiola and Derry, 2020; Mena et al., 2016). Future studies could thus attend to how decision-makers influence identity statements to eliminate what they deem 'undesirable' memories (cf. Anteby & Molnar, 2012).

Desired future image might further influence organizational memory as decision-makers, comparing identity to postalgic and/or dystopian visions, categorize that identity as simply 'good' or 'bad.' Such thinking reflects Suddaby and colleagues' (2023) focus on the extradiegetic components of historical myths: given our societal understanding of the tropes embedded within storytelling (i.e., nostalgia, postalgia, etc.), the specific details of a story, deemed intradiegetic details, become less important to their impact than the extradiegetic ones, which merely reflect general emotional valence and temporal orientation. In other words, as decision-makers consider where their organization is (identity) against where they would like it to go (desired future image), they are less likely to concern themselves with the nuances of their organization's identity than whether it is one they want their organization to continue embracing or discard (cf. Dutton & Dukerich, 1991). If we are to accept that organizational identity already reflects a distillation of organizational memory, then this additional filtration process would further strip organizational memory of its detail.

Such simplifications reach a potential endpoint following the broadcasting of organizational strategy, wherein decision-makers—now two steps removed from organizational memory—present a vision of where the organization has been and should go (Suddaby et al., 2023). With audiences focused more on the tropes embedded within such presentations than on their past-oriented details—and with decision-makers' penchant for presenting only those details that support their desired strategy (Coraiola & Derry, 2020)—all that officially remains of organizational memory at this point might be a general valence and a handful of details. Such a 'stripping of memory' would explain the ability of decision-makers to engage in rhetorical history, as they can now more easily manipulate largely forgotten elements of the past (Do & Lyle, 2022). Such a grim outlook for organizational memory highlights the need to study intraorganizational oral histories and the groups that retain them, as they likely serve as the last line of defense in keeping such memories alive (Coraiola et al., 2023).

In sum, organizational identity holds a powerful influence over both individual and collective outcomes in organizations, wielding the potential to bolster, reshape, or even erase aspects of organizational life (Foroughi, 2020). This influence speaks to the continued importance of identity as an organization-level construct, one with boundless potential for future scholars to explore.

A mnemonic theory of organizations?

My argument in this chapter has focused on placing memory at the center of organizational experience: influenced by the past, authored by organization members, and reified and simplified on its way to influencing organizational identity, desired future image, and strategy. While my reach will not exceed these connections here, this centralizing of memory in organizational experience begs the question of whether memories serve as the touchstone of organizational reality. The host of influential organizational scholarship rooting identity and strategy—amongst the most populous concepts investigated by the two branches of organizational scholars (organizational theory and strategy—Hatch & Schultz, 2017; Ravasi et al., 2019; Suddaby et al., 2010, 2016)—in mnemonic processes suggests that what organizations remember, forget, and/or represent has an outsized influence on our organizations (Hoon et al., 2023). It may thus be worth exploring the utility of a novel theory—a mnemonic theory—focused squarely on explaining organizations (and those within them) through memory. While such a theory lies outside the scope of this chapter, it is my view that its potential demands attention.

Conclusion

During the fall of 2017, at the behest of my advisor, I reached out to a group of scholars operating in the organizational memory and identity spaces to organize a symposium titled "The Intersection of Memory and Identity" for the Academy of Management annual meeting. While merely reflecting a burgeoning scholarly interest of mine, its timing now appears prescient, as scholars—myself included—have increasingly sought to explain the connections between these two constructs in the proceeding years. In this chapter I have sought to position them processually, arguing for an amendment to our definition of organizational identity to better reflect what it appears to be: the distillation of organizational memory into labels and meanings. I hope this alteration encourages greater attention from a wider web of scholars on the intricate dynamics associated with the past and places greater theoretical attention on memories of that past as cornerstones of organizational life.

References

Alvesson, M., Ashcraft, K. L., & Thomas, R. (2008). Identity matters: Reflections on the construction of identity scholarship in organization studies. *Organization*, *15*(1), 5–28. https://doi.org/10.1177/1350508407084426

Anteby, M., & Molnar, V. (2012). Collective memory meets organizational identity: Remembering to forget in a firm's rhetorical history. *Academy of Management Journal*, *55*(3), 515–540. https://doi.org/10.5465/amj.2010.0245

Ashforth, B. E., & Reingen, P. H. (2014). Functions of dysfunction: Managing the dynamics of an organizational duality in a natural food cooperative. *Administrative Science Quarterly*, *59*(3), 474–516

Ashforth, B. E., Schinoff, B. S., & Brickson, S. L. (2020). "My company is friendly," "Mine's a rebel": Anthropomorphism and shifting organizational identity from "what" to "who." *Academy of Management Review*, *45*(1), 29–57. https://doi.org/10.5465/amr.2016.0496

Ashforth, B. E., Schinoff, B. S., & Rogers, K. M. (2016). "I identify with her," "I identify with him": Unpacking the dynamics of personal identification in organizations. *Academy of Management Review*, *41*(1), 28–60. https://doi.org/10.5465/amr.2014.0033

Assmann, J. (2011). *Cultural memory and early civilization: Writing, remembrance, and political imagination*. Cambridge University Press. https://doi.org/10.1017/CBO9780511996306

Bartunek, J. M., Rousseau, D. M., Rudolph, J. W., & DePalma, J. A. (2006). On the receiving end: Sensemaking, emotion, and assessments of an organizational change initiated by others. *The Journal of Applied Behavioral Science*, *42*, 182–206. https://doi.org/10.1177/0021886305285455

Basque, J., & Langley, A. (2018). Invoking Alphonse: The founder figure as a historical resource for organizational identity work. *Organization Studies*, *39*(12), 1685–1708. https://doi.org/10.1177/0170840618789211

Battilana, J., Besharov, M., & Mitzinneck, B. (2017). On hybrids and hybrid organizing: A review and roadmap for future research. In R. Greenwood, C. Oliver, T. B. Lawrence, & R. E. Meyer (Eds.), *The Sage handbook of organizational institutionalism* (2nd ed., pp. 133–169). Sage. https://doi.org/10.4135/9781446280669.n6

Battilana, J., & Dorado, S. (2010). Building sustainable hybrid organizations: The case of commercial microfinance organizations. *Academy of Management Journal, 53*(6), 1419–1440. https://doi.org/10.5465/amj.2010.57318391

Besharov, M. L. (2014). The relational ecology of identification: How organizational identification emerges when individuals hold divergent values. *Academy of Management Journal, 57*(5), 1485–1512. https://doi.org/10.5465/amj.2011.0761

Booth, C., Clark, P., Delahaye, A., Procter, S., & Rowlinson, M. (2007). Accounting for the dark side of corporate history: Organizational culture perspectives and the Bertelsmann case. *Critical Perspectives on Accounting, 18*(6), 625–644. https://doi.org/10.1016/j.cpa.2007.03.012

Brickson, S. L. (2005). Organizational identity orientation: Forging a link between organizational identity and organizations' relations with stakeholders. *Administrative Science Quarterly, 50*(4), 576–609. https://doi.org/10.2189/asqu.50.4.576

Cannon, S. M., & Kreutzer, K. (2018). Mission accomplished? Organizational identity work in response to mission success. *Human Relations, 71*(9), 1234–1263. https://doi.org/10.1177/0018726717741677

Caprar, D. V., Walker, B. W., & Ashforth, B. E. (2022). The dark side of strong identification in organizations: A conceptual review. *The Academy of Management Annals, 16*(2), 759–805. https://doi.org/10.5465/annals.2020.0338

Casey, A. (2019). *Organizational identity and memory: A multidisciplinary approach*. Routledge. https://doi.org/10.4324/9781315669786

Chiles, T. H., Meyer, A. D., & Hench, T. J. (2004). Organizational emergence: The origin and transformation of Branson, Missouri's musical theaters. *Organization Science, 15*(5), 499–519. https://doi.org/10.1287/orsc.1040.0095

Chreim, S. (2005). The continuity–change duality in narrative texts of organizational identity. *Journal of Management Studies, 42*(3), 567–593. https://doi.org/10.1111/j.1467-6486.2005.00509.x

Connerton, P. (1989). *How societies remember*. Cambridge University Press. https://doi.org/10.1017/CBO9780511628061

Connerton, P. (2009). *How modernity forgets*. Cambridge University Press. https://doi.org/10.1017/CBO9780511627187

Coraiola, D. M., & Derry, R. (2020). Remembering to forget: The historic irresponsibility of US Big Tobacco. *Journal of Business Ethics, 166*(2), 233–252. https://doi.org/10.1007/s10551-019-04323-4

Coraiola, D. M., Foster, W. M., Mena, S., Foroughi, H., & Rintamäki, J. (2023). Ecologies of memories: Memory work within and between organizations and communities. *The Academy of Management Annals, 17*(1), 373–404. https://doi.org/10.1007/s10551-019-04323-8

Corley, K. G., & Gioia, D. A. (2004). Identity ambiguity and change in the wake of a corporate spin-off. *Administrative Science Quarterly, 49*(2), 173–208. https://doi.org/10.2307/4131471

Crawford, B., Coraiola, D. M., & Dacin, M. T. (2022). Painful memories as mnemonic resources: Grand Canyon Dories and the protection of place. *Strategic Organization, 20*(1), 51–79. https://doi.org/10.1177/1476127020981353

Cutcher, L., Dale, K., & Tyler, M. (2019). 'Remembering as forgetting': Organizational commemoration as a politics of recognition. *Organization Studies, 40*(2), 267–290. https://doi.org/10.1177/0170840617727776

Dacin, M. T., Munir, K., & Tracey, P. (2010). Formal dining at Cambridge colleges: Linking ritual performance and institutional maintenance. *Academy of Management Journal, 53*(6), 1393–1418. https://doi.org/10.5465/amj.2010.57318388

Do, B., & Lyle, M. C. B. (2022). Memory-based change management: Using the past to guide the future. *Organizational Psychology Review, 12*(3), 306–331. https://doi.org/10.1177/20413866221093512

Do, B., Lyle, M. C. B., & Walsh, I. J. (2019). Driving down memory lane: The influence of memories in a community following organizational demise. *Organization Studies, 40*(9), 1307–1329. https://doi.org/10.1177/0170840618765573

Dutton, J. E., & Dukerich, J. M. (1991). Keeping an eye on the mirror: Image and identity in organizational adaptation. *Academy of Management Journal*, *34*(3), 517–554. https://doi.org/10.2307/256405

Eury, J. L., Kreiner, G. E., Treviño, L. K., & Gioia, D. A. (2018). The past is not dead: Legacy identification and alumni ambivalence in the wake of the Sandusky scandal at Penn State. *Academy of Management Journal*, *61*(3), 826–856. https://doi.org/10.5465/amj.2015.0534

Farchi, T., Dopson, S., & Ferlie, E. (2023). Do we still need professional boundaries? The multiple influences of boundaries on interprofessional collaboration. *Organization Studies*, *44*, 277–298. https://doi.org/10.1177/01708406221074146

Fleming, C. M. (2012). White cruelty or Republican sins? Competing frames of stigma reversal in French commemorations of slavery. In M. Lamont & N. Mizrachi (Eds.), *Responses to stigmatization in comparative perspective* (pp. 488–505). Routledge.

Foroughi, H. (2020). Collective memories as a vehicle of fantasy and identification: Founding stories retold. *Organization Studies*, *41*(10), 1347–1367. https://doi.org/10.1177/0170840619844286

Foroughi, H., & Al-Amoudi, I. (2020). Collective forgetting in a changing organization: When memories become unusable and uprooted. *Organization Studies*, *41*(4), 449–470. https://doi.org/10.1177/0170840619830130

Foroughi, H., Coraiola, D. M., Rintamäki, J., Mena, S., & Foster, W. M. (2020). Organizational memory studies. *Organization Studies*, *41*(12), 1725–1748. https://doi.org/10.1177/0170840620974338

Foster, W. M., Suddaby, R., Minkus, A., & Wiebe, E. (2011). History as social memory assets: The example of Tim Hortons. *Management & Organizational History*, *6*(1), 101–120. https://doi.org/10.1177/1744935910387027

Gioia, D. A., & Chittipeddi, K. (1991). Sensemaking and sensegiving in strategic change initiation. *Strategic Management Journal*, *12*(6), 433–448. https://doi.org/10.1002/smj.4250120604

Gioia, D. A., Patvardhan, S. D., Hamilton, A. L., & Corley, K. G. (2013). Organizational identity formation and change. *The Academy of Management Annals*, *7*(1), 123–193. https://doi.org/10.5465/19416520.2013.762225

Gioia, D. A., Schultz, M., & Corley, K. G. (2000). Organizational identity, image, and adaptive instability. *Academy of Management Review*, *25*(1), 63–81. https://doi.org/10.2307/259263

Gioia, D. A., & Thomas, J. B. (1996). Identity, image, and issue interpretation: Sensemaking during strategic change in academia. *Administrative Science Quarterly*, *41*, 370–403. https://doi.org/10.2307/2393936

Greve, H. R., & Rao, H. (2014). History and the present: Institutional legacies in communities of organizations. *Research in Organizational Behavior*, *34*, 27–41. https://doi.org/10.1016/j.riob.2014.09.002

Halbwachs, M. (1950). *The collective memory*. Presses Universitaires de France.

Hatch, M. J., & Schultz, M. (2002). The dynamics of organizational identity. *Human Relations*, *55*(8), 989–1018. https://doi.org/10.1177/0018726702055008181

Hatch, M. J., & Schultz, M. (2017). Toward a theory of using history authentically: Historicizing in the Carlsberg Group. *Administrative Science Quarterly*, *62*(4), 657–697. https://doi.org/10.1177/0001839217692535

Hernes, T. (2007). *Understanding organization as process: Theory for a tangled world*. Routledge. https://doi.org/10.4324/9780203934524

Hernes, T., & Schultz, M. (2020). Translating the distant into the present: How actors address distant past and future events through situated activity. *Organization Theory*, *1*(1). https://doi.org/10.1177/2631787719900999

Hoon, C., Brinkmann, J., & Baluch, A. M. (2023). Narrative memory work of employees in family businesses: How founding stories shape organizational identification. *Family Business Review*, *36*(1), 37–62. https://doi.org/10.1177/08944865231159475

Howard-Grenville, J., Metzger, M. L., & Meyer, A. D. (2013). Rekindling the flame: Processes of identity resurrection. *Academy of Management Journal*, *56*(1), 113–136. https://doi.org/10.5465/amj.2010.0778

Jones, C., Lee, J. Y., & Lee, T. (2019). Institutionalizing place: Materiality and meaning in Boston's North End. In P. Haack, J. Sieweke, & L. Wessel (Eds.), *Microfoundations of* institutions (pp. 211–239). Emerald. https://doi.org/10.1108/S0733-558X2019000065B016

Kreiner, G. E., Hollensbe, E., Sheep, M. L., Smith, B. R., & Kataria, N. (2015). Elasticity and the dialectic tensions of organizational identity: How can we hold together while we are pulling apart? *Academy of Management Journal, 58*(4), 981–1011. https://doi.org/10.5465/amj.2012.0462

Lawrence, T. B., & Phillips, N. (2019). *Constructing organizational life: How social-symbolic work shapes selves, organizations, and institutions.* Oxford University Press. https://doi.org/10.1093/oso/9780198840022.001.0001

Lowenthal, D. (1985). *The past is a foreign country.* Cambridge University Press.

Lubinski, C. (2018). From 'history as told' to 'history as experienced': Contextualizing the uses of the past. *Organization Studies, 39*, 1785–1809. https://doi.org/10.1177/0170840618800116

Lyle, M. C. B., Eckardt, R., Corley, K. G., & Lepak, D. (2023). Gravity's pull: The identity related motives and outcomes of hiring stars. *Human Resource Management Review, 33*(2), 100932. https://doi.org/10.1016/j.hrmr.2022.100932

Lyle, M. C. B., Hockensmith, A. S., & Cocieru, O. C. (2024). Applying a wide-angle lens: De-centering work organizations in organization studies. *Strategic Organization, 22*(3), 609–619. https://doi.org/10.1177/14761270231156110

Lyle, M. C. B., Hockensmith, A. S., & Walsh, I. J. (2024). Up in smoke? The lingering influence of history on community identity dynamics. *Strategic Organization, 22*(4), 825–851. https://doi.org/10.1177/14761270231169103

Lyle, M. C. B., Walsh, I. J., & Coraiola, D. M. (2022). What is NORML? Sedimented meanings in ambiguous organizational identities. *Organization Studies, 43*(12), 1991–2012. https://doi.org/10.1177/01708406211057725

Mantere, S. (2013). What is organizational strategy? A language-based view. *Journal of Management Studies, 50*(8), 1408–1426. https://doi.org/10.1111/joms.12048

Mantere, S., Schildt, H. A., & Sillince, J. A. (2012). Reversal of strategic change. *Academy of Management Journal, 55*(1), 172–196. https://doi.org/10.5465/amj.2008.0045

Mena, S., Rintamäki, J., Fleming, P., & Spicer, A. (2016). On the forgetting of corporate irresponsibility. *Academy of Management Review, 41*(4), 720–738. https://doi.org/10.5465/amr.2014.0208

Olick, J. K. (1999). Collective memory: The two cultures. *Sociological Theory, 17*(3), 333–348. https://doi.org/10.1111/0735-2751.00083

Parker, P. S. (2002). Negotiating identity in raced and gendered workplace interactions: The use of strategic communication by African American women senior executives within dominant culture organizations. *Communication Quarterly, 50*(3–4), 251–268. https://doi.org/10.1080/01463370209385663

Patvardhan, S. D., Gioia, D. A., & Hamilton, A. L. (2015). Weathering a meta-level identity crisis: Forging a coherent collective identity for an emerging field. *Academy of Management Journal, 58*(2), 405–435. https://doi.org/10.5465/amj.2012.1049

Pratt, M. G. (2000). The good, the bad, and the ambivalent: Managing identification among Amway distributors. *Administrative Science Quarterly, 45*(3), 456–493. https://doi.org/10.2307/2667106

Pratt, M. G., & Rosa, J. A. (2003). Transforming work-family conflict into commitment in network marketing organizations. *Academy of Management Journal, 46*(4), 395–418. https://doi.org/10.2307/30040635

Ravasi, D., Rindova, V., & Stigliani, I. (2019). The stuff of legend: History, memory, and the temporality of organizational identity construction. *Academy of Management Journal, 62*(5), 1523–1555. https://doi.org/10.5465/amj.2016.0505

Ravasi, D., & Schultz, M. (2006). Responding to organizational identity threats: Exploring the role of organizational culture. *Academy of Management Journal, 49*(3), 433–458. https://doi.org/10.5465/amj.2006.21794663

Rowlinson, M., Booth, C., Clark, P., Delahaye, A., & Procter, S. (2010). Social remembering and organizational memory. *Organization Studies*, *31*(1), 69–87. https://doi.org/10.1177/0170840609347056

Sasaki, I., & Ravasi, D. (2024). Historical consciousness and bounded imagination: How history inspires and shapes innovation in long-lived firms. *Academy of Management Discoveries*, *10*(1), 63–90. https://doi.org/10.5465/amd.2021.0184

Schultz, M., & Hernes, T. (2013). A temporal perspective on organizational identity. *Organization Science*, *24*(1), 1–21. https://doi.org/10.1287/orsc.1110.0731

Smith, W. K., & Besharov, M. L. (2019). Bowing before dual gods: How structured flexibility sustains organizational hybridity. *Administrative Science Quarterly*, *64*(1), 1–44. https://doi.org/10.1177/0001839217750826

Souza, A. S., Overkott, C., & Matyja, M. (2021). Categorical distinctiveness constrains the labeling benefit in visual working memory. *Journal of Memory and Language*, *119*, 104242. https://doi.org/10.1016/j.jml.2021.104242

Suddaby, R., & Foster, W. M. (2017). *History and organizational change*. Sage. https://doi.org/10.1177/0149206316675031

Suddaby, R., Foster, W. M., & Quinn Trank, C. (2010). Rhetorical history as a source of competitive advantage. In J. A. C. Baum & J. Lampel (Eds.), *The globalization of strategy research* (pp. 147–173). Emerald.

Suddaby, R., Foster, W. M., & Quinn Trank, C. (2016). Re-membering: Rhetorical history as identity work. In M. G. Pratt, M. Schultz, B. E. Ashforth, & D. Ravasi (Eds.), *The Oxford handbook of organizational identity* (pp. 297–316). Oxford University Press.

Suddaby, R., Israelsen, T., Mitchell, J. R., & Lim, D. S. (2023). Entrepreneurial visions as rhetorical history: A diegetic narrative model of stakeholder enrollment. *Academy of Management Review*, *48*(2), 220–243. https://doi.org/10.5465/amr.2020.0010

Suddaby, R., & Jaskiewicz, P. (2020). Managing traditions: A critical capability for family business success. *Family Business Review*, *33*(3), 234–243. https://doi.org/10.1177/0894486520942611

Szpunar, P. M., & Szpunar, K. K. (2016). Collective future thought: Concept, function, and implications for collective memory studies. *Memory Studies*, *9*(4), 376–389. https://doi.org/10.1177/1750698015615660

Trouillot, M. R. (2015). *Silencing the past: Power and the production of history*. Beacon Press.

Vinitzky-Seroussi, V. (2002). Commemorating a difficult past: Yitzhak Rabin's memorials. *American Sociological Review*, *67*(1), 30–51. https://doi.org/10.1177/000312240206700102

Wadhwani, R. D., Suddaby, R., Mordhorst, M., & Popp, A. (2018). History as organizing: Uses of the past in organization studies. *Organization Studies*, *39*(12), 1663–1683. https://doi.org/10.1177/0170840618814867

Wagner-Pacifici, R., & Schwartz, B. (1991). The Vietnam Veterans Memorial: Commemorating a difficult past. *American Journal of Sociology*, *97*(2), 376–420. https://doi.org/10.1086/229783

Walsh, I. J., & Bartunek, J. M. (2011). Cheating the fates: Organizational foundings in the wake of demise. *Academy of Management Journal*, *54*(5), 1017–1044. https://doi.org/10.5465/amj.2008.0658

Walsh, I. J., & Glynn, M. A. (2008). The way we were: Legacy organizational identity and the role of leadership. *Corporate Reputation Review*, *11*, 262–276. https://doi.org/10.1057/crr.2008.20

Ybema, S. (2004). Managerial postalgia: Projecting a golden future. *Journal of Managerial Psychology*, *19*(8), 825–841. https://doi.org/10.1108/02683940410568284

Ybema, S. (2014). The invention of transitions: History as a symbolic site for discursive struggles over organizational change. *Organization*, *21*(4), 495–513. https://doi.org/10.1177/1350508414527255

Zerubavel, E. (2003). Calendars and history: A comparative study of the social organization of national memory. In J. K. Olick (Ed.), *States of memory: Continuities, conflicts, and transformations in national retrospection* (pp. 315–337). Duke University Press. https://doi.org/10.1215/9780822384687-012

Zucker, L. G. (1988). *Institutional patterns and organizations: Culture and environment*. Ballinger.

Trevor Israelsen and Roy Suddaby
Chapter 3
Inheritance as an organizational purpose

Intergenerational transmission is a central theme in several major theories of organization. For example, intergenerational transmission has been theorized, variously, as a means of institutionalizing organizations (e.g., Ocasio, 2023; Sasaki et al., 2019; Zucker, 1977), fostering organizational culture (e.g., Harrison & Carroll, 1991; Hatch, 2004; Schein, 1983), constructing organizational identity (e.g., Joshi et al., 2010; Kreiner & Murphy, 2016; Schultz & Hernes, 2013), and perpetuating organizational values (e.g., Frake & Harmon, 2023; Jaskiewicz et al., 2015; Suddaby, Ng, et al., 2023).

While existing scholarship sees intergenerational transmission as a *means* of perpetuating organizational phenomena, we see that intergenerational transmission and inheritance can become *ends* in themselves against which organizations either flourish or flounder. That is, we observe that some organizations consider transmission and inheritance to be a *core organizational purpose.* In such cases, the idea of inheritance becomes a "vocabulary of motive" (Mills, 1940) for justifying the organization's existence (see, e.g., Suddaby, Manelli, et al., 2023).

Consider the following examples:

- The Buddy Holly Center, located in Lubbock, Texas, is dedicated to "preserving, collecting and promoting the legacy of Buddy Holly and the Music of Lubbock and West Texas" (Buddy Holly Center, 2024).
- When pressed to sell a family farm, its owners note that the "real purpose" of the farm is "to teach the kids how to work," to, thereby, perpetuate core family values (e.g., Gómez-Mejía et al., 2009).
- The stated purpose of the Hershey Trust Company (a fiduciary for the Hershey Company, The Milton Hershey School, Hershey Entertainment and Resorts, and other entities) is "to advance the legacy of Milton and Catherine Hershey in perpetuity through excellence in asset management and trust administration" (Hershey Trust Company, 2024).
- The Catechism of the Catholic Church (1997) states: "In order to preserve the Church in the purity of the faith handed on by the apostles, Christ who is the Truth willed to confer on her [the Church] a share in his own infallibility. By a 'supernatural sense of faith' the People of God, under the guidance of the Church's living Magisterium, 'unfailingly adheres to this faith'" (Para. 889).
- The Stonemason's Guild of St. Stephen traces its origins "back to the first 'Gild Moot' called by King Athelstan in 936 A.D. and much of the Guild structure, including some rules, are rooted, earlier still, in the Clodian Laws of 55 B.C. . . . The ancient, skilled techniques, often employing hand tools, remain central to our

teaching and practice. . . . Our unique history and culture is of great importance to us" (Stonemason's Guild, 2024).
- The stated purpose of the organization FamilySearch is to "inspire people everywhere to connect with their family—across generations," and the organization is "dedicated to preserving important family records and making them freely accessible online" (FamilySearch, 2024).

What each of these examples has in common is an idealized statement of organizational purpose premised on the perceived *intrinsic value* of inheritance. Such rhetoric construes inheritance as more than instrumental—as something bigger than a means for the accomplishment of other organizational objectives. Inheritance, we suggest, can be central to the core purpose of an organization. Indeed, inheritance is an implicit element of the organizational purpose rhetoric employed by a wide array of organizational forms including, for example, family-owned businesses, philanthropic foundations, museums, religious organizations, business trusts, crafts-based ventures, educational institutions, political regimes, indigenous communities, biographical organizations, and iconic corporations. Yet we know very little about how inheritance operates as a justification for an organization's existence.

In this chapter, we explore how, when, and with what effects organizations construe inheritance as organizational purpose. We conceptualize inheritance as a process of transmitting and managing residuals (including assets, values, and power) across generations. In this chapter, we use the term *residual* to refer generally to that which lingers or remains across generations. Yet, we also observe that this 'forward reach' through time (i.e., the transmission of residuals from past to present) is enabled in critical ways by the 'backward reach' of actors who retrospectively construct and reconstruct the world in the ongoing present (i.e., historical consciousness of the past in the present). We use the term *historical conflation* to explain these multitemporal dynamics wherein inheritance is constituted as a justification for an organization's existence. Specifically, our concept of historical conflation helps to explain how diverse actors—who are distributed across wide spans of space and time—see themselves as part of something bigger than their own lives and interests, such that they work to preserve, pass down, and receive across generations. Before introducing the concept of historical conflation, however, it is necessary to first review prior research on the phenomena of intergenerational transmission and inheritance.

Inheritance

Inheritance is a prominent topic of study in disciplines such as law (Busch et al., 2022; Cunliffe & Erreygers, 2013; Friedman, 2009; Kendrick, 2011; Miller & McNamee, 1998; Mumford, 2007), philosophy (e.g., Brassington, 2019; de Tocqueville, 1835/1945; Halliday, 2018; Mill, 1848/1961; Pedersen & Bøyum, 2020), anthropology (Boyd & Richerson, 2005; Goody, 1976; Hann, 2008; Ingold, 2016; Kroeber, 1962), economics (Braun & Stuhler, 2018; Erreygers & Vandevelde, 1997; Piketty & Saez, 2013), sociology (Beckert, 2007, 2008; Bourdieu, 1998; Clignet et al., 2018; Collier, 1948; Glass et al., 1986; McNamee & Miller, 1989; Weber, 2019), gerontology (Angel & Mudrazija, 2011; Kohli, 2004), and evolutionary biology (Lewens, 2015; Mendel, 1865/2013; Pontarotti, 2015; Sukhoverkhov & Gontier, 2021), but is a much less prominent concept in organizational theory (e.g., Vermeulen, 2018). Across such disciplines, the word *inheritance* has two interrelated meanings: First, it refers to the present residuals left behind by past generations. Such residuals can take several different forms ranging, for example, from property, assets, and status to values, traits, and identities. Second, the term refers to the *processes* through which such residuals are transmitted and managed from one generation to the next. In this chapter, as noted, we define inheritance as a process of transmitting and managing residuals (including assets, values, and power) across generations.

Similar concepts

Inheritance is related to other concepts such as tradition, legacy, lineage, and heritage. The term *tradition* is used to connote how practices (sometimes labeled "traditia") are carried forward across generations through processes (sometimes labeled "tradere") and by actors with vested interests in such practices (sometimes labeled "custodians") (e.g., Dacin et al., 2019; Shils, 1981; Suddaby & Jaskiewicz, 2020). The term *legacy* is used to connote how past actors (sometimes labeled "legators," "legacy senders," or "organizational ghosts") are carried forward and remembered by subsequent actors (sometimes labeled "legatees" or "legacy receivers") (e.g., Bednar & Brown, 2023; Colquitt et al., 2023; Radu-Lefebvre et al., 2024).

Like the concepts of tradition and legacy, the term *inheritance* refers to processes through which residuals left behind by past generations are transmitted to subsequent generations. Indeed, legacy is sometimes understood as a form of inheritance that is associated with a specific individual or collective actor from the past. Tradition is likewise understood as a form of inheritance, but one whose point of origin has been forgotten or de-emphasized. Together, legacy and tradition comprise common dynamics involved in the transmission and management of residuals from past generations.

The concept of *heritage* shares with inheritance a common etymology (along with concepts such as hereditary, heritability, and heir). These concepts all locate in the present the act of receiving some residual from the past. The concept of heritage refers to a specific way in which residuals left behind from past generations are selected and specifically designated for preservation by a social entity—often by a society or culture (e.g., Caust & Vecco, 2017).

The concept of *lineage* typically refers to the specific institutional vehicle of hereditary (often biological, family) relations through which intergenerational transmission and inheritance can occur (Durkheim, 1921). However, inheritance is not exclusively a family matter (Vermeulen, 2018), is not limited to sociobiological considerations (Lewens, 2015), and, as we argue in this chapter, is often nested and distributed across a variety of different forms of economic, social, and political organization.

Inheritance is, thus, a term that denotes how present actors work to manage their relationship with the residuals left behind from past generations after they are gone. It is, thus, important to note that the concept of inheritance used in this chapter assigns primary agency in the transmission of such residuals to actors in the present. Indeed, we argue using the concept of "historical conflation" that inheritance involves a type of perdurance that "lies not in the transmission, across generations, of an already constructed world but in the continual bringing forth, or production, of a world that—from generation to generation—is ever in formation" (Ingold, 2022, p. S37).[1] In the remainder of this chapter, we introduce the concept of historical conflation and explain how it operates as an organizational purpose that involves managing residuals (such as assets, values, and power) across generations. We first describe the historical origins of inheritance as an organizational purpose.

The historical origins of inheritance as organizational purpose

The notion of inheritance—as the management of residuals left behind by past generations—is a very old one. Inheritance appears in ancient texts such as *The Epic of Gilgamesh* (which mentions brothers dividing an inheritance) or *The Iliad* and *The Odyssey* (which focus on the heritability of land, wealth, and reputation within family lineage). Inheritance and related concepts also appear in sacred texts. The Hebrew Bible uses the concept of "birthright" to connote both a material transmission from parent to child and a sign of a covenant (or spiritual bequeathment) between G-d and the descendants of Abraham. The Four Books of Confucianism emphasize the importance of intergenerational filial piety to parents, elders, and ancestors. The Daozang

---

[1] Ingold (2022) adopts a different view of inheritance, wherein the term connotes that "whatever is inherited is received essentially un-changed and intact, as an undivided totality" (p. S34). The differences are threefold. First, whereas Ingold (2022) views inheritance as a sending-receiving *event*, we theorize inheritance as a more extended process that involves the transmission and management of residuals left behind by past generations. Second, whereas Ingold (2022) views inheritance as *perfect* transmission, in this chapter we instead introduce the concept of "historical conflation" to explain how the transmission associated with such residuals appears to be much more seamless (and effortless) than it actually is. Third, whereas Ingold (2022) is primarily concerned with "*ecological* inheritance," in this chapter we focus primarily on the social construction of inheritance as a human social-organizational process.

highlights the importance of transmitting Taoist teachings across generations from masters to disciples. The Hindu Dharmashastras include detailed rules regarding the succession and distribution of property. The New Testament uses the concept of inheritance to both teach about the importance of forgiveness (e.g., the prodigal son) and to describe the ultimate rewards of righteousness (e.g., 'inheriting' eternal life). The Quran also contains detailed instructions regarding the rights of heirs and the importance of the equitable distribution of the estates of the deceased.

As is obvious from the range of different uses and points of emphasis, the notion of inheritance is a flexible concept that can be applied to explain the perdurance of various types of phenomena over time. Indeed, this very semantic flexibility provided by the concept of inheritance was helpful in the conceptual formulation and invention of modern legal institutions and organizational forms. That is, the ancient idea of inheritance provided a conceptual architecture through which legal entities such as trusts, foundations, and ultimately joint stock companies were invented as institutions that can persist beyond the involvement or lifetimes of their founders.

In *Power and the Structure of Society*, Coleman (1974) explained how our modern notions of trusts and corporations originated in legal disputes surrounding property ownership in churches. It was clear to legal scholars that priests did not own all of the land or assets of the church; they were only stewards of such assets. And yet, the law required an owner. The solution was to

> declare the saint for whom the church was named as the owner. Thus many centuries after their deaths, St. Peter and St. Paul and St. James became extensive property owners. The law had found a solution. When property associated with St. Paul's church was transferred, the seller would be St. Paul, while the guardian of St. Paul's property, who acted to protect his interests, was the priest currently installed in St. Paul's church. (p. 17)

In this way, the legal doctrine of "the trust" emerged that would (in the context of religious organizations) allow for a distinction between owners (e.g., grantors), stewards (e.g., trustees), and the congregation (e.g., beneficiaries). The original application of this doctrine was to codify a social structure wherein predecessors could transmit assets to their heirs in a manner that could be recognized as legally binding (e.g., Bove & Langa, 2021). Over time, this same logic of inheritance was applied beyond families and churches to other entities such as hospitals and universities (e.g., Friedman, 2009).

Inheritance has long been recognized as something bigger than the intergenerational perpetuation of capital. It was obvious, for example, in the perpetuation of property by medieval churches that the priest was not the authority per se but was standing in a chain of priesthood that was transmitted intergenerationally. This chain of authority was bigger than the priest and, perhaps because of the practices of celibacy within the Christian church, bigger also than the lineage of any specific family.

Ideas about the inheritance of authority were also at the very fabric of medieval political systems. Kings, for example, maintained legitimacy by virtue of a noble lineage that bestowed a 'divine right' to act as sovereign authorities over their kingdoms

(Weber, 2019). In some cases, however, this legitimacy came into question—leading to early theorization regarding the notion of inheritance (Coleman, 1974). When kings were too young, too old, or otherwise incapable of making authoritative decisions, it became important to differentiate between the king as an individual and the king as an instantiation of a sovereign lineage. The resulting legal theory of the "corporate sole" held that political inheritance had a perdurance that extended some degrees beyond the flesh-and-blood person of the monarch. As Coleman (1974) wrote:

> The king had two bodies, the physical body and the body politic. The 'body politic,' who . . . knew no minority, no infirmity, no old age, knew neither birth nor death . . . [with] an explicit separation of 'The Crown' from the particular king who was the current possessor of the Crown . . . a separation of the idea of the monarchy from the particular monarch. (pp. 19–20)

In such examples, the notion of inheritance takes the form of legacy (e.g., St. Peter) or tradition (e.g., the body politic), which provide the conceptual infrastructure for institutions (e.g., the church, the monarchy). Over the centuries, the underlying notion of inheritance (as codified in the institutions of priesthood, monarchy, and trusts) evolved and was manifest in different forms to include philanthropic foundations, guilds, etc. More recently, patterns of inheritance have been adapted for use within more formal, bureaucratic systems (e.g., Weber, 2019), such as joint stock companies and modern corporations.

Today, inheritance is often commingled with other purposes. Yet it also retains a sense of independent value that asserts itself in organizational debates about purpose. Such debates occur, for example, in organizations such as multigenerational family businesses (e.g., inheritance and profit), trusts (e.g., inheritance and wealth preservation), foundations (e.g., inheritance and philanthropy), family offices (e.g., inheritance and asset management), monarchies (e.g., inheritance and power), churches (e.g., inheritance and salvation), museums (e.g., inheritance and knowledge), and other organizations. While such organizations clearly negotiate various vocabularies of motive (Mills, 1940), they also construe residuals left behind by past generations as having intrinsic value—thereby prizing the mechanics of intergenerational transmission perhaps, at times, beyond even the technical requirements of the task at hand (e.g., Selznick, 2011). As noted, we seek to explain how this occurs: how diverse actors—who are distributed across wide spans of space and time—come to see themselves as part of something bigger than their own lives and interests, such that they work to preserve, pass down, and receive across generations.

The role of historical conflation in inheritance

One of the core challenges involved in studying inheritance as an organizational purpose is that residuals from past generations are often nested and distributed across a variety of different entities and organizations in the present. Trusts, for example, are organizations. But they are not organizations in the way that we are used to thinking about organizations as discrete, bounded, formal legal entities—such as corporations, associations, or clubs. They are organizations that bring together different entities (individuals or organizations) in the roles of grantor, trustee, and beneficiary (Bove & Langa, 2021). Inheritance brings together and compresses the interests of multiple interfacing entities—weaving a fabric across both time and space.

Inheritance involves weaving individual stories that are distributed over wide spans of time into a tapestry that blends lives and values together back across generations. In order to observe and study inheritance as an organizational purpose, we first need a concept that can explain how diverse actors—who are distributed across wide spans of space and time—see themselves as part of something bigger than their own lives and interests, such that they work to preserve, pass down, and receive across generations. We use the term *historical conflation* to explain how this occurs.

Historical conflation involves the use of figurative language (such as synecdoche and metonymy)[2] to blend objects of discourse together. The Cambridge Dictionary (2024) defines conflation as "the act or process of combining two or more separate things into one whole, especially pieces of text or ideas." To conflate means to blend or fuse to form a composite. In its prevailing colloquial usage, conflation is typically seen as a fallacy that occurs when cognitive biases cloud the exercise of better judgment.

However, in this chapter, we use the term *historical conflation* in a specific technical sense where conflation is not a priori negative and can be generative—even a force for good in the world. We thus use the label historical conflation in a value-neutral sense to denote a symbolic process of weaving the identities and motives of different entities together to comprise a conceptual-institutional system. What the notion of historical conflation provides to our understanding of inheritance is a conceptual architecture that explains how actors and entities who are distributed across wide spans of historical time see themselves as being bound together. As a practice, historical conflation provides grounds upon which present actors make claims on the residuals that are left behind after mortal lives. That is, historical conflation provides a sociocognitive link that orients individual thought and action toward entities in the distant past and future.

---

[2] Synecdoche is a figure of speech in which a part is made to represent the whole or vice versa. Metonymy, by contrast, is a figure of speech that substitutes the name of one thing for that of another with which is it associated.

While historical conflation is an abstract concept, organizations provide concrete and often taken-for-granted vocabularies for rationalizing the process of conflation. Trusts, for example, provide a legal vocabulary for conflating the motives of grantors, trustees, and beneficiaries. Family businesses, similarly, operate on the conflation of motive and identity between founders and their successors. Private philanthropic foundations provide a language that rationalizes synecdoche between philanthropists and the social entity of the foundation. Biographical museums (such as presidential libraries, celebrity museums, etc.) also act as institutional frameworks for stretching a legacy through time. Perhaps the most extreme form of conflation is that which occurs within a political dynasty—where disparate elements of a political regime are routinely described as if they were acts of a sovereign ruler.

In this way, historical conflation is a sociocognitive structure that binds actors of different generations together to carry forward the residuals left behind by generations distributed over disparate times and contexts. We now explore how organizations provide vocabularies of historical conflation for transmitting and managing three illustrative types of present residuals left behind by past generations: (1) assets, (2) values, and (3) power.

Inheritance and the conflation of assets

Assets are a common type of residual left behind by past generations. Assets that are subject to transmission and inheritance can take a number of different forms. These include financial assets such as cash, stocks, and bonds; real assets such as land, buildings, and commodities; and intangibles such as intellectual property and brand equity.

The inheritance of assets often takes the form of legacy, wherein an identifiable legator is understood to transmit assets to legatees who are entrusted with their ownership or control. The means of this entrustment vary depending on the type of organization—including family lineage, trusts, foundations, and corporations—through which the transmission is facilitated. Because such entities are often nested together in processes of inheritance, it is important to define the respective vocabularies through which they provide a legally and pragmatically acceptable justification for the transmission of assets across generations. Only by doing so can their complex, nested interactions be adequately understood.

The institution of family lineage provides one such vocabulary for conflating entities of different generations. Family lineage is a set of sociobiological relations that extends across generations to comprise descent from a common ancestry (Durkheim, 1921). Family lineage is among the most ancient of institutions and is often understood as the primary vehicle through which societies and social structures reproduce themselves across generations (Mead, 1934/2015; Zimmerman, 2023). Families reproduce society both biologically through procreation and also culturally through early childhood processes of socialization. Despite this, we often forget that the notion of "reproduction" in family lineage is itself a figure of speech.

In his 2012 book *Far from the Tree: Parents, Children and the Search for Identity*, Andrew Solomon argues that narratives of intergenerational family continuity are sometimes veiled attempts to immortalize or perpetuate personal identity.

> There is no such thing as reproduction. When two people decide to have a baby, they engage in an act of production, and the widespread use of the word reproduction for this activity, with its implication that two people are but braiding themselves together, is at best a euphemism to comfort prospective parents before they get in over their heads. In the subconscious fantasies that make conception look so alluring, it is often ourselves that we would like to see live forever, not someone with a personality of his own. (Solomon, 2012, p. 1)

The notion of family lineage is not only a biological fact but also a deeply institutionalized vocabulary for conflating the identities of parents and children across successive generations.

The vocabulary of family lineage is so effective that most legal systems around the world are built around the concept of family lineage as the default means of distributing assets across generations (Beckert, 2007). As previously noted, in some cultures, such as those influenced by feudal or tribal systems, inheritance rights based on lineage are deeply embedded in traditional customs and laws (Beckert, 2008). Despite this, modern legal systems also provide mechanisms for individuals to determine the distribution of their assets through wills, trusts, and other estate planning tools, allowing them to deviate from strict familial inheritance patterns if they choose to do so (Friedman, 2009).

The rules through which entities of different generations are conflated differ slightly in the context of a trust as compared to the context of family lineage. The defining characteristic of a trust is the organization of assets between grantors, trustees, and beneficiaries. Grantors, trustees, and beneficiaries may be distributed over vast spans of space and time (Bove & Langa, 2021). This is most likely when trusts take the form of irrevocable trusts and testamentary trusts, which, unlike living trusts or revocable grantor trusts, externalize assets beyond the direct control of individuals and often across generations (Bove & Langa, 2021). In this way, trusts bring a defined assemblage of people together in an organized mobilization of assets over time and space.

What is particularly interesting about the vocabulary of grantor, trustee, and beneficiary is the flexibility it provides in the conflation of entities and motives in the management of assets. Grantors, trustees, and beneficiaries can be individuals, but they can also be families (either conjugal or lineal). Furthermore, the language of grantor, trustee, and beneficiary can be used to bring together organizations—and sometimes very large organizations—as owners or controllers of assets. So, for example, American chocolatier Milton Hershey established an irrevocable trust and, thereby, designated a board of trustees as owners of the controlling interests of the

Hershey Company, where a beneficiary of this arrangement was an orphanage. He described this arrangement by saying, "I have no heirs—that is, no children, so I have decided to make the orphan boys of America my heirs" (Young, 1923, p. 4).

We can all think of examples of cases where the vocabulary of grantors, trustees, and beneficiaries is, as in Hershey's case, intended as a force for good in the world. However, trusts—like other organizations—can also be used for less than noble purposes. During the Gilded Age in the United States, for example, trusts became a favored instrument for the monopolistic business practices of so-called "robber barons" (Beckert, 2007, 2008). It is for this reason that antimonopoly legislation in the United States carries the label "anti-trust laws" (Clignet et al., 2018).

Despite this, many trusts retain freedoms that more formal organizations (such as corporations) do not have. While regulations vary, some trusts can be established simply by the signature of a single individual (sometimes even without witnesses or notaries). Many trusts are not required to be legally registered and are often not required to file reports to regulators (e.g., Bove & Langa, 2021).

Philanthropic foundations provide an additional vocabulary, alongside family lineage or trusts, for conflating entities, assets, and systems and stretching these over extended periods of time. The concept of the foundation was invented as a means of perpetuating organization beyond its founder. In the late 14th century, the English word *foundation* simply meant "that which is founded" and was applied to entities such as colleges or hospitals that had financial endowments to support them (Online Etymology Dictionary, 2024). It was only in the 15th century that the term was used to refer specifically to benevolent or charitable purposes.

Today, the term philanthropic foundation is used to describe a formal organization that is legally registered for charitable purposes and is supported by assets provided by its founder and sometimes others (Silk & Lintott, 2011). In this way, foundations provide a vocabulary and legal instrument for conflating a founder with his or her assets and extending this relationship through time beyond the founder's lifetime (Manelli et al., 2023). This process of inheritance involved in philanthropic foundations is often more formalized than the transmission of assets through family lineages or trusts (e.g., Silk & Lintott, 2011). Despite this, the intergenerational transmission of assets through philanthropic foundations is not as heavily regulated as corporations.

Corporations can adopt inheritance as an organizational purpose. Indeed, the legal entity of the corporation was invented with the express purpose of perpetuating the organization beyond the lifetime of its founders (Coleman, 1974). This process is illustrated by family-owned corporations. The ownership and control of family-owned businesses are regularly transmitted to successors within owning families across two or three generations. Some families are even able to own and control businesses for hundreds of years. Because such failures of intergenerational transmission are a common reason for the failure of businesses, intergenerational succession within families is an important strategic consideration within family-owned firms (e.g., Miller et al., 2003; Suddaby & Jaskiewicz, 2020). Like the concept of family lineage, the concept of intrafamily succession provides a vocabulary that rationalizes the conflation of successive generations within a family.

A family office is "an organization that is dedicated to providing tailored and holistic service to respond to [a] family's needs, in order to maintain transgenerational control over the financial, human, and socioemotional wealth of the family" (De Massis et al., 2021, p. 352). Family offices are, perhaps, the latest arrival on the scene of organizational forms dedicated specifically to the management of asset inheritance (e.g., Rivo-López et al., 2017). Not surprisingly, given this recency, family offices have yet to establish an overarching vocabulary for legitimating the intergenerational transmission of assets. Despite this, family offices bring together experts in the management and control of vast amounts of wealth. George Marcus (1992) uses the term *surrogate* to refer to individuals or entities (such as family offices) that act as proxies or substitutes for the direct management of wealth by family members within a wealthy business dynasty across generations. He writes that such surrogates "have both a sociological reality for family members and a totally separate, but parallel, technical reality for specialists, particularly within the legal system"; across generations, this surrogate comes to be viewed by family members "as a monolithic legacy which controls extended family relationships more than it is controlled by them" (Marcus, 1992, p. 25). The metaphor of surrogacy may, thus, provide an emergent vocabulary of historical conflation for explaining the role that wealth management experts play in the intergenerational transmission of assets.

Inheritance and the conflation of values

The phenomenon of inheritance is not limited to the intergenerational transmission of assets. Some organizations are dedicated specifically to the perpetuation of specific values across generations in the form of tradition, heritage, or legacy. Religious organizations, for example, are theorized as a means of bringing people together as stewards of a chain of memory that reaches from the distant past into the present and future (Hervieu-Léger, 2000). In addition, many museums, arts organizations, heritage organizations, and craft-based organizations see their purpose as the preservation of values from the past.

One of the core challenges involved in the effort to transmit values over time is the tension that arises between values (as abstract ideals) and their carriers (as concrete, situated entities). Values are, by definition, bigger than their carriers and more broadly applicable than any specific situation or desirable world state (Kraatz et al., 2020). Selznick (1994), for example, worked to understand "the conditions and processes which frustrate ideals or instead give them life and hope" (p. x). This tension between values and their carriers is illustrated by the phenomenon in which elites within organizations work to co-opt values ("Bolshevism," "democratic grassroots," etc.) for purposes that seem, at times, distant from the idealized end states indicated by values themselves.

One way of transmitting values is by blurring the distinction between ideals and their human carriers. This can involve stretching individuals through time and space by conflating their actions (which are necessarily limited in consciousness, time, and virtue) with the broader motives and actions of institutions. Thus, Milton S. Hershey becomes a moral legacy—a representation of higher motives crystallized in organizations such as the Milton S. Hershey School, which as the beneficiary of the Hershey Trust (fiduciary of the chocolate firm, Hershey Company) uses the inherited wealth to educate orphans and needy children (D'Antonio, 2006). By so doing, the actions of many stakeholders over the decades are conflated with the actions of a hero who is infused with extra significance and meaning. In this manner, Milton Hershey becomes more than a natural person—he becomes a narrative character to whom values are ascribed and from whom inspiration is drawn for moral and ethical behavior in the present. The conflation of values is, thus, a practice that involves collapsing distinctions between unlimited values and their limited carriers.

Values can be transmitted in organizations by encapsulating them in individuals who serve as the characters (heroes and villains) of a tale of good and evil. Because values are, by definition, better than their carriers and bigger than specific situations, the narrative choice to cast limited individuals as representations of unlimited values requires substantial creativity and artistic license. Sometimes we have no better way of transporting values than by personifying them. And, within the Western literary canon, heroic protagonists are, almost invariably, superhuman (Campbell, 2008; Frazer, 1922; Frye, 2006). Such literary characters are prescient and hypermuscular and sometimes even cheat death. But flesh-and-blood persons depend heavily on others and have limited attention and mortality. In this sense, one risk involved in conflating individuals with broader institutions is that the values of entire institutions can be called into question simply by identifying the limitations of those characters with whom values are conflated.

As noted, values transcend specific situations. However, values must be carried out and transmitted in specific situations. This dualism means that situations must somehow be blurred with other past and future situations that can elevate human activity to a broader, transhistorical realm of metaphysical meaning. This is accomplished not only by collapsing distinctions between values and their carriers but also by the use of narratives to conflate events with other events. This involves "the conflation of time past and time present, [in which] the mere act of remembering is invested with the power to see and perhaps shape the future" (Ballenger, 1997, p. 790). Morality tales "take the form of a narrative conflation of various epochs . . . into a timeless continuum, thus undermining the belief in a linear developmental personal and historical narrative" (Beispiel, 2008, p. 3). The conflation of events involves temporal compression. Stories take values from the past and make them relevant in the present.

This enables the mobility of values over time—imposing the future on the past and vice versa.

In this way, the intergenerational transmission of values is often made possible through complex assemblages of stories set within an overarching frame narrative (e.g., Fletcher, 2021). This process of weaving stories together for the preservation and transmission of values is illustrated in the discourse of ancient civilizations ranging from Mesopotamia (e.g., 'Epic of Gilgamesh'), to India (e.g., the Vedas), to Palestine (e.g., the Bible), to Greece (e.g., the Iliad/Odyssey). A story told a single time to a passive audience is much less powerful than a chorus of voices, captivated by a story, that tells that story again and again to new audiences. This process of weaving stories together over time bundles stories together to enable organizations to extend and carry values through time.

Some organizations—including, for example, churches, mosques, synagogues, monasteries, temples, volunteer groups, interfaith organizations, museums, arts organizations, and social movements—provide a vocabulary for weaving stories, values, and their human carriers together over time. Sacred texts, for example, are typically organized around overarching epics that reveal an existential problem for humankind, such as sin, suffering, death, self-sufficiency, pride, or self-centeredness. The epics posit a metaphysical solution—salvation, nirvana, peace, submission, etc.—and thereby sacralize core values, such as mercy, humility, propriety, devotion, and connection. Sacred texts, thus, provide grounds for individuals to understand themselves within a broader cosmology that is inherited across generations—a process that is enabled by religious organizations.

Outside of the context of religious organizations, similar mechanisms of narrative conflation are used to carry values over time. It is often said, for example, that while the United States has a troubled past, the arc of American history bends toward freedom—meaning that stories used to describe American history are often characterized by an optimistic metanarrative focused on the gradual integration of an ever more diverse polyphony of voices who took up early American ideals of equality and appropriated these ideas to new circumstances, often despite fierce opposition from the original promoters of freedom (Foner, 1999). In this manner, organizations dedicated to civics education—including liberal arts universities—work to weave together historical narratives into assemblages that can not only neutralize value-based threats to national identity but also preserve and carry forward values in the real world.

The core point here is that values are bigger than their carriers, and yet the carriers play a critically important, albeit imperfect, role in giving life to (and/or frustrating) values. However, in order for values to be transmitted and carried forward through time, historically situated actors must find ways to carry transhistorical values. This can be accomplished through story bundles that provide accepted vocabularies for blending entities and events together within an overarching frame narrative. Thus, biographical organizations (such as biographical museums, libraries, or archives) whose purpose is to perpetuate the legacies of past political leaders, social activists, celebrities, or entrepreneurs utilize a vocabulary of historical conflation that infuses past heroes with surplus value and metaphysical content and, thereby, construe them as having a legacy of values that reaches down into the present.

Inheritance and the conflation of power

The central preoccupation of Max Weber's *Economy and Society* (1922/2019) was the underlying forms of power used by leaders to coordinate human action in society. The key challenge was how to make raw power seem legitimate and palatable. He argued that this occurs in three ways: charisma, bureaucracy, and tradition. Charisma is powerful but inherently unstable since it is held by flesh-and-blood persons within finite lifetimes. However, Weber theorized that the power of charismatic leaders can be routinized after their death. In his theorization, this routinization occurs either through formal organizations or through traditional authority (Weber, 2019). Formal organizations (bureaucracies) legitimize power through explicit rules. The legitimacy of traditional authority, by contrast, is "based on, and believed in, by virtue of the sanctity of long-established orders and ruling power that have existed 'time out of mind'" (Weber, 2019, p. 355).

Despite this, formal organizations do play a role in the intergenerational transmission of residuals—including the intergenerational transmission of power. One very effective way to legitimate power in the present is by weaving oneself into an already established tradition or legacy for which one acts as custodian or steward. Weber (2019, p. 227) alluded to this when he noted that in traditional authority, "rules which in fact are innovations can be legitimized only by the claim that they have been 'valid of yore,' but have only now been recognized by means of wisdom" (p. 227). In this sense, Weber (2019, p. 359) theorized that traditional authority was derived from ancient ideas about lineage and argued that such power is premised on a "superficial analogy to the household" (Weber, 2019, p. 229). Wielding such power in legitimate ways is premised on the ability to be "strictly bound by tradition" (Weber, 2019, p. 231). This is sometimes achieved through the idea of interpretive originalism—where stewards of organizations such as philanthropic foundations, trusts, or even political regimes legitimate decisions by interpreting 'the will of the founder.'

Monarchies are an extreme example of intergenerational power. Monarchies, and other elite dynasties, share some characteristics with other lineage-based forms of inheritance, only they reach more deeply into the fabric of the societies in which they operate. Whereas the core inheritance for most business-owning families is material assets, monarchies inherit not only wealth but also titles. Inherited monarchic lineage grants extreme political power. At their apex, monarchic dynasties were so powerful that they were used to not only command empires but also demarcate historical eras (e.g., the Ming dynasty). In this way, the term *dynasty* is itself a form of synecdoche in which a lineage is substituted for a political regime.

Today, elite family dynasties have a more complex path for achieving and maintaining power. If they live in nondemocratic societies, they can very well do so through traditional political channels, but even then, dynasts must often supplement their legitimacy through economic success. This is because dynastic power is often centrifugal—most descendants are forced toward the peripheries of traditional authority, and it takes enormous effort and social skill for such descendants to maintain access to the core of inherited power (Israelsen, 2023).

Family dynasties living in democratic societies must find other ways to establish and command power. They can do so through corporations. They can do so through philanthropy or celebrity. They can do so through political elections. Economic achievement is one way for elites to exhibit charisma and thereby reproduce authority across generations (de Pina-Cabral & De Lima, 2020). Even in the 21st century, the power of elite family dynasties remains unparalleled by any other status group in many parts of the world (Israelsen, 2023).

Conclusion

While we may often associate inheritance with the distant past, organizations dedicated to preserving some economic, cultural, and political inheritance remain important forces for good and bad in our time. Inheritance is a source of enormous challenges in our age of increasing inequalities. Yet inheritance also plays an important role in binding people together in intergenerational projects that existed before they were born and will, if they are good stewards, continue after they die. Inheritance provides a mechanism and process for the intergenerational transmission of legacies, traditions, and heritage and thereby helps to constitute the human condition as something that is shared beyond individual lives and goals.

In management studies, we have become accustomed to the notion that organizations resolve strategic questions using prospective discourse laden with future-oriented idioms. However, when an organization adopts the stewardship of residuals from past generations as its purpose, the retrospective notion of inheritance becomes the primary idiom used to justify strategic decisions within that organization. When organizations seek to justify innovation, they do so by construing it as consistent with some deeper, newfound understanding about the past.

Similarly, within such organizations, stakeholder commitment is typically established on the sanctity of age-old traditions or on the legacies of past heroes. Such commitment may, for example, involve a sense of belonging as "the visible expression of a lineage which the believer expressly lays claim to and which confers membership of a spiritual community that gathers past, present and future believers" (Hervieu-Léger, 2000, p. 81). Honoring the legacies of past heroes involves a similarly metaphysical extension of the mind beyond finite human lifespans to draw past individuals beyond their mortal lifespan to construe the legator as a proxy for the institution as a whole. In extreme cases, the virtue or charisma of a past leader is treated as an existential imperative for holding the very fabric of the institution together.

In this chapter, we have argued that the transmission and management of present residuals of past generations comprise a central purpose for many organizations around the world. We have introduced the notion of "historical conflation" as a concept that helps to explain how such organizations manage to bring together and compress entities across time and space into a narrativized tapestry that blends lives and values together across generations. Both concepts demand further refinement as we work toward a more general framework for understanding intergenerational transmission and inheritance in and by organizations.

References

Angel, J. L., & Mudrazija, S. (2011). Aging, inheritance, and gift-giving. In R. Binstock, L. George, & J. Schulz (Eds.), *Handbook of aging and the social sciences* (pp. 163–173). Academic Press. https://doi.org/10.1016/B978-0-12-380880-6.00012-5

Ballenger, B. (1997). Methods of memory: On Native American storytelling. *College English, 59*(7), 789–800. https://doi.org/10.58680/ce19973653

Beckert, J. (2007). The longue durée of inheritance law: Discourses and institutional development in France, Germany, and the United States since 1800. *European Journal of Sociology. Archives Européennes de Sociologie, 48*(1), 79–120. https://doi.org/10.1017/S0003975607000306

Beckert, J. (2008). *Inherited wealth*. Princeton University Press. https://doi.org/10.1515/9780691187402

Bednar, J. S., & Brown, J. A. (2023). Organizational ghosts: How "ghostly encounters" enable former leaders to influence current organizational members. *Academy of Management Journal, 67*(3), 737–766. https://doi.org/10.5465/amj.2022.0622

Beispiel, C. (2008). *(Re-)constructing her-/his history: Forms and functions of problematising time in Virginia Woolf's Orlando* (Thesis, University of Duisburg Essen).

Bourdieu, P. (1998). *The state nobility: Elite schools in the field of power*. Stanford University Press.

Bove, A. A., Jr., & Langa, M. (2021). *The complete book of wills, estates & trusts: Advice that can save you thousands of dollars in legal fees and taxes*. St. Martin's Griffin.

Boyd, R., & Richerson, P. J. (2005). *The origin and evolution of cultures*. Oxford University Press. https://doi.org/10.1093/oso/9780195165241.001.0001

Brassington, I. (2019). On rights of inheritance and bequest. *The Journal of Ethics, 23*(2), 119–142. https://doi.org/10.1007/s10892-019-09283-5

Braun, S. T., & Stuhler, J. (2018). The transmission of inequality across multiple generations: Testing recent theories with evidence from Germany. *Economic Journal (London), 128*(609), 576–611. https://doi.org/10.1111/ecoj.12453

Buddy Holly Center. (2024). *Buddy Holly Center*. Retrieved June 15, 2024, from https://ci.lubbock.tx.us/departments/buddy-holly-center/home

Busch, H. C. S., Halliday, D., & Gutmann, T. (Eds.). (2022). *Inheritance and the right to bequeath: Legal and philosophical perspectives*. Taylor & Francis.

Cambridge Dictionary. (2024). *Conflation*. Cambridge University Press. Retrieved June 15, 2024, from https://dictionary.cambridge.org/us/dictionary/english/conflation

Campbell, J. (2008). *The hero with a thousand faces* (Vol. 17). New World Library.

Catechism of the Catholic Church. (1997). *English translation of the Catechism of the Catholic Church for the United States of America*. U.S. Catholic Conference.

Caust, J., & Vecco, M. (2017). Is UNESCO World Heritage recognition a blessing or burden? Evidence from developing Asian countries. *Journal of Cultural Heritage, 27*, 1–9. https://doi.org/10.1016/j.culher.2017.02.004

Clignet, R., Beckert, J., & Harrington, B. (2018). *Death, deeds, and descendants: Inheritance in modern America*. Routledge. https://doi.org/10.4324/9780203793749

Coleman, J. S. (1974). *Power and the structure of society*. W. W. Norton & Company.

Collier, K. G. (1948). The inheritance of values. *The Sociological Review, 40*(1), 97–112. https://doi.org/10.1111/j.1467-954X.1948.tb02282.x

Colquitt, J. A., Sabey, T. B., Pfarrer, M. D., Rodell, J. B., & Hill, E. T. (2023). Continue the story or turn the page? Coworker reactions to inheriting a legacy. *Academy of Management Review, 48*(1), 11–31. https://doi.org/10.5465/amr.2019.0084

Cunliffe, J., & Erreygers, G. (Eds.). (2013). *Inherited wealth, justice and equality*. Routledge.

D'Antonio, M. (2006). *Hershey: Milton S. Hershey's extraordinary life of wealth, empire, and utopian dreams*. Simon and Schuster.

Dacin, M. T., Dacin, P. A., & Kent, D. (2019). Tradition in organizations: A custodianship framework. *The Academy of Management Annals, 13*(1), 342–373. https://doi.org/10.5465/annals.2016.0122

De Massis, A., Kotlar, J., & Manelli, L. (2021). Family firms, family boundary organizations, and the family-related organizational ecosystem. *Family Business Review, 34*(4), 350–364. https://doi.org/10.1177/08944865211052195

de Pina-Cabral, J., & De Lima, A. P. (Eds.). (2020). *Elites: Choice, leadership and succession*. Routledge. https://doi.org/10.4324/9781003135845

de Tocqueville, A. (1945). *Democracy in America*. Vintage Books. (Original work published 1835)

Durkheim, É. (1921). La famille conjugale. *Revue Philosophique de la France et de l'Etranger, 91*, 1–14.

Erreygers, G., & Vandevelde, T. (Eds.). (1997). *Is inheritance legitimate?: Ethical and economic aspects of wealth transfers*. Springer Science & Business Media. https://doi.org/10.1007/978-3-662-03343-2

FamilySearch. (2024). *About FamilySearch*. Retrieved June 15, 2024, from https://www.familysearch.org/en/about/

Fletcher, A. (2021). *Wonderworks: The 25 most powerful inventions in the history of literature*. Simon & Schuster.

Foner, E. (1999). *Story of American freedom*. WW Norton & Company.

Frake, J., & Harmon, D. (2023). Intergenerational transmission of organizational misconduct: Evidence from the Chicago Police Department. *Management Science*. http://dx.doi.org/10.2139/ssrn.3948012

Frazer, J. G. (1922). *The golden bough*. https://doi.org/10.1007/978-1-349-00400-3

Friedman, L. M. (2009). *Dead hands: A social history of wills, trusts, and inheritance law*. Stanford University Press.

Frye, N. (2006). *The great code: The Bible and literature* (Vol. 19). University of Toronto Press.

Glass, J., Bengtson, V. L., & Dunham, C. C. (1986). Attitude similarity in three-generation families: Socialization, status inheritance, or reciprocal influence? *American Sociological Review, 51*, 685–698. https://doi.org/10.2307/2095493

Gómez-Mejía, L. R., Haynes, K. T., Núñez-Nickel, M., Jacobson, K. J., & Moyano-Fuentes, J. (2007). Socioemotional wealth and business risks in family-controlled firms: Evidence from Spanish olive oil mills. *Administrative Science Quarterly, 52*(1), 106–137. https://doi.org/10.2189/asqu.52.1.106

Goody, J. (1976). *Production and reproduction: A comparative study of the domestic domain* (No. 17). Cambridge University Press.

Halliday, D. (2018). *Inheritance of wealth: Justice, equality, and the right to bequeath*. Oxford University Press. https://doi.org/10.1093/oso/9780198803355.001.0001

Hann, C. (2008). Reproduction and inheritance: Goody revisited. *Annual Review of Anthropology, 37,* 145–158. https://doi.org/10.1146/annurev.anthro.37.081407.085222

Harrison, J. R., & Carroll, G. R. (1991). Keeping the faith: A model of cultural transmission in formal organizations. *Administrative Science Quarterly, 36,* 552–582. https://doi.org/10.2307/2393274

Hatch, M. J. (2004). Dynamics in organizational culture. In M. S. Poole & A. H. Van de Ven (Eds.), *Handbook of organizational change and innovation* (pp. 190–211). Oxford University Press.

Hershey Trust Company. (2024). *Hershey Trust Company: Over 100 years of strength, heritage, and stability.* Retrieved June 15, 2024, from https://www.hersheytrust.com/

Hervieu-Léger, D. (2000). *Religion as a chain of memory.* Rutgers University Press.

Ingold, T. (2016). *Lines: A brief history.* Routledge. https://doi.org/10.4324/9781315625324

Ingold, T. (2022). Evolution without inheritance: Steps to an ecology of learning. *Current Anthropology, 63*(S25), S32–S55.

Israelsen, T. (2023). *Entrepreneurial conflation in American business dynasties* (Doctoral dissertation, University of Victoria).

Jaskiewicz, P., Combs, J. G., & Rau, S. B. (2015). Entrepreneurial legacy: Toward a theory of how some family firms nurture transgenerational entrepreneurship. *Journal of Business Venturing, 30*(1), 29–49. https://doi.org/10.1016/j.jbusvent.2014.07.001

Joshi, A., Dencker, J. C., Franz, G., & Martocchio, J. J. (2010). Unpacking generational identities in organizations. *Academy of Management Review, 35*(3), 392–414.

Kendrick, L. (2011). The Lockean rights of bequest and inheritance. *Legal Theory, 17*(2), 145–169. https://doi.org/10.1017/S1352325211000085

Kohli, M. (2004). Intergenerational transfers and inheritance: A comparative view. *Annual Review of Gerontology & Geriatrics, 24*(1), 266–289.

Kraatz, M. S., Flores, R., & Chandler, D. (2020). The value of values for institutional analysis. *The Academy of Management Annals, 14*(2), 474–512. https://doi.org/10.5465/annals.2018.0074

Kreiner, G. E., & Murphy, C. (2016). Organizational identity work. In M. G. Pratt, M. Schultz, B. E. Ashforth, & D. Ravasi (Eds.), *Oxford handbook of organizational identity* (pp. 276–296). Oxford University Press.

Kroeber, A. L. (1962). General features of culture. In *Culture: A critical review of concepts and definitions* (pp. 159–190). Cambridge University Press.

Lewens, T. (2015). *Cultural evolution: Conceptual challenges.* Oxford University Press. https://doi.org/10.1093/acprof:oso/9780199674183.001.0001

Manelli, L., Magrelli, V., Kotlar, J., Messeni Petruzzelli, A., & Frattini, F. (2023). Building an outward-oriented social family legacy: Rhetorical history in family business foundations. *Family Business Review, 36*(1), 143–168. https://doi.org/10.1177/08944865231157195

Marcus, G. E. (1992). *Lives in trust: The fortunes of dynastic families in late twentieth-century America.* Westview Press.

McNamee, S. J., & Miller, R. K., Jr. (1989). Estate inheritance: A sociological lacuna. *Sociological Inquiry, 59*(1), 7–29. https://doi.org/10.1111/j.1475-682X.1989.tb01077.x

Mead, G. H. (2015). *Mind, self & society.* University of Chicago Press. (Original work published 1934) https://doi.org/10.7208/chicago/9780226112879.001.0001

Mendel, G. (2013). *Mendel's principles of heredity* (Transl. W. Bateson). Courier Corporation. (Original work published 1865)

Mill, J. S. (1961). *Principles of political economy.* Augustus M. Kelley. (Original work published 1848)

Miller, D., Steier, L., & Le Breton-Miller, I. (2003). Lost in time: Intergenerational succession, change, and failure in family business. *Journal of Business Venturing, 18*(4), 513–531. https://doi.org/10.1016/S0883-9026(03)00058-2

Miller, R., & McNamee, S. J. (1998). *Inheritance and wealth in America.* Springer Science and Business Media. https://doi.org/10.1007/978-1-4899-1931-1

Mills, C. W. (1940). Situated actions and vocabularies of motive. *American Sociological Review, 5*(6), 904–913. https://doi.org/10.2307/2084524

Mumford, A. (2007). Inheritance in socio-political context: The case for reviving the sociological discourse of inheritance tax law. *Journal of Law and Society, 34*(4), 567–593. https://doi.org/10.1111/j.1467-6478.2007.00405.x

Ocasio, W. (2023). Institutions and their social construction: A cross-level perspective. *Organization Theory, 4*(3), 26317877231194368. https://doi.org/10.1177/26317877231194368

Online Etymology Dictionary. (2024). *Foundation*. Harper. Retrieved June 17, 2024, from https://www.etymonline.com/search?q=foundation

Pedersen, J., & Bøyum, S. (2020). Inheritance and the family. *Journal of Applied Philosophy, 37*(2), 299–313. https://doi.org/10.1111/japp.12389

Piketty, T., & Saez, E. (2013). A theory of optimal inheritance taxation. *Econometrica, 81*(5), 1851–1886. https://doi.org/10.3982/ECTA10712

Pontarotti, G. (2015). Extended inheritance from an organizational point of view. *History and Philosophy of the Life Sciences, 37*, 430–448. https://doi.org/10.1007/s40656-015-0088-4

Radu-Lefebvre, M., Davis, J. H., & Gartner, W. B. (2024). Legacy in family business: A systematic literature review and future research agenda. *Family Business Review, 37*, 08944865231224506. https://doi.org/10.1177/08944865231224506

Rivo-López, E., Villanueva-Villar, M., Vaquero-García, A., & Lago-Peñas, S. (2017). Family offices: What, why and what for. *Organizational Dynamics, 46*(4), 262–270. https://doi.org/10.1016/j.orgdyn.2017.03.002

Sasaki, I., Ravasi, D., & Micelotta, E. (2019). Family firms as institutions: Cultural reproduction and status maintenance among multi-centenary shinise in Kyoto. *Organization Studies, 40*(6), 793–831. https://doi.org/10.1177/0170840618818596

Schein, E. H. (1983). The role of the founder in creating organizational culture. *Organizational Dynamics, 12*(1), 13–28. https://doi.org/10.1016/0090-2616(83)90023-2

Schultz, M., & Hernes, T. (2013). A temporal perspective on organizational identity. *Organization Science, 24*(1), 1–21. https://doi.org/10.1287/orsc.1110.0731

Selznick, P. (1994). *The moral commonwealth: Social theory and the promise of community*. University of California Press. https://doi.org/10.1525/9780520354753

Selznick, P. (2011). *Leadership in administration: A sociological interpretation*. Quid Pro Books.

Shils, E. (1981). *Tradition*. University of Chicago Press.

Silk, R. D., & Lintott, J. W. (2011). *Managing foundations and charitable trusts: Essential knowledge, tools, and techniques for donors and advisors* (Vol. 145). John Wiley & Sons. https://doi.org/10.1002/9781118531617

Solomon, A. (2012). *Far from the tree: Parents, children, and the search for identity*. Scribner.

Stonemason's Guild. (2024). *The Stonemason's Guild of St. Stephen*. Retrieved June 15, 2024, from https://www.stonemasonsguild.com/

Suddaby, R., & Jaskiewicz, P. (2020). Managing traditions: A critical capability for family business success. *Family Business Review, 33*(3), 234–243. https://doi.org/10.1177/0894486520942611

Suddaby, R., Manelli, L., & Fan, Z. (2023). Corporate purpose: A social judgement perspective. *Strategy Science, 8*(2), 202–211. https://doi.org/10.1287/stsc.2023.0185

Suddaby, R., Ng, W., Vershinina, N., Markman, G., & Cadbury, M. (2023). Sacralization and the intergenerational transmission of values in Cadbury. *Family Business Review, 36*(3), 296–314. https://doi.org/10.1177/08944865231188788

Sukhoverkhov, A. V., & Gontier, N. (2021). Non-genetic inheritance: Evolution above the organismal level. *Bio Systems, 200*, 104325. https://doi.org/10.1016/j.biosystems.2020.104325

Vermeulen, F. (2018). A basic theory of inheritance: How bad practice prevails. *Strategic Management Journal, 39*(6), 1603–1629.

Weber, M. (2019). *Economy and society: A new translation*. Harvard University Press. https://doi.org/10.4159/9780674240827

Young, J. (1923, November 18). Hershey, unique philanthropist: His munificent gift to orphan boys a long cherished idea. *New York Times*. https://www.nytimes.com/1923/11/18/archives/hershey-unique-philanthropist-his-munificent-gift-to-orphan-boys-a.html

Zimmerman, C. C. (2023). *Family and civilization*. Simon and Schuster.

Zucker, L. G. (1977). The role of institutionalization in cultural persistence. *American Sociological Review, 42*, 726–743. https://doi.org/10.2307/2094862

Micki Eisenman and Andrea Casey
Chapter 4
Constructing legacy: Managing legacy in discursive and embodied ways

Legacy is a construct that is evoked in scholarly work on organizational memory and rhetorical history (e.g., Coman & Casey, 2022; Lubinski, 2018; Lubinski & Gartner, 2023; Ravasi et al., 2019; Suddaby et al., 2016, 2020; Suddaby, Israelsen, Mitchell, et al., 2023; Suddaby, Israelsen, Bastien, et al., 2023), but which we argue is not sufficiently precise as a theoretical construct in organizational research. In general, the construct of legacy is used to reference how a collective understanding of the past, particularly regarding significant events or individuals, can be perceived as a force that constrains or enables organizational choices in the present and future. In this sense, it echoes the concept of collective memory. But, legacy is often perceived in organizational research in a more strategic framing because a common perception of legacy is in the context of path dependency, highlighting that past choices, reflected in recollections of these events or individuals, affect the range of possible strategic options organizations have in the present and as they imagine their futures (Suddaby, 2016).

Our goal in this chapter is to advance the theorization of legacy and, subsequently, to put forth an approach for how it might be used and managed by organizations. To do so, we define legacy as a collective understanding of a past event or individual that is significant in the present. Based on this significance, it becomes a force that affects present choices. This definition highlights that legacy is not only a form of collective memory in which a group of people interpret the past in similar ways, but also an aspect of the past that is significant because these people believe it affects their current strategic options. In this sense, while collective memory explains affinities within social groups, we highlight legacy as a concept that pertains to managers and organizations because it is strategically relevant. Subsequently, we suggest understanding legacy as a potential tool managers might strive to control, even if not all aspects of an organization's legacy can be intentionally influenced.

To develop this argument, we highlight that scholars have tied legacy to a collective understanding intentionally constructed through interactions of key stakeholders. However, what is collectively understood and how this understanding evolves is less clear than the benefits of this understanding, which are often articulated in terms of significant events in an organization's history such as the organization's founding and how core organizational identity claims emerge (Walsh & Glynn, 2008) or ties to rep-

---

Acknowledgments: Micki Eisenman acknowledges the support of The Israel Science Foundation (grant No. 1910/22).

resentational material artifacts such as those preserved in corporate museums (Nissley & Casey, 2002; Ravasi et al., 2019; Walsh & Glynn, 2008). Thus, advancing these ideas requires us to elaborate what an event is and who is the collective that understands it as significant. Further, as we will explain below, this collective understanding is both cognitive and emotional, and its meaning is transmitted discursively, through stories told within the organization and narratives about its past. Further, legacy is not necessarily monolithic and may affect subgroups within an organization (Colquitt et al., 2023). Of further importance is that legacy, although typically tied to strategic benefits, is not necessarily constructive and positive and may often carry negative weight that limits strategic choices or forces firms to deal with a tarnished reputation resulting from choices of past managers (e.g., Booth et al., 2007; Rowlinson & Hassard, 1993). Our argument in this chapter is that understanding legacy in this more nuanced way illuminates how it might be managed.

We begin with an elaboration of the idea of an event. An event is a discrete, yet ongoing, aspect of the organization's past that describes something about the activities of the organization, its founder or other key individuals, or a group of organizations that interact, such as the development of a new technology or a key strategic choice that set an organization, or field, on its present course. Importantly, an event is both discrete, in that it happened in the past and people understand it as such, but at the same time is ongoing as it is connected to other key events, and its significance has evolving relevance in the present (Wagner-Pacifici, 2016). Information about an event is transmitted through narratives, materials such as symbolic artifacts, or embodied sensations such as gestures (Wagner-Pacifici, 2010). Events have meaning in organizational contexts because they can lead to structural changes (Sewell, 1996) and they can, more or less consciously, suggest a framework for understanding relationships among people, objects, or ideas (cf. Colquitt et al., 2023).

We clarify with an example: Steve Jobs is collectively understood as an influential founder, and his ideas about the significance of a closed operating system and an emphasis on aesthetic design are considered by members of the organization to be significant events. They are discrete in the sense that they happened in the past in the context of a design choice or a strategic statement made by Jobs. But they are ongoing in the sense that they put in place an ethos of careful design and a closed ecosystem that not only guide the firm's present strategic choices, but are also considered by members of the organization to be the source of the firm's success and central to its distinctive identity, for example as manifested by the advertising tag "Think Different!" A more complex legacy may evolve as these discrete events become connected to other events as they are recalled.

Next, we posit that collective understanding of an event as significant both constitutes the significance of the event and constitutes the collective itself in an ongoing way. Thus, our answer to the question of how the collective understanding of an event is relevant is that an event is meaningful when a group, such as members of an organization, associates present strategic choices with the meanings associated with this event. More specifically, when a group has a shared collective interpretation of the event, these collective interpretations generate a sense of affinity, positive or negative, among those sharing the interpretation, and the event becomes a powerful strategic tool. It can, for example, affect the identity of members of an organization (Schultz & Hernes, 2013) or their thoughts about strategically positioning or repositioning their firm (Hatch & Schultz, 2017; Ravasi et al., 2019). The relationship between legacy, as a form of collective memory, and organizational identity also surfaces in research where organizational identity is based on why the events were chosen and how the legacies evolve (Casey, 2019; Ravasi et al., 2019).

As we expand upon below, the strategic potency of such past events is tied to the ways in which they are aligned with institutionalized cultural myths and ideas that are cognitively legitimate and related emotions. As these myths and ideas may change over time, the potency of a legacy might not be stable over time. A full development of these ideas allows us to advance the understanding of the legacy construct. Thus, a primary contribution of our chapter is expounding a set of ideas that are tied to recent developments in organizational memory studies (Foroughi et al., 2020; Rowlinson et al., 2010), such as the growing body of work enhancing the accuracy of constructs related to organizational memory and its applications (e.g., Casey, 2019, on identity; Coman & Casey, 2022, on history; Lubinski & Gartner, 2023, on generation; Suddaby & Jaskiewicz, 2020, on traditions). Additionally, we emphasize the ways legacy is transmitted not only through the texts that narrate its underlying ideas but also through material artifacts that underlie the relationships among those sharing the legacy. Thus, we continue work that examines other modalities of memory and memory-based social affinities (e.g., Crawford et al., 2022; Eisenman & Frenkel, 2021; Foroughi, Eisenman, & Parsley, forthcoming).

Second, we advance our understanding of managing legacy. Specifically, we articulate that legacy may be intentionally managed by maintaining it in ways that make it useful for organizations to balance continuity and change, yet the importance of authenticity needs to be considered in this process. We also highlight that legacy might be affected in unintentional ways. We theorize how organizations could respond to what might threaten legacy and the need for preemptive management of its unintentional erosion. In this context, we offer a proscriptive framework that highlights some ways further theorizing might apply our ideas.

In what follows, we first theorize the importance of legacy as a collective understanding of a past significant event or individual that creates affinities among those understanding its significance in similar ways and explain such collective understanding as both cognitive and embodied. In the next section, we theorize how legacy is sustained, highlighting that this happens through both discursive and material mechanisms that allow the collective understanding to be transmitted over time. Having theorized legacy and the mechanisms that sustain it allows us to address, in a final section, what firms might do to maximize the strategic potential of their legacies. Based on our theorization, we highlight that legacy might be intentionally affected and utilized. We also highlight that legacy might change in ways that are unintentional and elaborate what firms might do in this case.

The conceptualization of legacy

What is clear in organizational research is that legacy is a shared understanding of the past that is carried over to the present in that it is accepted by members of an organization or frames a debate among them about the identity of the organization or its strategic directions (e.g., Hatch & Schultz, 2017; Ravasi et al., 2019). It is often associated with an origin point in an organization's past, such as an important individual or a significant event. In this sense, it is an imprinting made by a key executive or other stakeholder that continues to impact an organization, as a firm or broader societal group, through enduring meanings that are collectively understood in a way that continues to have influence after the individual's demise or departure (cf. Colquitt et al., 2023) and ultimately may come to represent characteristics or the identity of the organization itself. For instance, Foster et al.'s (2011) study of the Tim Horton Company showed how organizational members drew from the founder, Tim Horton, to establish legitimacy across a larger audience as they expanded business and reputation in new and different markets. In this sense, aspects of the founder's personal history as a hockey player were the foundation of a discursive effort to position the organization as "Canadian." However, this study did not elaborate on the collective understanding of the legacy and how it sustained the organization, but focused on how the understanding was strategically useful to the firm. As such, legacy overlaps with the idea of rhetorical history that emphasizes how the past can be used as a basis for discursive arguments that serve the firm's strategic goals (Suddaby et al., 2010).

Other studies have also discussed the strategic importance of the relationship between founders and legacies and highlighted that this relationship may be viewed as a constraint or a foundation upon which to build the future (Ogbonna & Harris, 2001). In particular, a founder's initial strategic vision may continue to influence the decisions of successive managers. This work suggested that the consequences of a strategic legacy are connected to the flexibility of that legacy and managers' awareness of its influence (Ogbonna & Harris, 2001, p. 25). In this regard, it is important to mention that while some legacies are launched with the intent to affect future choices, such as the founding documents of a museum such as the Freer Gallery (Coman & Casey, 2022), others are more emergent outcomes of retrospective sensemaking (Colquitt et al., 2023).

More generally, legacy overlaps with rhetorical history to the extent that it is used to conceptualize the tension between continuity and change (Suddaby & Jaskiewicz, 2020). Legacy, as suggested by the above examples, gives people within an organization an ongoing sense of purpose and continuity. Lubinski and Gartner (2023), for example, showed how family firms refer to core ideas from the past to suggest that current members of the firm are continuations of a longstanding, and therefore legitimate, generational lineage. Staying the course and maintaining continuity in this context offer a powerful sense of direction for current members of the firm. However, the past can also burden present choices. In this case, members of the family firm were careful to articulate strategic change as a reinvention or reevaluation of past choices. To succeed in benefiting from an established legacy while managing change, they argued that newer generations need to articulate their proposed shift in the context of the longstanding legacy.

Legacy as constitutive of mnemonic communities

To move beyond the articulation that legacy is an idea or set of choices from the past carried over to impact the present, we posit that legacy should be understood as an affinity, positive or negative, among people within an organization that is based on their collective understanding of a past event and the ways in which it gives meaning to the past, present, and future. The literature has highlighted this idea in the context of firms that look to the texts generated by their founders to understand the events that have shaped the organization. Sasaki, Kotlar, Ravasi, and Vaara (2020), for example, showed that longstanding Japanese family firms used discursive statements made by founders to make strategic decisions in the present. Similarly, Hatch and Schultz (2017) also explored the meaning and importance of the phrase *Semper Ardens* ("Always Burning") in their study of Carlsberg and showed how the discovery of this statement affected strategic decision-making and aligned members of the organization. Lastly, Schultz and Hernes (2013) showed that finding a plaque with the phrase "only the best is good enough" oriented the firm toward a (re-)commitment to excellence.

Our definition of legacy pushes us to highlight the affinity created within the organization in these cases. Remembering the past is not merely an evocation of past events, but a social opportunity to establish membership in social groups—mnemonic communities—and acquire the identity of the group by becoming versed in its memories and assuming them as one's own (Halbwachs, 1950/1980; Suddaby et al., 2016; Zerubavel, 2003). Put differently, it is important to understand legacy as a collective understanding that can orient a mnemonic community. While organizational theorists do not fully understand how such groups emerge, we do know that central to this emergence is people's perceptions that they are tied to events that are meaningful to them. Moreover, these affinities allow members of the mnemonic community to develop a shared set of values and practices that create continuity between the community's past and its aspirational future. Thus, it is not the words on the plaque that allowed the founder to shape the firm years after his departure, but the affinity that these words created among members of Lego interacting with each other and searching, together, for a sense of where the firm should head (Schultz & Hernes, 2013). Barring such affinity, the words would not have the power to create a strategic sense for the firm.

Building on these ideas, we highlight legacy as a form of collective memory, emphasizing a shared collective interpretation that ties members of a mnemonic community together. In organizational contexts, such mnemonic communities are then groups of people, within or across organizations, that attribute similar interpretations and meanings to events from the past and use these interpretations to think about the present and future of their organizations. These individuals understand a past discrete event as having meaning, and they view this event as ongoing because they use it to guide and constrain their present choices. This emphasis is important: it allows us to suggest that unlike our understanding of rhetorical history, where aspects of the past are put to present strategic use through their articulation in a way that resonates as authentic (Foster et al., 2011), legacy is a concept that ties the past, as an event with meaning, to the community of people ascribing this meaning and forming a community based on such shared interpretation of meaning. Put differently, meaningful events in an organization's past are the basis for constituting mnemonic communities that preserve the relevance of this meaning in the present. Thus, legacy both constitutes and is constituted by the mnemonic communities that ascribe to it.

To push this conceptualization of legacy further, we add another dimension. For a legacy to have the potency to underlie the affinities that tie people to each other and to their organizations, the inherent ideas a legacy represents must align with cultural myths and institutionalized ideas and values that have cognitive legitimacy. Cognitive legitimacy refers to the extent to which ideas are considered valid and normative in a particular institutional and cultural context (Meyer & Rowan, 1977). This idea is relevant to the theorization of legacy because events will resonate as meaningful to the extent that they are well aligned with myths and institutionalized values. In particular, Suddaby, Israelsen, Mitchell, et al. (2023) emphasized that the past can be utilized more effectively to the extent that historical claims are well linked to beliefs or myths that resonate with the collective memories of the community that is the audience for these claims. More generally, then, because legacy draws from an organization's past, it has a broad palette of memory assets from which to draw to potentially meet the needs and aspirations of a diverse group of internal and external stakeholders. When organizations evoke and retell events that are central to legacy, these descriptions of the past gain objective reality as social facts (Suddaby, Israelsen, Bastien, et al., 2023). This is a powerful insight that highlights the strategic potency of crafting and maintaining legacies. Meaningful events that have significance in ongoing ways can guide organizational decisions to a greater extent when they are perceived as objective social facts rather than crafted interpretations. To the extent that organizations do this well and authentically, they can craft a past that institutionalizes their own existence. Using our previous examples, Job's approach to a tightly bound operating system and user-friendly design resonates with the institutionalized myth that technological innovation is a sign of positive progress. As we argue below, changes to such institutionalized ideas are likely to affect legacy.

The transmission of legacy through time

Our articulation of legacy as a continual evocation of a past event, by a collective within an organization, implies that legacy is a set of interpretations that travel through time. This transmission is often carried by various organizational artifacts such as rituals, ceremonies, stories, language, or objects (Colquitt et al., 2023). We build on these ideas and theorize that this transmission is both discursive and embodied. Past studies have highlighted the importance of the discursive transmission of legacy, one based on the ability to narrate ideas directly through written texts, stories, documents, or representational objects. For example, longstanding Japanese family firms turn to documents containing statements by firm founders to understand how the firm can find guidance for present choices in ideas the founder articulated and use these documents to balance the need for continuity and change (Sasaki et al., 2020). Similarly, Basque and Langley (2018) showed how a Québécois firm referenced its founder to maintain the firm's identity. Ravasi et al.'s (2019) study showed how strategic decisions at Vespa were made in consultation with the firm's archives, ensuring that present choices remained aligned with what present members of the firm considered key past choices. And Hatch and Schultz (2017) showed how a carving on a factory wall was interpreted as an authentic text that helped present-day strategists understand how to fortify the Carlsberg brand in a way that they sensed was aligned with the firm's legacy.

In these examples, discrete events tied to the firm's founders or early decisions made by management remained relevant through their discursive manifestations, and present members of the firms could consult these texts (see also Lubinski & Gartner, 2023; Maclean et al., 2018). The preservation of these texts over time allowed members of the legacy-based mnemonic community to reestablish their affinity toward each other through their ongoing interpretation of these texts as having meaning for their community. But legacy is not only a set of ideas that is manifested discursively.

Whereas the above examples focused on the cognitive aspects of collective understanding based on shared interpretations of an event that was represented and remembered through its narration, we posit that collective understanding of past events also manifests as an emotional resonance. Embodied reactions to material artifacts can create powerful affinities between people and between people and organizations (Crawford et al., 2022; Eisenman & Frenkel, 2021; Foroughi et al., 2024). For example, these ideas are core to corporate museums as they engage with diverse stakeholders and consumers through their interactive exhibits featuring their products over time

(Casey, 2019). They offer visitors the opportunity to relate their product and critical events in the organization's history with the significant events in their country, the world and, at times, the individual consumer. These museum experiences often include visitors taking action. At the World of Coke in Atlanta, for example, visitors can drink the product and tell a story of a memorable event in their own lives and how Coke played a part. At Crayola Factory, visitors can color pictures of their lives and smell the scent of a newly opened box of crayons. Similarly, Hershey's Chocolate World smells like Hershey's chocolate throughout and connects visitors with the product and memories from their lives (Casey, 2019).

Building on these insights, we argue that ideas, even when they are nonverbalized, can create affinities that tie people, within or across organizations, to an event and to the ongoing interpretations of its meaning. For example, Do, Lyle, and Walsh (2019) examined the legacy of the defunct Studebaker Corporation by examining how buildings left vacant after the demise of the corporation, which had been central to the city's economic vitality, evoked a sensation that helped members of the community understand how they might use the firm's legacy to launch an urban revitalization initiative. Their study showed how the interpretations of what Studebaker meant to the city of South Bend, Indiana—as a firm that was tied to the lives of many inhabitants and the source of their income, rather than as a firm with a set of articulated strategic choices—set a collective understanding about the potential future development of South Bend. Their analysis highlights how the material features of an area of the city are tied to the understanding of the past and the affinities it created. The insight we draw from this study is that material modalities can transmit ideas and emotions, even if these ideas are not cognitively narrated, because they can manifest in embodied ways. We apply these ideas to our conceptualization of legacy and suggest that a legacy is also an affinity that is sensed.

The management of legacy

Having understood legacy as a collective understanding of a past event or individual that has meaning in the present, and as a collective interpretation that underlies a sense of affinity among those sharing the interpretation, we move to assessing how and to what extent legacy can be managed. As stated above, legacy has various strategic benefits that can extend over long durations in organizational contexts, and it is important to understand the extent to which it can be intentionally applied. Importantly, while many references to legacy perceive it as monolithic, Colquitt et al. (2023) highlighted that legacies may vary in magnitude and that they may affect smaller or larger groups of people within the organization or can be more or less durable in their ability to transfer across time. In addition, multiple legacies exist in organizations, with some that may align and reinforce each other and others that are in conflict. Here, Lubinski (2018) argued for a more contextualized understanding of historical claims that views them as subject to validation, change, or refinement as they are negotiated among diverse audiences. She highlighted the potential for 'rhetorical frictions,' noting the need for "continuous and skillful history revisions to mitigate emerging conflicts in their reception" (Lubinski, 2018, p. 1785).

These arguments suggest that managers could benefit from taking an active approach to thinking about legacy. To elaborate on such agency, we first argue that, as legacy is transmitted discursively and materially, it should be managed by managing the texts and artifacts that allow its transmission. Second, we highlight that, because legacy is interpreted as more powerful and authentic to the extent that it is well aligned with institutionalized cultural myths, it should be managed by inquiring about and engaging with the environment through interactions with key stakeholders (internal and external) for changes to the institutionalized cultural myths in which these ideas are embedded. We elaborate on these ideas in the following paragraphs.

Managing discursive transmission

Recent studies have clarified how firms might actively manage their use of the past and capitalize on their legacies, often through ongoing engagement, inquiry, reflection, adaptation, and interpretation of texts tied to the founder of the organization (e.g., Basque & Langley, 2018; Sasaki et al., 2020; Suddaby & Jaskiewicz, 2020). Firms and managers in family businesses, for example, use organizational texts to strategically realize a sense of identity and purpose by evoking the generational lineage of current family members and highlighting the continuity of the firm. For each era, while management was embedded in the longstanding family history, it was also attuned to broader sociocultural and macroeconomic changes that required adaptation of the legacy (Lubinski & Gartner, 2023).

As we explained, legacy, as well as the affinity on which it is based, is grounded not only in a collective understanding of meanings, but also in an emotional resonance among people. In this context, mnemonic devices, such as portraits or statues of founders, can also evoke the underlying events on which a legacy draws because they are based on representations of events and ideas (Eisenman & Frenkel, 2021). Emotional resonance, however, is likely to be tied to ceremonies and rituals and other interactive processes of commemoration or co-remembering (Schwartz, 2000, 2005), as these lead to more embodied understandings of the relationship between an organization, its members, and the past (Connerton, 1989; Howard-Grenville et al., 2013). Such objects work as texts that are not necessarily interpreted consciously, but which still anchor mnemonic understandings (Crawford et al., 2022; De Vaujany & Vaast, 2014). They do so by connecting aspects of the organization's past with various symbols and generating ritualistic frameworks, such as ceremonies, that engage individual participation and thereby foster identification and affinity that reestablish membership in the mnemonic community (Suddaby et al., 2010).

It follows that organizations should keep alive texts, stories, traditions, and ceremonies that work to remind members of the organization of the critical legacies. Arguably, to the extent that organizations have more tangible artifacts that reiterate the stories underlying the legacy, the legacy is likely to be more durable in terms of its ability to be transmitted over long periods of time (Colquitt et al., 2023). This is important because we conceptualize legacy as the basis for an affinity tying members of an organization (or groups of organizations) together. As we highlighted, the legacy constitutes the mnemonic community that uses the legacy to reinforce its resource base (e.g., its identity in the context of its ability to maintain continuity or its ability to determine its strategy in the context of change and innovation). The vitality of the mnemonic community then gives the legacy its strategic potency. To maintain this cycle and its benefits, the artifacts representing and evoking the legacy, and reminders of its underlying details, should be accessible in an ongoing way to members of the organization (Wagner-Pacifici, 2016).

Organizations engage in this process by setting up archives or museums that highlight these details (e.g., Basque & Langley, 2018; Foster et al., 2020; Maclean et al., 2018; Nissley & Casey, 2002; Rowlinson & Hassard, 1993). These ideas imply that to the extent that texts and artifacts are preserved and can be accessed, the information about the events that underlie the legacy can be retrieved and evoked. However, explicit stories, which legitimate specific actors and events (Maclean et al., 2012), reduce the interpretative flexibility of the legacy. Because we understand legacy as more potent to the extent that it is aligned with institutionalized cultural myths, and because we know that these ideas vary over time, we argue that it is important to tie legacy to artifacts that offer greater flexibility. Organizations must therefore be mindful to select and preserve texts that represent the legacy but also allow leeway for more interpretations that adapt to changes in norms and diverse stakeholders over time.

Our argument is evidenced by recent studies. For example, Hatch and Schultz (2017) showed how an inscription on a factory wall with the phrase *Semper Ardens* ("Always Burning") was used to express historical truths about Carlsberg's legacy, in that it set in motion an orienting affinity among present members of Carlsberg. At the same time, the meaning of this phrase is quite vague; beyond offering an orienting affinity in the present, it holds no clear strategic dictums. Instead, the emotional resonance of this carving, and the sense that it was "authentic" to the organization, is what enabled the strategic orientation of the firm. Additionally, Cappelen and Strandgaard-Pedersen (2021) showed how a culinary movement in Turkey established a common meaningful past it could utilize strategically by being intentionally ambiguous and remembering certain aspects of the past while forgetting others to tie the movement to aspects of the region's history that were more or less desirable. They demonstrated how these practices of balancing the past and present discursively led to strategic benefits that would not have materialized had the movement taken a less ambiguous approach to retelling its history and expressing its origins. Further, they showed that chefs maintained this ambiguity through their artifacts—the actual dishes—that balanced a sense of familiarity with a sense of novelty. These efforts allowed broader identification with the emergent field that was able to sidestep sociopolitical issues that may have limited the potential affinities to this culinary movement.

Subsequently, organizations need to maintain a delicate balance when creating repositories of legacy-related information. Organizations can use their legacies to demonstrate how current choices are related to a clear strategic past (Lubinski & Gartner, 2023) when these legacies echo cultural tropes and well-known myths (Suddaby, Israelsen, Mitchell, et al., 2023). But, organizations should consider that when legacy-related information is vague, organizational members can evoke the past while simultaneously allowing for novelty that is perceived as authentic and that resonates with diverse members. Thus, we argue that it is beneficial to maintain some level of ambiguity in retelling stories that transmit organizational legacies. We posit that legacies are more durable when they facilitate or engage in this interpretative flexibility as part of the "situated nature of historical rhetoric" (Lubinski, 2018, p. 1785).

Managing embodied transmission

While the above paragraphs treated material mnemonic devices, such as portraits or wall carvings, as discursive, an important distinction here is that some mnemonic devices are the basis for relational affinities among members of an organization (Eisenman & Frenkel, 2021). Such affinities are based on sensory reactions to the device rather than on conscious narrative interpretations of it, and in this sense, they are more open and flexible. For example, De Vaujany and Vaast (2014, 2016) showed how a new university housed in a set of buildings previously used by NATO, and as such imbued with historic significance, built on the past uses of the space. The university evoked these past uses and their potential effect on the new university but did not articulate them in a "closed" way. This approach afforded the university the freedom to develop various strategic initiatives that tied the space's past to the university's future.

Thus, although aesthetic responses to material artifacts are individual responses, they can set in motion unconsciously coordinated activity that is expressed through the body rather than verbalized; subsequently, they are potentially very powerful in their capacity to tie people together (Eisenman & Frenkel, 2021). To explain, Eisenman and Frenkel argued that mnemonic devices can be classified as more or less contemporary, and this distinction has implications for engaging with the organization's history. For example, bronze statues of founders are primarily mnemonic devices that are representational, as they evoke particular individuals and their (typically) personal history. Further, classical bronze statues are likely devices that were common in past centuries, and the embodied response to them is tied to a sense that they are carried over from a distant past. This tension offers an interesting balance to be managed: The close representation of the person limits the interpretative flexibility, but the absence of a contemporary design distances the person and the ideas he represents from the people currently in the organization. Thus, the organization in this case can actively choose to evoke the person represented by the statue when the ideology he represents is useful to maintaining the legacy and can also actively distance the present organizational interactions from this person by highlighting that time has passed and diminished the relevance of this ideology. These ideas were articulated in the context of statues depicting founders of organizations or benefactors of universities that were slave owners. Organizations can actively align with aspects of these individuals' personalities, work ethics, or ideals and can also articulate a clear break from these ideas by the fact that the representation of these individuals is an old artifact rather than a current one. To exemplify, Decker (2014) showed how changes in architectural styles of banks in Ghana were deliberately used to articulate a break from the colonial past. Drawing on these ideas, we suggest that in putting in place material artifacts that evoke the legacy which have very contemporary designs, organizations can generate affinities that are very contemporary because these devices are by definition recent and current. Moreover, they can use such mnemonic devices to communicate a break with past traditions and representations.

As also discussed in the Eisenman and Frenkel (2021) study, mnemonic devices can vary in terms of their aesthetic richness—their potential to elicit sensory responses based on their aesthetic features, such as color, texture, shape, and so on. Aesthetically rich mnemonic devices orient mnemonic communities by eliciting affinities based on intimate embodied experiences. At the same time, they are typically nonrepresentational and as such have greater interpretative flexibility. An example in this context is the stadium studied by Howard-Grenville et al. (2013); it generated affinities and maintained the legacy of Eugene, Oregon, and its university as an institution with key abilities and achievements in track and field athletics. These affinities were based not (only) on a discursive articulation of the legacy and key people and events that enabled it, but on the memory of the sensory experience of being in a packed stadium and watching sporting events and particular athletes. The underlying idea conveyed by Eisenman and Frenkel is that the power of sitting with others in a crowded stadium, being exposed to their bodily odors, and cheering together is a powerful way to evoke a legacy and keep it current in ways the town or university can utilize strategically.

We extend this insight to highlight that participation in organizational rituals can create affinities to the organization, based on the sensory reactions people have during their participation, and in the absence of a direct coupling between the ritual and its interpretative meanings. Therefore, we argue that efforts to manage legacies can benefit from the creation and maintenance of rituals and ceremonies that tie people to the organization in embodied ways.

Monitoring cultural alignment

While the above paragraphs imply that legacy can be intentionally managed through the transmission of discursive and material mnemonic devices, this section highlights that legacy is more potent to the extent that it is well aligned with institutionalized cultural myths. As explained above, an organization's references to the past and their strategic appropriation resonate as more authentic and relevant to the organization's identity and strategic choices when they are well aligned with institutionalized cultural myths, values, and norms (Suddaby, Israelsen, Mitchell, et al., 2023). This idea implies that the use of the past is contextual, and its resonance varies over time in correlation with its alignment with broader social ideas. However, these myths, as a set of ideas and values that are shared across society, do not change in ways any one organization can control or affect. Thus, we suggest that organizations can maintain agency by inquiring, reflecting, and engaging with these cultural myths through ongoing interaction with key internal and external stakeholders to assess shifts so that they can preempt a possible erosion of their legacies.

To expand, we return to the example of the New Anatolian cuisine (Cappelen & Strandgaard-Pedersen, 2021). Here, we posit that organizations benefit by monitoring their sociocultural environments and aligning the stories underlying their legacies with prevailing cultural myths. Their study showed how actors historicized their past with a degree of discretionary freedom. In the case of this movement, chefs were cognizant of both the negative evaluation of the Ottoman Empire as a colonialist relic and of the current Turkish government and worked to create narratives that positioned the movement as both predating the colonial past and as more cross-regional than tied to current Turkish borders. In so doing, they elicited broad-ranging identification instead of succumbing to contestation that might carry over from controversy over the current Turkish regime (i.e., Erdoğan's Turkey).

As another example, Lubinski and Gartner (2023) showed that legacies may be intentionally tied to broad-scale societal developments. In this study, they articulated that the firm existed throughout periods of societal change and that sociotechnological developments affected the craft and expertise of the firm. A key insight in their analysis is that values change over time and, therefore, the transmission of legacy needs to be attuned to these changes to resonate as meaningful in the present and be considered by members of the organization as a useful guide toward the future. Another key insight is that some narrative structures give texts an eternal quality that allows them to evoke emotional resonance in an ongoing way. Specifically, a fairy tale–like structure or a connection to basic crafts allows the stories to extend across time. Similarly, when the past is closely tied to clear myths or to very distant pasts, they can also be the basis for transmitting legacies in ongoing ways. In these ways, Lubinski and Gartner highlighted the idea that aspects of organizational legacies are tied to well-established myths, and to the extent that these myths are highly institutionalized, a particular organization's legacy increases in relevance and potency. Moreover, to the extent that a legacy is tied to a broader institutional myth, this legacy is likely to be more durable and less easily challenged.

Generalizing from these studies, the importance of alignment with institutionalized cultural myths and cognitively legitimate ideas allows us to propose that legacy may be affected in unintentional ways and that managers might use this understanding to control legacy to an extent. Primarily, we propose that organizations need to monitor their environments to assess an overall change in norms and values, often by monitoring regulatory changes. We view such efforts as a preemptive approach to managing legacy erosion. In this context, we advocate that organizations should engage in strategic analyses that examine political, economic, regulatory, sociocultural, or technological shifts in their competitive environment. For example, it would benefit organizations to monitor societal events such as the *Rhodes Must Fall* movement prompting the toppling of statues depicting influential organizational figures who were also slave owners on university campuses (Suddaby, Israelsen, Bastien, et al., 2023), and to anticipate that certain outcomes that could highlight aspects of their legacy are not well aligned with institutionalized cultural norms. In this case, we suggest that organizations emphasize different aspects of their pasts or enhance the ambiguity of their discursive efforts before the normative shift diminishes the potency of their legacy by devaluing it or reducing its authenticity. To the extent that organizations do not do this monitoring, they may face a potential legacy crisis. In the example of university founders who were slave owners, legacy is based on the meanings present members of the organization attribute to these founders. In present times, these meanings are now subject to negative evaluation, leading members of the organization to question their identification within the mnemonic community of the university. We suggest that managing legacy is therefore tied to monitoring changes in cultural norms and values and assessing shifts in the cognitive legitimacy of ideas. In so doing, organizations can preempt an erosion of their legacy.

Another direction for this preemptive monitoring is an ongoing assessment of industries in terms of their birth and growth. As industries grow and inhabit more firms, their degree of cognitive legitimacy increases (Carroll & Hannan, 1989). Organizations active in fields with high degrees of cognitive legitimacy have a broader range of institutionalized ideas with which to align, while organizations active in newer fields with less established cognitive legitimacy are more restricted (Cappelen & Strandgaard-Pedersen, 2021; Lander et al., 2022). To actively manage legacy, we argue that organizations should understand the extent of cognitive legitimacy their field enjoys as well as the extent to which their organization is isomorphic with the field's norms. Subsequently, organizations should select well-established ideas as the basis for their discursive efforts when they are established actors in fields with high degrees of cognitive legitimacy—typically older, larger, and rapidly growing industries. And, they should pursue more ambiguous and interpretatively flexible articulations of their legacies when they are actors in newer industries that do not yet enjoy high levels of cognitive legitimacy or when they are fairly marginal to the industry. This flexibility will allow them leeway to develop their legacies in ways that resonate as authentic and foster identification with the social groups that have affinities toward the legacy.

Conclusion

This chapter puts forth a theorization of legacy that defines legacy as a collective understanding of a past event or individual that is significant in the present and shapes present choices in organizations. Legacies have both cognitive and emotional components, and their meaning is transmitted through stories. Our theorization suggests that there are obvious aspects of legacy that could be actively managed. In particular, as legacy is transmitted through texts and tangible artifacts, organizations can work to create and control them (e.g., Colquitt et al., 2023; Lubinski & Gartner, 2023; Suddaby & Jaskiewicz, 2020). At the same time, the potency of a legacy is tied to how well it is aligned with institutionalized cultural myths and ideas. While many studies have highlighted that legacies should echo institutionalized myths (e.g., Lubinski & Gartner, 2023; Suddaby, Israelsen, Mitchell, et al., 2023), we highlight two implications of this insight. First, in designing and maintaining the artifacts that transmit legacy, organizations are better off selecting artifacts with greater interpretative flexibility. Second, organizations should monitor their environments to identify shifts in ideas that are cognitively legitimate and adapt when these ideas shift.

References

Basque, J., & Langley, A. (2018). Invoking Alphonse: The founder figure as a historical resource for organizational identity work. *Organization Studies*, *39*(12), 1685–1708. https://doi.org/10.1177/0170840618789211

Booth, C., Clark, P., Delahaye, A., Procter, S., & Rowlinson, M. (2007). Accounting for the dark side of corporate history: Organizational culture perspectives and the Bertelsmann case. *Critical Perspectives on Accounting*, *18*(6), 625–644. https://doi.org/10.1016/j.cpa.2007.03.012

Cappelen, S. M., & Strandgaard-Pedersen, J. (2021). Inventing culinary heritage through strategic historical ambiguity. *Organization Studies*, *42*(2), 223–243. https://doi.org/10.1177/0170840620918382

Carroll, G. R., & Hannan, M. T. (1989). Density dependence in the evolution of populations of newspaper organizations. *American Sociological Review*, *54*, 524–541. https://doi.org/10.2307/2095875

Casey, A. (2019). *Organizational identity and memory: A multidisciplinary approach*. Routledge. https://doi.org/10.4324/9781315669786

Colquitt, J., Sabey, T. B., Pfarrer, M. D., Rodell, J. B., & Hill, E. T. (2023). Continue the story or turn the page? Coworker reactions to inheriting a legacy. *Academy of Management Review, 48*(1), 11–31. https://doi.org/10.5465/amr.2019.0084

Coman, S., & Casey, A. (2022). *New directions in organizational and management history*. De Gruyter. https://doi.org/10.1515/9783110693539

Connerton, P. (1989). *How societies remember*. Cambridge University Press. https://doi.org/10.1017/CBO9780511628061

Crawford, B., Coraiola, D. M., & Dacin, M. T. (2022). Painful memories as mnemonic resources: Grand Canyon Dories and the protection of place. *Strategic Organization, 20*(1), 51–79. https://doi.org/10.1177/1476127020981353

De Vaujany, F.-X., & Vaast, E. (2014). If these walls could talk: The mutual construction of organizational space and legitimacy. *Organization Science, 25*, 713–731. https://doi.org/10.1287/orsc.2013.0858

De Vaujany, F. X., & Vaast, E. (2016). Matters of visuality in legitimation practices: Dual iconographies in a meeting room. *Organization, 23*(5), 763–790.

Decker, S. (2014). Solid intentions: An archival ethnography of corporate architecture and organizational remembering. *Organization, 21*(4), 514–542.

Do, B., Lyle, M. C., & Walsh, I. J. (2019). Driving down memory lane: The influence of memories in a community following organizational demise. *Organization Studies, 40*(9), 1307–1329. https://doi.org/10.1177/0170840618765573

Eisenman, M., & Frenkel, M. (2021). Remembering materiality: A material-relational approach to organizational memory. *Organization Theory, 2*(3), 26317877211029666. https://doi.org/10.1177/26317877211029666

Foroughi, H., Coraiola, D. M., Rintamäki, J., Mena, S., & Foster, W. M. (2020). Organizational memory studies. *Organization Studies, 41*(12), 1725–1748

Foroughi, H., Eisenman, M., & Parsley, S. (2024). Old skool spinning and syncing: Memory, technologies, and occupational membership in a DJ community. *Journal of Management Studies*, joms.13086. https://doi.org/10.1111/joms.13086

Foster, W. M., Coraiola, D. M., Quinn-Trank, C., & Bastien, F. (2020). Unpacking organizational remembering. In K. Bruce (Ed.), *Handbook of research on management and organizational history* (pp. 256–274). Edward Elgar. https://doi.org/10.4337/9781788118491.00021

Foster, W. M., Suddaby, R., Minkus, A., & Wiebe, E. (2011). History as social memory assets: The example of Tim Hortons. *Management & Organizational History, 6*(1), 101–120. https://doi.org/10.1177/1744935910387027

Halbwachs, M. (1950/1980). *The collective memory*. Harper.

Hatch, M. J., & Schultz, M. (2017). Toward a theory of using history authentically: Historicizing in the Carlsberg Group. *Administrative Science Quarterly, 62*(4), 657–697. https://doi.org/10.1177/0001839217692535

Howard-Grenville, J., Metzger, M. L., & Meyer, A. D. (2013). Rekindling the flame: Processes of identity resurrection. *Academy of Management Journal, 56*(1), 113–136. https://doi.org/10.5465/amj.2010.0778

Lander, M. W., Roulet, T. J., & Heugens, P. P. (2022). Tempering temperance? A contingency approach to social movements' entry deterrence in Scottish whisky distilling, 1823–1921. *Academy of Management Journal, 66*(5), 1384–1410. https://doi.org/10.5465/amj.2019.1411

Lubinski, C. (2018). From 'history as told' to 'history as experienced': Contextualizing the uses of the past. *Organization Studies, 39*(12), 1785–1809. https://doi.org/10.1177/0170840618800116

Lubinski, C., & Gartner, W. B. (2023). Talking about (my) generation: The use of generation as rhetorical history in family business. *Family Business Review, 36*(1), 119–142. https://doi.org/10.1177/08944865231152283

Maclean, M., Harvey, C., & Chia, R. (2012). Sensemaking, storytelling and the legitimization of elite business careers. *Human Relations, 65*, 17–40. https://doi.org/10.1177/0018726711425616

Maclean, M., Harvey, C., Sillince, J. A. A., & Golant, B. D. (2018). Intertextuality, rhetorical history and the uses of the past in organizational transition. *Organization Studies, 39*(12), 1733–1755. https://doi.org/10.1177/0170840618789206

Meyer, J. W., & Rowan, B. (1977). Institutionalized organizations: Formal structure as myth and ceremony. *American Journal of Sociology, 83*(2), 340–363. https://doi.org/10.1086/226550

Nissley, N., & Casey, A. (2002). The politics of the exhibition: Viewing corporate museums through the paradigmatic lens of organizational memory. *British Journal of Management, 13*(s2), S35–S45. https://doi.org/10.1111/1467-8551.13.s2.4

Ogbonna, E., & Harris, L. C. (2001). The founder's legacy: Hangover or inheritance? *British Journal of Management, 12*(1), 13–31.

Ravasi, D., Rindova, V., & Stigliani, I. (2019). The stuff of legend: History, memory, and the temporality of organizational identity construction. *Academy of Management Journal, 62*(5), 1523–1555. https://doi.org/10.5465/amj.2016.0505

Rowlinson, M., Booth, C., Clark, P., Delahaye, A., & Procter, S. (2010). Social remembering and organizational memory. *Organization Studies, 31*(1), 69–87.

Rowlinson, M., & Hassard, J. (1993). The invention of corporate culture: A history of the histories of Cadbury. *Human Relations, 46*(3), 299–326. https://doi.org/10.1177/001872679304600301

Sasaki, I., Kotlar, J., Ravasi, D., & Vaara, E. (2020). Dealing with revered past: Historical identity statements and strategic change in Japanese family firms. *Strategic Management Journal, 41*(3), 590–623. https://doi.org/10.1002/smj.3065

Schultz, M., & Hernes, T. (2013). A temporal perspective on organizational identity. *Organization Science, 24*(1), 1–21. https://doi.org/10.1287/orsc.1110.0731

Schwartz, B. (2000). *Abraham Lincoln and the forge of national memory*. University of Chicago Press.

Schwartz, B. (2005). The new Gettysburg Address: Fusing history and memory. *Poetics, 33*(1), 63–79. https://doi.org/10.1016/j.poetic.2005.01.003

Sewell, W., Jr. (1996). Historical events as transformations of structure: Inventing revolution at the Bastille. *Theory and Society, 25*(6), 841–881. https://doi.org/10.1007/BF00159818

Suddaby, R. (2016). Toward a historical consciousness: Following the historic turn in management thought. *M@n@gement, 19*, 46–60. https://doi.org/10.3917/mana.191.0046

Suddaby, R., Coraiola, D., Harvey, C., & Foster, W. (2020). History and the micro-foundations of dynamic capabilities. *Strategic Management Journal, 41*(3), 530–556. https://doi.org/10.1002/smj.3058

Suddaby, R., Foster, W. M., & Trank, C. Q. (2010). Rhetorical history as a source of competitive advantage. In A. C. Joel & J. Lampel (Eds.), *The globalization of strategy research* (Advances in Strategic Management, Vol. 27, pp. 147–173). Emerald Group. https://doi.org/10.1108/S0742-3322(2010)0000027009

Suddaby, R., Foster, W. M., & Trank, C. Q. (2016). Re-membering: Rhetorical history as identity work. In M. G. Pratt, M. Schultz, B. E. Ashforth, & D. Ravasi (Eds.), *The Oxford handbook of organizational identity* (pp. 297–316). Oxford University Press.

Suddaby, R., Israelsen, T., Bastien, F., Saylors, R., & Coraiola, D. (2023). Rhetorical history as institutional work. *Journal of Management Studies, 60*(1), 242–278. https://doi.org/10.1111/joms.12860

Suddaby, R., Israelsen, T., Mitchell, J. R., & Lim, D. S. (2023). Entrepreneurial visions as rhetorical history: A diegetic narrative model of stakeholder enrollment. *Academy of Management Review, 48*(2), 220–243. https://doi.org/10.5465/amr.2020.0010

Suddaby, R., & Jaskiewicz, P. (2020). Managing traditions: A critical capability for family business success. *Family Business Review, 33*(3), 234–243. https://doi.org/10.1177/0894486520942611

Wagner-Pacifici, R. (2010). Theorizing the restlessness of events. *American Journal of Sociology, 115*(5), 1351–1386. https://doi.org/10.1086/651299

Wagner-Pacifici, R. (2016). Reconceptualizing memory as event: From "difficult pasts" to "restless events." In A. L. Tota & T. Hagen (Eds.), *Routledge international handbook of memory studies* (pp. 44–49). Routledge.

Walsh, I. J., & Glynn, M. A. (2008). The way we were: Legacy organizational identity and the role of leadership. *Corporate Reputation Review, 11*(3), 262–276. https://doi.org/10.1057/crr.2008.20

Zerubavel, E. (2003). Calendars and history: A comparative study of the social organization of national memory. In J. K. Olick, J. Adams, & G. Steinmetz (Eds.), *States of memory: Continuities, conflicts, and transformations in national retrospection* (pp. 315–337). Duke University Press.

Part II: **Organizational legacy in the broader ecology**

Peter Trümmel, Vittoria Magrelli, Paola Rovelli, Alfredo De Massis, and Christof Rissbacher

Chapter 5
Embedded legacy and the role of entrepreneurial family firms in business ecosystems: The Aspiag case

Legacies within business ecosystems

Legacy is a widely used construct that holds implications for individuals (e.g., Achtenhagen et al., 2022), families (e.g., Hammond et al., 2016), and organizations (e.g., Suddaby, 2016). In the specific context of entrepreneurial families (EFs),[1] which own and run the predominant type of organization—i.e., family businesses—legacy can explain why such businesses endure for multiple generations (Jaskiewicz et al., 2015). Defined as "a psychological, relational, and historical concept whose nature is immaterial and only comes to life through direct interaction with senders belonging to a prior generation or through artifact-mediated interaction with senders located in the past" (Radu-Lefebvre et al., 2024, p. 23), legacy is (a) a psychological concept, because it is attributed a value; (b) a relational concept, because its emergence depends on interactions between generations; and (c) a historical concept, because those interactions can span from the past into the present. Within EFs, legacy is passed down to the next generations with the aim not only of intergenerational continuity but also maintenance of the interconnections among the family's history, culture, and geographic origins (Thompson et al., 2009). In such a way, legacy serves as a motivator, especially for the next generation of the EF, and gives firms a sense of direction for entrepreneurship (Jaskiewicz et al., 2015). Admittedly, legacy is not exclusively beneficial, with the possibility of being perceived as a burden that is transmitted to the following generations (Wade-Benzoni & Tost, 2009). Moreover, how useful elements of a legacy are to the recipients influences the extent and selection of surviving legacy elements (Colquitt et al., 2023). Legacy can thus be molded by different actors and developed and transformed over time by generations (Sharma & Manikutty, 2005), demonstrating enduring yet malleable traits (Barbera et al., 2018) that can serve both internal and external stakeholders (Manelli et al., 2023).

---

[1] An entrepreneurial family is "a group of individuals related by kinship, adoption, or affinity (by marriage or other relationship) who jointly own and/or manage multiple assets, following a shared vision for how such assets should collectively create value across generations" (De Massis et al., 2021, p. 360).

https://doi.org/10.1515/9783111631462-006

While EFs are dominant and relevant contributors to a local economy (Aldrich & Cliff, 2003; Baù et al., 2019), their legacies forge organizational identity[2] and bind EFs to their territory (e.g., Lumpkin & Bacq, 2022; Suddaby, 2016). Yet, despite such multifaceted connections with their environment, legacies have mostly been investigated in isolation, i.e., at the individual, familial, or organizational level, disregarding the existence and interconnections of multiple actors and legacies in a shared geographic, historic, and socioeconomic context. Such oversight is consequential since effective actions must be embedded in social structures to realize their competitive advantage (Granovetter, 1985). EFs are a particularly relevant group of interacting actors that shape the socioeconomic composition and development of a territory (Bichler et al., 2022). Hence, if the focus shifts from the actors to their relationships (i.e., relational agency; Burkitt, 2016), we need to shift our attention from isolated cases of legacies to multiple locally embedded, socially, and economically interconnected systems of legacies. Thus, to understand how interconnected legacies that are locally embedded develop entrepreneurial relevance for their respective EFs, stakeholders, and the territory at large, we turn to their relationships within an established business ecosystem.

Existing literature on EFs' embeddedness provides strong arguments for how and why EFs are significant contributors to a territory's development and how such embeddedness serves EFs themselves. For example, recent research has shown that the local embeddedness of EFs profoundly affects entrepreneurial processes (i.e., opportunity recognition, venture creation, or resource mobilization) due to their embedded social relationships (Aldrich & Cliff, 2003), contributing to the regional economy (Baù et al., 2019) and civic wealth creation (Lumpkin & Bacq, 2022). However, this stream of literature has thus far left aside the EFs' roots of a legacy in a territory (Lumpkin & Bacq, 2022). At the same time, literature on legacy points out that the interconnection among generations is a key aspect of the successful use and transmission of legacy over time (e.g., Barbera et al., 2018; Colquitt et al., 2023). For example, Ge and colleagues (2022) found EFs' operations to be based on traditions, grounding an EF in the past and a broader cultural heritage of a region when they target external stakeholders' strategic use of history to tap into the respective sources of competitive advantage (e.g., acceptance by broader communities, reputation for longevity, innovation through tradition). Yet, this stream of literature has prioritized the study of single legacies, isolated from other actors with legacies of their own. Others have previously pointed out that a family's "legacy emerges through the complex social interactions and exchanges among individual family members" and their regional environment (Hammond et al., 2016, p. 1214; Manelli et al., 2023). In fact, Coraiola et al. (2023) encouraged the application of an ecological lens to examine such complex systems of interactions among individuals and communities that span time through shared memories

---

[2] Organizational identity refers to the enduring and distinctive essence, features, and behaviors of an organization (Albert & Whetten, 1985).

(i.e., "memory work"). Hence, both streams of literature emphasize that EFs do not operate in isolation and are instead interconnected with their territorial and sociohistorical surroundings. Thus, we shift the focus of inquiry from individual EF legacies to the dynamic relationships among EFs' legacies and their territory, embedded in business ecosystems.

In the past decade, there has been continued scientific interest in the phenomenon of business ecosystems (Fuller et al., 2019)—i.e., "dynamic group[s] of largely independent economic players that create products or services that together constitute a coherent solution for customers" (Reeves & Pidun, 2022, p. xiii)—approaching them as dynamic and complex rather than static entities (e.g., Arthur, 2021). Recently, studies on the development of business ecosystems have focused on understanding the interdependencies among local organizations and how these actors give rise to their respective businesses (e.g., Iansiti & Levien, 2004; Reeves & Pidun, 2022). The purpose of a business ecosystem is to create and share value through the joint efforts and activities of interdependent partners (Adner, 2017; Iansiti & Levien, 2004). Each player indeed draws from the collaborations with other players in the business ecosystem (Tsou et al., 2018)—thus becoming partners—which involves providing or exchanging financial or technological resources (Iansiti & Levien, 2004; Zahra & Nambisan, 2012), capabilities (Pidun, Reeves, & Zoletnik, 2022), and institutions (Clarysse et al., 2014). Research has shown that the scope of such business ecosystems often focuses on market niches and/or geographically well-defined territories (Clarysse et al., 2014; Pidun et al., 2022a, 2022b). As such, scholars have placed great emphasis on geographic locality to develop knowledge about its causal effects on competitive advantage within a region (e.g., Iansiti & Levien, 2004).

The purpose of this chapter is to show how the relationships among legacies of EFs can influence the business ecosystem to which they belong. In so doing, we integrate the literature on business ecosystems (e.g., Fuller et al., 2019) and family business legacy (e.g., Barbera et al., 2018) based on assumptions of relational agency, which Burkitt (2016) unraveled as the agency that unfolds across time and space, within the social relations between interacting parties that are dialogically, polyphonically, and emotionally interconnected. This focus on interconnectedness is warranted since EFs have grown strong roots in their geographic location through their family businesses, for their lives have continuously merged with their territory (Baù et al., 2019), allowing for business ecosystems to emerge due to their local embeddedness (Aldrich & Cliff, 2003; Baù et al., 2019). Due to their historically grown connections to their territory, family businesses' past and present entrepreneurial activity gives rise to and maintains the dynamics that form local business ecosystems (e.g., Adner, 2017; Arthur, 2021; Lumpkin & Bacq, 2022; Suddaby, 2016). To develop a conceptualization of such dynamics, we draw from multiple cases of EFs affiliated with the retail network of Aspiag Services Srl (hereafter: *Aspiag*). Aspiag is a prominent food retailer located in northeastern Italy that manages the Despar brand. Specifically, Aspiag is active in the regions of Trentino–Alto Adige, Veneto, Emilia-Romagna, and Friuli–Venezia Giulia. In these geographically defined local territories, Aspiag holds an orchestrating role (e.g., procurement, supply, distribution, and marketing; Pidun et al., 2022a) within a business ecosystem of independent affiliated EFs that run stores under the brand of Despar. With this chapter, we contribute to an understanding of legacy's role in a territory's local history and economy, i.e., how interconnected EFs in a business ecosystem generate efficiency through legacy, engage in exchange among legacies, and leverage legacy to (commercially) navigate their territory. Hence, we provide an alternative perspective on the organizing power that a multitude of legacies can have over a dominant form of organization (Fuller et al., 2019; Moore, 1993).

The remainder of this chapter is structured as follows. First, we describe our research setting, presenting the case of Aspiag as a business ecosystem that envelops embedded cases of individual EFs' legacies tied to the business ecosystem's development. Second, we present our findings on how legacies within a business ecosystem interrelate. We conceptualize how these relationship dynamics shape a business ecosystem in a territory. Finally, we conclude by presenting our contributions to theory and practice.

An embedded case study of Aspiag and its affiliates

To investigate how relationships among EFs' legacies shape the structure of a business ecosystem, we needed to understand which parties take which role and how they interconnect with one another. We adopted a case study approach (Stake, 1978, 1995), which allows for an in-depth exploration of the relationships that constitute the business ecosystem. We treated each relationship between Aspiag and its affiliated EFs as embedded cases within the network of relationships, providing an understanding of the dynamics of interconnected legacies in this particular business ecosystem. Studying these embedded cases, we reveal the ways in which the complex web of relationships among legacies influences and is influenced by the network.

Research setting

Our study focused on the business ecosystem that included Aspiag and its affiliated EFs. Aspiag is a food retailer that belongs to SPAR Austria and manages the Despar brand in Northeast Italy. SPAR was founded in the Netherlands in 1932 by Adriaan J. Van Well, who understood that the union of numerous small wholesalers could significantly shape the European economic landscape of the 1930s (Aspiag Service Srl., 2023). The name initially chosen was "Spar," which is an acronym that, when translated into English, means "harmonious cooperation provides benefit to all." From the Netherlands, SPAR expanded first to Belgium and then throughout the rest of Europe

(Austria, Italy, Slovenia, Croatia), reaching as far as countries in Africa and Asia. In 1954, Hans F. Reisch established the first SPAR organization in Austria and by the end of the 1950s, there were independently operating SPAR retailers throughout Austria. The SPAR Voluntary Union, subsequently Despar Italia, was founded in 1960 (Aspiag Service Srl., 2023).

Today, SPAR is present in almost all Italian regions with three types of store formats to meet the needs of its customers with different habits and lifestyles: Despar, characterized by quality, good assortment, and excellence in fresh food and service; Eurospar, with a wide assortment of food and nonfood items; and Interspar, with large square footage and assortment aimed at meeting all customer needs. In Italy, the Despar brand is managed by six different independent partners (the largest of which is Aspiag) that are unified in the Limited Liability Consortium Despar Italia, situated in Casalecchio di Reno (Bologna), which ensures conformity with the corporate identity. Each member operates its business in a predefined geographic area, having a license to use the Despar brand and managing its own logistics platforms and outlets in the territory. Consortium Despar Italia protects the brand, has direct contact with SPAR International, and takes care of the development of branded products and promotions. In 2022, the structure of Aspiag included 255 direct branches and 306 affiliates, with a turnover of 2.32 billion Euros (Aspiag Service Srl, 2022).

Methodological approach

We analyzed interconnected legacies by looking at cases (Stake, 1978, 1995) of relationships within the business ecosystem composed of Aspiag and its affiliated EFs in Northeast Italy. We considered each relationship between individual affiliates and Aspiag as an embedded case within the network of relationships. As such, we engaged in collecting archival data to reconstruct the origins and developments of relationships and their dynamics, while also collecting observational data from ethnographic interviews with affiliated EF and Aspiag employees. The collected data provided an understanding of the individual EFs' legacy and connection to their surrounding territory, the content and quality of their connection to Aspiag, and how the collective of legacies shapes the business ecosystem at large. Table 5.1 summarizes the collected data and its purpose within our analysis (Patton, 2002).

Throughout our data collection, we interviewed affiliated EFs that had (a) long-standing and continuous relationships with Aspiag (e.g., some reaching back to the very beginning of SPAR's operations in Italy), and (b) strong ties to the territory (i.e., families that originate from that region). We also interviewed informants from Aspiag (regional managers and consultants), who provided deep insights into the territory and their affiliated EFs. Regional managers were selected based on their assignment to the regions in which selected affiliated EFs operated. For instance, some of the regional managers had continuously worked with the interviewed affiliated EFs since

Table 5.1: Data and Its Analytical Purposes.

Data	Source	Use in analysis
Interviews	– 3 EFs from South Tyrol – 1 EF from Emilia-Romagna – 1 EF from Friuli-Venezia Giulia – 7 Aspiag informants (regional managers and consultants) *26 interviews; 26 interviewees; 18 hours of recorded interviews*	– Provided insights into the territory, EF legacies, and Aspiag's management of affiliates and territory – Enabled us to capture relationships, their dynamics, their origins, and perceptions thereof
Pictures	– Of places (e.g., SPAR stores) – Of events – Of historic documents (e.g., family trees) *30 pictures*	– Provided an understanding of space, references to the local territory, product display, and assortment
Observations	– Researcher notes on interviews, places, events, and personal experience	– Provided subjective impressions of other data – Enabled us to corroborate data and facilitate data interpretation
Archival material	– Aspiag marketing material – Reports (e.g., annual and sustainability reports) – Books (e.g., jubilee book) *341 pages of documents*	– Provided additional contextual and historical insights – Enabled us to enrich and triangulate our data

Note: EF, entrepreneurial family.

they began their careers with Aspiag. Consultants, as the other category of Aspiag informants, were interviewed because of their knowledge about both the regions and the affiliated EFs in the respective regions; for one of the regions, we could not identify a fitting consultant as an Aspiag informant. Ultimately, we conducted 26 interviews: nine interviews with seven informants within Aspiag (e.g., regional managers, human resource managers, top executives, consultants), and 17 interviews with five affiliated EFs (19 informants), amounting to roughly 18 hours of audio material. In addition, we participated as observers in two Aspiag "end of the year" meetings attended by the affiliated EFs of two specific regions (Emilia Romagna and Trentino Alto-Adige) and were given access to archival material from Aspiag and some of the affiliated families. As a secondary data source, we collected more than 300 pages of archival documents related to the EFs and Aspiag. In addition to personal notes on meetings, interviews, places, and events, we took 30 pictures of historical documents (e.g., old photographs of stores, places, or events) and places (e.g., old rooms of former stores, current stores, and store features) when we visited families at their stores and homes.

By analyzing our data set through a grounded theory approach (Corbin & Strauss, 1990; Gioia et al., 2013; Patton, 2002), we developed our understanding of how legacy shapes relationships in a business ecosystem. According to the legacy definition of Radu-Lefebvre et al. (2024), which highlights that legacy is a psychological, historical, and relational construct, we considered pieces of information that revealed anything about an EF's past historical elements of legacy (e.g., family stories). We recognized pieces of information about EFs' reflections on values and norms, their business mindset, and the future as psychological elements of legacy. Pieces of information about how EFs connected to their internal members and their environment across generations represented relational elements of legacy. When looking at the relationships among EFs and with Aspiag, we focused on informants' characterizations of their connections to one another.

In particular, we began to organize our data based on the relationships they referred to. We identified three levels of relationships within the business ecosystem of Aspiag and its affiliated EFs. First, there was the relationship between Aspiag and its affiliated EFs. Second, there were relationships at the level of the families, both within individual EFs and among EFs. Lastly, there were relationships at the level of the territory: each family had its unique connection to its region. Through this organization of data, we were able to establish credibility through triangulation and member checks (Guba, 1981). Moreover, this step of organizing our data facilitated the subsequent analysis. In a second step, we began to dive deeper into our data, familiarizing ourselves with individual EFs and their relationships at the previously identified levels. We iteratively coded our data case by case to uphold a structured process. This step delivered a codebook and a list of interesting and relevant quotes. Lastly, we followed the grounded theory approach (Glaser & Strauss, 2017) to structure our data based on emerging themes and, ultimately, aggregated categories as the highest abstraction of our data. In this last step, we considered codes and themes across cases and relationships, embracing dependability. Throughout the process, the research team came together frequently to discuss data interpretation, coding, clustering, and abstractions for the sake of confirmability (Guba, 1981). Table 5.2 presents our final data structure with examples of empirical evidence, emergent themes, and aggregated categories.

Findings

Legacies in a territory

Through our data analysis, we were able to see how different components of the EFs' legacy (psychological, historical, relational; Radu-Lefebvre et al., 2024) play out at the different relationship levels (*"Families–Territory," "Families," "Aspiag–Families"*;

Table 5.2: Data Structure.

Level of relationship	Exemplary evidence	Emergent theme	Aggregate category
Aspiag families (EFs)	RM 2: "Even when there is a severe problem, they [EF 3] have always behaved in a polite, responsible, and civil manner."	Respectful partnership	**Efficiency:** Aspiag taps into the commercial potential of territory through families; families have access to established system of services and distribution.
	EF 3 recounted multiple stories of when and how their respective Aspiag regional manager is always available to discuss problems or new ideas for products, shop set-ups, or other collaborations.		
	RM 1: "I believe that the advantage for Aspiag [is] a certain capillarity to cover even areas or territories that might not seem so attractive from a commercial point of view."	Families tapping into territorial opportunities for Aspiag	
	EF 3: "These are local suppliers of products and we have control over what of them to include in your range of products."	Aspiag shares authority and services with families	
	Aspiag services: logistics, marketing, branding, design (architecture and interior), organizational infrastructure, "Aspiag Academy" (an educational initiative to foster relationships with affiliates)		

Category	Quotes		
Families (relationships within and among EFs)	EF 3: "We have known them [EF 4] ever since we joined Aspiag. They always have a story to tell and we always learn something from them." EF 1: "I wanted to see a few things. So I went away for 2 weeks to a store in Veneto to see . . . their food counter. I have always been interested in learning things, not only through courses." In EF 3 and 4, the oldest children (next generation) have begun to help out or even work full-time in the store.	Interfamilial network provides learning and support (i.e., access to other families' legacies) Intrafamilial network provides workforce and continuity (i.e., succession and legacy)	**Exchange:** Network of affiliation (horizontal) and family ties (vertical) enable mutual benefits for families, both from Aspiag resources (e.g., logistics, educational services) and families' territorial resources (e.g., knowledge, legacy).
Families (EFs) – Territory	EF 4: "We have had this store in this village since 1872. Everybody knows us." EF 1: "Always linked to the territory, [we] have been attentive to the selection of local companies, offering an assortment of quality products linked to Friulian tradition and culture."	(Family) history in the territory	**Leverage:** Family's legacy enables EF to commercially navigate the territory.
	Consultant 1: "They have the ability to read that territory and to invent and innovate for that territory."	Family holds (tacit) knowledge about the territory	
	Consultant 2: "And above all, the difference is that Aspiag is very tied to the territory. While there are many other franchises in Italy, the uniqueness of Aspiag is that when they enter a territory and approach an entrepreneur to become a Despar associate, they also say, 'Teach me what is done in your territory, so that I can bring it to my branches as well.'"	Territory holds commercial opportunities	

Note: EF, entrepreneurial family; RM, regional manager.

Table 5.3) within the business ecosystem of Aspiag. Based on the information shared by EFs, their legacies encompassed psychological components of values, e.g., trust, respect, and commitment to Aspiag and their territory (i.e., local suppliers) and their way of valuing local traditions (e.g., Friulian traditions) or family artifacts (e.g., their sentimental presentation of old pictures). Historical components of legacy emerged as stories about past generations' business activities, family stories, or accounts of their territory's development over the years that often originated several decades earlier. Some of these historical components manifested in the EFs' tacit knowledge about their territory (e.g., in their intricate understanding and navigation of their territory). Relational components presented themselves as descriptions and characterizations of enduring connections and relationships to former EF generations, to other actors from a territory (e.g., local communities, suppliers), and to Aspiag.

Based on our data, we found that the affiliated EFs drew from their respective pasts—i.e., the learning and experience of previous generations—and the relationships and traditions that previous generations established with the territory, Aspiag, and other affiliated EFs. Specifically, legacies were based on EFs having been locally embedded, on entrepreneurial pasts and visions for the future, and on traditions that connected the EFs with their surrounding territories and ways of doing business. As an informant from EF 3 stated:

> It is not only that we have our roots here, that we are connected to the region; we have our traditions and they come from the family and this region. We are part of [local territory] and for now, we would like to keep the business going. And then we take it from there.

This shows that an EF's legacy plays a pivotal role in the EF's relationship to a territory, as well as its relationship to its business and, by extension, to Aspiag. In the following section, we elaborate on the three identified levels of relationship and how they shaped the business ecosystem.

Roles of legacies in a business ecosystem

As presented in Table 5.3, we identified three levels of relationships that shaped the business ecosystem encompassing Aspiag, its affiliated EFs, and the territory in which Aspiag and the EFs operated. Namely, levels of relationships appeared between the territory and affiliated EFs (*Families–Territory*), within and among affiliated EFs (*Families*), and between Aspiag and its affiliated EFs (*Aspiag–Families*). These levels were not only distinct due to the parties involved in these relationships but were also related to different (a) purposes of these relationships within the business ecosystem, (b) roles the involved parties took within these relationships, and (c) foundations of these relationships.

Table 5.3: Relationships Within a Business Ecosystem.

Level of relationship	Foundation of relationship	Roles of involved relationship parties	Role of legacy within relationship
EFs–Territory	(Family) history in the territory	– EF holds (tacit) knowledge about the territory – Territory holds commercial opportunities	**Leverage of legacies**: EFs' legacy enables EFs to commercially navigate the territory.
EFs	Affiliation Family ties	– Inter-familial network provides learning and support (i.e., access to other EFs' legacies) – Intra-familial network provides workforce and continuity (i.e., succession and legacy)	**Exchange among legacies**: Network of affiliation (horizontal) and family ties (vertical) enables mutual benefits for families, both from Aspiag resources (e.g., logistics, educational services) and EFs' territorial resources (e.g., knowledge, history, relationships to territory).
Aspiag–EFs	Respectful partnership	– Families harvesting territorial opportunities – Aspiag shares authority and services with families	**Efficiency through legacies**: Aspiag taps into the commercial potential of the territory through EFs (e.g., their tacit knowledge, relationships to territory); EFs have access to established system of services and distribution.

Note: EF, entrepreneurial family.

Leverage of legacies. At the first level were the relationships that the affiliated EFs had with the territory. The purpose of relationships at this level was for EFs to leverage historic and relational components of their legacies to commercially navigate the territory. Specifically, EFs' intricate knowledge of the territory (of people, communities, history, preferences, customs, and traditions) enabled them to recognize commercial opportunities and adapt business practices. Especially through their traditions and enduring connections to their local communities, EFs felt connected and embedded in the territory, and they possessed a deep and often tacit understanding of their territory. Through this understanding, EFs could "read" the territory, as an Aspiag consultant and former affiliate put it:

> A 200-square-meter store can exist in that small village that feeds that family for five generations because they have the ability to read that territory and to invent and innovate for that territory.

In these relationships with the territory, the territory held (or constrained) the commercial opportunities for the business ecosystem. It also provided feedback to the EFs through changes in demand, behavior, and revenue concerning the family's performance. In turn, the EF held tacit and explicit knowledge about the territory that they then used to navigate it.

The foundation for relationships at this level was the family's history (e.g., stories of parents or grandparents founding and running the business or their social position in local communities) in its territory and the resulting embeddedness in this territory. Because the interviewed EFs all had longstanding origins in their region, they had personal connections to the local population, knew about the development, history, and traditions of the territory, and were part of this territory even before they began their affiliation with Aspiag. As an informant from EF 4 stated, "We have had this store in this village since 1872. Everybody knows us."

Exchange among legacies. At the second level, there were relationships within and among EFs. The purpose of these relationships among different EFs was the exchange of knowledge (e.g., advice, contact information for suppliers) and the sharing of information (e.g., through councils). Within affiliated EFs, family members exchanged past knowledge and experiences, i.e., elements of their legacy and their workforce. Through these exchanges within and among EFs, a network of interconnected EFs within a territory was formed, enabling EFs to mutually benefit from Aspiag resources (e.g., logistics, educational services) and territorial resources (e.g., knowledge, elements of legacy).

In this network of relationships, on the one hand, the intrafamilial relationships and exchanges provided for the continuity of psychological, historical, and relational legacy components and of the business ecosystem at large. On the other hand, the interfamilial network of relationships allowed access to other EFs' legacies, e.g., historical legacy components in the form of past knowledge and experience and relational components of EFs' deep connection to local communities, both of which could be helpful to other affiliated EFs. As an informant from EF 3 commented:

> We always learn something. Because it's mostly events or small trips that we go to and we usually sit together. We don't just talk about business. . . . It's often things that someone else knows a bit more about and we talk a lot. So there's always a lively exchange.

The foundations for the relationships at this level were based on kinship for the intrafamilial relationships among family members. The foundation of interfamilial relationships was their contractual connection to Aspiag. However, relationships among affiliated EFs also encompassed a strong personal bond that went beyond contractual ties. The EFs built bonds based on a feeling of a shared history, territory, and industry. Due to these personal bonds, affiliated EFs were in frequent and spontaneous contact, without Aspiag's involvement. Specifically, there was a lively and continuous exchange of information among EFs surrounding official events and gatherings initiated and organized by Aspiag where EFs met. This informal exchange was relevant because it was consequential for business practices, i.e., one EF could make use of another EF's legacy components, both relational (connections to local communities) and historical (knowledge and past experiences). For example, ad hoc obstacles, e.g., disruptions in supply, complications with local regulations, or mishaps in business processes, could be circumvented or removed by asking for advice directly from other affiliated EFs. This advice could often be applied directly and spread current best practices within the network without depending on Aspiag's resources or services. For instance, when telling us more about how EFs connect and stay in contact, EF 3 told us that the EFs chat and call one another via their phones over long distances. Aspiag also organized events and trips at which EFs came together.

Efficiency through legacies. At the third level were relationships between Aspiag and the affiliated EFs. The purpose of this level of relationship was the efficient profiteering off of a territory's commercial opportunities. The generated profits benefited both Aspiag and its affiliated EFs. The efficiency was rooted in the EFs' deep connection to the territory and their intimate knowledge of it, i.e., knowing what kind of products, innovations, and practices work best, and the most effective use of Aspiag's provided infrastructure and services. Hence, legacy became a facilitator for efficient commercial operations in a territory, as it provided the family with both the connection to the territory, i.e., profitable local products and suppliers, and knowledge about the territory, i.e., about customer preferences for the shopping experience (e.g., avoiding self-checkout cashiers, weighing of fresh fruits) and products (e.g., tourists looking for traditional local products, locals looking for established and locally known brands and products). A regional manager described this economic rationale with Aspiag's inability to cover all locally distinct needs of customers:

> Today, because of the structure we have, we are unable to have all the suppliers that everyone needs, so we leave a certain part of freedom in the purchase, in the management of these products, and indeed, from a point of view, we also recommend contacting small producers in the area precisely because of . . . not being able to satisfy the consumption and needs of all consumers.

In this relationship, Aspiag provided affiliated EFs with organizational structure and services related to logistics, supply chain management, marketing, and training, among others. In addition, Aspiag gave affiliates a fair share of authority in how to run their business. In turn, the affiliated EFs realized the commercial opportunities of the territory through their intricate connection to their surroundings, generating revenue and profit for the system.

This relationship was based on a respectful partnership wherein Aspiag took on the role of a steward to the affiliated EFs, who then depended on Aspiag's infrastructure to harvest the territory's economic potential in retail. During the past 50 years, Aspiag has tried to build bonds with the EFs affiliated with it (and thus were part of the business ecosystem). As one of the regional managers explained:

> We are dealing with families with whom we have built and want to continue to build a path of growth in the future, with families who rely completely on us, families who have absolute trust in us and with whom over the years we have built an important connection made up of personal relationships.

Correspondingly, an informant from EF 2 expressed gratitude for the supportive relationship with Aspiag, confirming that the relationship between Aspiag and its affiliated EFs was partnership-based:

> Support, training, and the example of art have been fundamental for the growth of the company and for the path it is taking, for business growth, but also for our growth. Why? They have always given us support at 360 degrees.

Relationships dynamics in a business ecosystem

Trying to understand the unfolding relationship dynamics within a business ecosystem, we looked at the relationships among Aspiag, as an orchestrating actor, and multiple EFs with individual legacies, as independent actors, within a territory. Most prominently, the EFs' historical and relational legacy components drove the dynamics of interconnectedness in the Aspiag business ecosystem. This network of relationships in Northeast Italy proved to be far from static. Rather, relationships on all levels shaped the business ecosystem. For instance, Aspiag was able to efficiently tap into a territory's commercial potential because of its respectful partnership with the affiliated EFs. Affiliated EFs exchanged knowledge, often in the form of advice, as examples of historical legacy components. Within affiliated EFs, family members exchanged workforce and career prospects (via succession) as relational legacy components. Also, EFs possessed deep connections to their territory because of their historical relations with local communities and other EFs within the business ecosystem, i.e., their locally embedded legacy. The EFs' embedded legacy, in turn, enabled them to navigate the commercial opportunities in their territory.

Overall, we found that the legacies of affiliated EFs dynamically shaped the relationships in this business ecosystem. On the one hand, our analysis shows that multiple EFs develop outward-oriented legacies—legacies that grow and develop relevance beyond the EFs and are therefore not exclusively transferred and shared within the boundaries of an EF, connecting them to their surrounding environment (Manelli et al., 2023). On the other hand, we also see how the legacies of individual EFs are interconnected through their historical ties within the business ecosystem they operate in, giving rise to dynamics of relationships that influence a business ecosystem's development (Burkitt, 2016; Iansiti & Levien, 2004).

Discussion and contributions

Our findings show that legacy takes different roles within the relationships that shape a business ecosystem. Empirically, we drew from a setting of an established business ecosystem that enveloped an orchestrating organization, multiple affiliated EFs, and their legacies in Northeast Italy. Through our analysis, we found three levels of relationships. *Families–Territory* relationships were based on the EF's family history in a territory. On this level, EFs leveraged their history and intricate connection to the territory to commercially navigate their surrounding territory. The *Families* relationships were based on interfamilial relationships of kinship and on interfamilial relationships of personal (and professional) bonds. On this relationship level, EFs exchanged legacy vertically (within EFs) and horizontally (among EFs). Vertical exchanges involved the sharing of psychological legacy components (e.g., values and visions) and historical legacy components (e.g., knowledge and past experiences) along kinship lines from past to present generations. These internal, vertical exchanges in themselves were part of the legacy's relational components (Radu-Lefebvre et al., 2024). Horizontal exchanges involved the sharing of historical legacy components (e.g., knowledge and past experiences) and relational components (e.g., enduring connection to a territory) shared among EFs across the business ecosystem network of affiliated EFs. This *Families* level encompasses the interconnectedness of EFs' legacies within the same business ecosystem. The *Aspiag–Families* relationships were based on contractual relationships. On this relationship level, Aspiag and its affiliated EFs generated commercial efficiency through the EFs' relational legacy components (i.e., the EFs' embeddedness in the business ecosystem) and their interconnected legacies (on the *Families* level) and historical legacy components (i.e., the EFs' intricate and tacit knowledge and understanding of their respective territory). Overall, we found that psychological, historical, and relational legacy components operate at different levels of relationships in a business ecosystem, building bridges across actors (i.e., Aspiag as orchestrating organization and EFs as affiliates), space (i.e., territories), and time (i.e., history).

While legacy is predominantly presented as a resource for organizations to draw from, we find that in the context of a business ecosystem, EFs catalyze their psychological, historical, and relational legacy components to create efficient, profitable relationships among business partners, enhance exchange among affiliates, and facilitate leveraging a firm's local embeddedness. Thus, not only does our study confirm that legacies are a source of competitive advantage (e.g., Sasaki et al., 2020; Suddaby & Jaskiewicz, 2020), but more importantly, we describe how legacy can do so, presenting legacy as a dynamic process functioning at multiple levels of its ecosystem (e.g., Taraday, 2013), rather than a static resource. Specifically, EFs tapped into the complex interconnections among affiliated EFs, Aspiag, and territories by using and relying on their different legacy components. As day-to-day situations and the wider context continued to change, they demanded flexible responses. The interconnectedness of legacies and their different roles at different levels provided adjustable solutions for the EFs and the business ecosystem. As such, legacy equipped EFs with useful inputs (e.g., historical legacy components) and business-enhancing mechanisms (e.g., relational legacy components), and it provided fruitful outputs (i.e., competitive advantage). In this vein of being a process, legacy becomes a catalyst for competitive advantage through the relational agency of the relationships among interacting actors within the business ecosystem. These relationships, in turn, emerge from the actors' embeddedness.

While it is widely acknowledged that EFs' embeddedness contributes to regional economic development (Aldrich & Cliff, 2003; Baù et al., 2019; Lumpkin & Bacq, 2022; Suddaby, 2016), we add to this research by showing that such contributions are, at least to some extent, grounded in EFs' ability to recognize and leverage their legacy and the benefits it offers to the business ecosystem around them. So far, legacy has attracted scholarly attention in terms of its content, involved parties, transmission, and contexts of existence, pointing out its social and economic relevance for EFs (Radu-Lefebvre et al., 2024), yet little has been known about the process of these attributes unfolding in a dynamic system of social and economic relationships (e.g., Rao et al., 2000), i.e., the role of embedded legacy in the contexts it exists and works in. Our findings complement existing knowledge about legacy, as we move beyond the isolated legacies of single families and instead look at their integration in a dynamic social, geographic, and commercial context.

These insights provide an alternative perspective on the current knowledge about business ecosystems, which assumes such systems to be rather static, ignoring the temporality of historically grown interdependencies of interacting EFs. This is a remarkable neglect of such ecosystems' origins and antecedents (Fuller et al., 2019; Iansiti & Levien, 2004; Moore, 1993), diminishing the illustrative power of the evolutionary metaphor (Mars et al., 2012). We highlight the relational dynamics between the partners within the ecosystem. We point out that the legacies of individual EFs interconnect, especially based on their historical legacy components (value, stories, past experiences) and relational legacy components (interactions between family generations and among EFs within the business ecosystem). Hence, we shift the focus from individual organizations to their interdependencies. This shift in attention is based on previous claims that actors and their actions must be "embedded in concrete, ongoing systems of social systems" to realize their competitive advantage (Granovetter, 1985, p. 487). Within social systems, interdependencies are the result that ultimately grounds agency in the relationships among interacting actors (i.e., relational agency; Burkitt, 2016). In fact, we aim to provide insights into how multiple legacies coexist and interrelate within the framework of a business ecosystem, as a prominent form of organizing (Fuller et al., 2019; Moore, 1993).

Ultimately, with our study, we show that legacy is not only relevant to a single EF that is concerned with a legacy's contents, involved parties, transmission, and contexts (Radu-Lefebvre et al., 2024). Rather, we are able to show that embedded legacy, as the historically grown relations and interconnectedness with other EFs' legacies that bind EFs to a territory, is also relevant for the development of an ecosystem and how such an ecosystem can benefit from a legacy's competitive advantage (Sasaki et al., 2020; Suddaby & Jaskiewicz, 2020).

Conclusion

With this chapter, we present the legacy of EFs as an integrated and interconnected process that works on different levels within a territory, stressing the embeddedness of legacy and the relational agency of the relationships among such legacies. With this shift in focus from actors to their dynamic relationships, we introduce the concept of relational agency (Burkitt, 2016) to discussions of collectively constructed histories (e.g., Anteby & Molnar, 2012; Suddaby et al., 2023; Suddaby, 2016) in organizations and their surrounding environments, especially in family businesses (Suddaby & Jaskiewicz, 2020). As such, we connect previously separate streams of literature. While business ecosystems are prevalently concerned with transactions and value creation (e.g., Adner, 2017; Iansiti & Levien, 2004), research on legacy has thus far focused on understanding its nature, development, and effects (e.g., Radu-Lefebvre et al., 2024). Hence, we introduce a dynamic view of the business ecosystem that takes into account the history of a territory, the actors therein, and ongoing social relations (Aldrich & Cliff, 2003; Baù et al., 2019; Burkitt, 2016; Granovetter, 1985; Thompson et al., 2009). Still, our findings and contributions are limited to contexts of business ecosystems wherein relationships are based on direct commercial relationships that serve the system's purpose. We cannot make any reliable claims as to how and why or to what extent legacies and the historical development of individual actors within a geographic region contribute to a local economy. For that, further research is needed to understand and evaluate the economic relevance of legacies, both in isolation and in settings of interdependency.

References

Achtenhagen, L., Haag, K., Hultén, K., & Lundgren, J. (2022). Torn between individual aspirations and the family legacy—individual career development in family firms. *Career Development International*, 27(2), 201–221. https://doi.org/10.1108/CDI-06-2020-0156

Adner, R. (2017). Ecosystem as structure: An actionable construct for strategy. *Journal of Management*, 43(1), 39–58. https://doi.org/10.1177/0149206316678451

Albert, S., & Whetten, D. A. (1985). Organizational Identity. In B. M. Staw & L. L. Cummings (Eds.), *Research in organizational behavior* (pp. 263–295). JAI Press.

Aldrich, H. E., & Cliff, J. E. (2003). The pervasive effects of family on entrepreneurship: Toward a family embeddedness perspective. *Journal of Business Venturing*, 18(5), 573–596. https://doi.org/10.1016/S0883-9026(03)00011-9

Anteby, M., & Molnar, V. (2012). Collective memory meets organizational identity: Remembering to forget in a firm's rhetorical history. *Academy of Management Journal*, 55(3), 515–540. https://doi.org/10.5465/amj.2010.0245

Arthur, W. B. (2021). Foundations of complexity economics. *Nature Reviews Physics*, 3(2), 136–145. https://doi.org/10.1038/s42254-020-00273-3

Aspiag Service Srl. (2022). *Report integrato 2021*. https://despartribuprod01.blob.core.windows.net/despartribu/sezioni/azienda/report_integrato_2021.pdf

Aspiag Service Srl. (2023). *Storia*. https://www.despar.it/it/storia/#gref

Barbera, F., Stamm, I., & DeWitt, R. L. (2018). The development of an entrepreneurial legacy: Exploring the role of anticipated futures in transgenerational entrepreneurship. *Family Business Review, 31*(3), 352–378. https://doi.org/10.1177/0894486518780795

Baù, M., Chirico, F., Pittino, D., Backman, M., & Klaesson, J. (2019). Roots to grow: Family firms and local embeddedness in rural and urban contexts. *Entrepreneurship Theory and Practice, 43*(2), 360–385. https://doi.org/10.1177/1042258718796089

Bichler, B. F., Kallmuenzer, A., Peters, M., Petry, T., & Clauss, T. (2022). Regional entrepreneurial ecosystems: How family firm embeddedness triggers ecosystem development. *Review of Managerial Science, 16*(1), 15–44. https://doi.org/10.1007/s11846-020-00434-9

Burkitt, I. (2016). Relational agency: Relational sociology, agency and interaction. *European Journal of Social Theory, 19*(3), 322–339. https://doi.org/10.1177/1368431015591426

Clarysse, B., Wright, M., Bruneel, J., & Mahajan, A. (2014). Creating value in ecosystems: Crossing the chasm between knowledge and business ecosystems. *Research Policy, 43*(7), 1164–1176. https://doi.org/10.1016/j.respol.2014.04.014

Colquitt, J. A., Sabey, T. B., Pfarrer, M. D., Rodell, J. B., & Hill, E. T. (2023). Continue the story or turn the page? Coworker reactions to inheriting a legacy. *Academy of Management Review, 48*(1), 11–31. https://doi.org/10.5465/amr.2019.0084

Coraiola, D. M., Foster, W. M., Mena, S., Foroughi, H., & Rintamäki, J. (2023). Ecologies of memories: Memory work within and between organizations and communities. *The Academy of Management Annals, 17*(1), 373–404. https://doi.org/10.5465/annals.2021.0088

Corbin, J., & Strauss, A. (1990). Grounded theory research: Procedures, canons and evaluative criteria. *Qualitative Sociology, 13*(1), 3–21. https://doi.org/10.1007/BF00988593

De Massis, A., Kotlar, J., & Manelli, L. (2021). Family firms, family boundary organizations, and the family-related organizational ecosystem. *Family Business Review, 34*(4), 350–364. https://doi.org/10.1177/08944865211052195

Fuller, J., Jacobides, M. G., & Reeves, M. (2019). The myths and realities of business ecosystems. *MIT Sloan Management Review, 60*(3), 1–9.

Ge, B., De Massis, A., & Kotlar, J. (2022). Mining the past: History scripting strategies and competitive advantage in a family business. *Entrepreneurship Theory and Practice, 46*(1), 223–251. https://doi.org/10.1177/10422587211046547

Gioia, D. A., Corley, K. G., & Hamilton, A. L. (2013). Seeking qualitative rigor in inductive research. *Organizational Research Methods, 16*(1), 15–31. https://doi.org/10.1177/1094428112452151

Glaser, B., & Strauss, A. (2017). *Discovery of grounded theory: Strategies for qualitative research*. Routledge. https://doi.org/10.4324/9780203793206

Granovetter, M. (1985). The problem of embeddedness. *American Journal of Sociology, 91*(3), 481–510. https://doi.org/10.1086/228311

Guba, E. G. (1981). Criteria for assessing the trustworthiness of naturalistic inquiries. *Educational Communication and Technology, 29*(2), 75–91. https://doi.org/10.1007/BF02766777

Hammond, N. L., Pearson, A. W., & Holt, D. T. (2016). The quagmire of legacy in family firms: Definition and implications of family and family firm legacy orientations. *Entrepreneurship Theory and Practice, 40*(6), 1209–1231. https://doi.org/10.1111/etap.12241

Iansiti, M., & Levien, R. (2004). Strategy as ecology. *Harvard Business Review, 82*(3), 68–78, 126.

Jaskiewicz, P., Combs, J. G., & Rau, S. B. (2015). Entrepreneurial legacy: Toward a theory of how some family firms nurture transgenerational entrepreneurship. *Journal of Business Venturing, 30*(1), 29–49. https://doi.org/10.1016/j.jbusvent.2014.07.001

Lumpkin, G. T., & Bacq, S. (2022). Family business, community embeddedness, and civic wealth creation. *Journal of Family Business Strategy, 13*(2), 100469. https://doi.org/10.1016/j.jfbs.2021.100469

Manelli, L., Magrelli, V., Kotlar, J., Messeni Petruzzelli, A., & Frattini, F. (2023). Building an outward-oriented social family legacy: Rhetorical history in family business foundations. *Family Business Review, 36*(1), 143–168. https://doi.org/10.1177/08944865231157195

Mars, M. M., Bronstein, J. L., & Lusch, R. F. (2012). The value of a metaphor: Organizations and ecosystems. *Organizational Dynamics, 41*(4), 271–280. https://doi.org/10.1016/j.orgdyn.2012.08.002

Moore, J. F. (1993). Predators and prey: A new ecology of competition. *Harvard Business Review, 71*(3), 75–86.

Patton, M. (2002). *Qualitative research & evaluation methods* (3rd ed.). Sage.

Pidun, U., Reeves, M., & Schüssler, M. (2022a). Do you need a business ecosystem? In M. Reeves & U. Pidun (Eds.), *Business ecosystems* (pp. 13–26). Walter de Gruyter. https://doi.org/10.1515/9783110775167-002

Pidun, U., Reeves, M., & Schüssler, M. (2022b). Why do most business ecosystems fail? In M. Reeves & U. Pidun (Eds.), *Business ecosystems* (pp. 35–46). Walter de Gruyter. https://doi.org/10.1515/9783110775167-004

Pidun, U., Reeves, M., & Zoletnik, B. (2022). What is your business ecosystem strategy? In M. Reeves & U. Pidun (Eds.), *Business ecosystems* (pp. 105–121). Walter de Gruyter. https://doi.org/10.1515/9783110775167-009

Radu-Lefebvre, M., Davis, J. H., & Gartner, W. B. (2024). Legacy in family business: A systematic literature review and future research agenda. *Family Business Review, 37*(1), 18–59. https://doi.org/10.1177/08944865231224506

Rao, H., Davis, G. F., & Ward, A. (2000). Embeddedness, social identity and mobility: Why firms leave the NASDAQ and join the New York Stock Exchange. *Administrative Science Quarterly, 45*(2), 268–292. https://doi.org/10.2307/2667072

Reeves, M., & Pidun, U. (2022). *Business ecosystems*. De Gruyter. https://doi.org/10.1515/9783110775167

Sasaki, I., Kotlar, J., Ravasi, D., & Vaara, E. (2020). Dealing with revered past: Historical identity statements and strategic change in Japanese family firms. *Strategic Management Journal, 41*(3), 590–623. https://doi.org/10.1002/smj.3065

Sharma, P., & Manikutty, S. (2005). Strategic divestments in family firms: Role of family structure and community culture. *Entrepreneurship Theory and Practice, 29*(3), 293–311. https://doi.org/10.1111/j.1540-6520.2005.00084.x

Stake, R. (1978). The case study method in social inquiry. *Educational Researcher, 7*(2), 5–8. https://doi.org/10.3102/0013189X007002005

Stake, R. E. (1995). *The art of case study research*. Sage.

Suddaby, R. (2016). Toward a historical consciousness: Following the historic turn in management thought. *M@n@gement, 19*(1), 46–60.

Suddaby, R., Israelsen, T., Mitchell, J. R., & Lim, D. S. (2023). Entrepreneurial visions as rhetorical history: A diegetic narrative model of stakeholder enrollment. *Academy of Management Review, 48*(2), 220–243. https://doi.org/10.5465/amr.2020.0010

Suddaby, R., & Jaskiewicz, P. (2020). Managing traditions: A critical capability for family business success. *Family Business Review, 33*(3), 234–243. https://doi.org/10.1177/0894486520942611

Taraday, H. (2013). Book review: Family Legacy and Leadership: Preserving True Family Wealth in Challenging Times. *Family Business Review, 26*(2), 200–202. https://doi.org/10.1177/0894486512474163

Thompson, B., Kellas, J. K., Soliz, J., Thompson, J., Epp, A., & Schrodt, P. (2009). Family legacies: Constructing individual and family identity through intergenerational storytelling. *Narrative Inquiry, 19*(1), 106–134. https://doi.org/10.1075/ni.19.1.07tho

Tsou, H. T., Chen, J. S., & Yu, Y. W. D. (2018). Antecedents of co-development and its effect on innovation performance: A business ecosystem perspective. *Management Decision, 57*(7), 1609–1637. https://doi.org/10.1108/MD-04-2018-0421

Wade-Benzoni, K. A., & Tost, L. P. (2009). The egoism and altruism of intergenerational behavior. *Personality and Social Psychology Review, 13*(3), 165–193. https://doi.org/10.1177/1088868309339317

Zahra, S. A., & Nambisan, S. (2012). Entrepreneurship and strategic thinking in business ecosystems. *Business Horizons, 55*(3), 219–229. https://doi.org/10.1016/j.bushor.2011.12.004

Hanna Aschhoff and Matthias Waldkirch
Chapter 6
Acquiring history? Foreign imprint management during postmerger integration

Organizational histories represent a unique resource that, at best, provide the basis for a competitive advantage that cannot be replicated or easily acquired (Suddaby et al., 2010, p. 148). How organizations handle their history is thus crucial to whether it becomes a boon or a bane for an organization. A key underlying assumption in the literature has been that organizations engage with their own history; yet, as organizations grow and merge with or acquire other firms, they might have to contend with history from outside their organizations. But how do organizations deal with histories that are not their own?

Recent studies in organizational research have sparked renewed interest in how organizations deal with histories and how and through which mechanisms the past in organizations endures or changes (de Cuyper et al., 2020; Ellis et al., 2016; Snihur & Zott, 2020). In particular, imprinting theory has contributed much to this discussion by investigating the persistence or decay of such historical features (Stinchcombe, 1965). Imprinting pays particular attention to how imprinters selectively incorporate elements into the organization during a sensitive moment of its existence that endures despite subsequent environmental changes (de Cuyper et al., 2020; Johnson, 2007, p. 101; Marquis, 2003, p. 656). We call imprints belonging to firms being acquired "foreign imprints." The term *foreign* implies not only that the imprint is external to the organization but also that it originates from a source unknown to the organization. We envision that foreign imprints can stem from different origins, such as a new geographic environment, a new industry, or as in our case, a new organizational partner.

The processes through which organizational imprints evolve beyond the founding stage, as the most impactful sensitive period, have only recently begun to spark interest (de Cuyper et al., 2020; Sinha et al., 2020) and hint at influential actors that can prioritize or modify imprints to serve new purposes (Sinha et al., 2020). Mergers and acquisitions (M&As) depict a fascinating and unique context to investigate how organizations utilize, transform, or leave behind foreign imprints. While we know that imprinted characteristics are persistent and enduring (Marquis & Tilcsik, 2013), recent studies have stated that imprints can also transform or even decay during periods of susceptibility (Simsek et al., 2015). M&As represent such an apparent discontinuity: Imprints from two organizations collide, restructuring and integration plans challenge essential characteristics, and actors suddenly have to deal not just with their own history but with the other firm's history and foreign imprints. As such, managers and other organizational actors become responsible for managing their imprints and those of their merger counterparts.

As "changing a core feature exposes an organization to great risk of mortality" (Carroll & Hannan, 2004, p. 64), it is no surprise that imprinting is related to one of the biggest reasons for acquisition failure: the inability to integrate two companies into one (Chatterjee et al., 1992; Nahavandi & Malekzadeh, 1988). On the one hand, a certain level of restructuring that might disrupt core imprints is often necessary to achieve desirable synergies. On the other hand, imprints are frequently tied to critical resources, knowledge, or technologies (Dias et al., 2023) that are worth retaining or even the reason for the acquisition in the first place. As such, this chapter investigates how organizations and their actors manage foreign imprints during M&A integration processes. To investigate our purpose, we draw on insights from a longitudinal single case study of a merger between two family firms with stable and old imprints and many instances of managers engaging with foreign imprints.

In our findings, we track the change of three foreign imprints and outline a two-stage process of how actors deal with foreign imprints. We show that organizations first engage in *foreign imprint stabilization and accentuation,* which unfold as *imprint conservation, restoration,* and *enactment.* These mechanisms allow actors to engage in *foreign imprint transformation,* encompassing *imprint appropriation, reformation,* and *substitution* (see Figure 6.1). These findings provide compelling new insights into how organizations deal with foreign histories and imprints and engage in foreign imprint management during M&A integration periods.

Theoretical background

Over the past decade, the study of how an organization's distant past influences its present and future has received growing attention. In organization studies, the concept of *rhetorical history* is primarily used to understand the "strategic use of the past as a persuasive strategy to manage key stakeholders of the firm" (Suddaby et al., 2010, p. 157; Suddaby & Foster, 2016). Studies applying a rhetorical history lens provide insights into how organizational actors use history through rhetorical strategies and narratives to further organizational agendas (Coraiola et al., 2023). Existing research in this area has highlighted how organizational members use rhetorical history to influence organizational strategy (Coman & Casey, 2020), maintain or legitimate present actions (Anteby et al., 2012; Suddaby & Jaskiewicz, 2020), protect brand identity (Foster et al., 2011), or impose meaning on the firm's past (Suddaby et al., 2010). As such, the emphasis lies on "historicizing" (Coraiola et al., 2023), the rhetorical practices through which actors utilize historical narratives.

Thus, there has been less focus on how histories are embedded in organizational processes and structures. Those practices allow the past to be remembered and potentially for specific meanings to be attached to it; one common outcome of such remembering processes is *organizational legacy*. While often treated as a near-factual property of organizations, legacies are subject to narrative processes, shaping what is continued and what remains in the past (Foroughi, 2020). For instance, organizational memory is oftentimes discursively contested, resulting in what is remembered and what is forgotten of organizational histories (e.g., Anteby et al., 2012; Foroughi & Al-Amoudi, 2020). As such, both concepts share a narrative focus and are subject to being employed and controlled by organizational members through discourse or action (Coman & Casey, 2020; Jenkins, 2003; White, 1984). However, legacy focuses more on transmitting past elements and their role in the present or future (Coman & Casey, 2020) and the tensions between organizational heritage preservation and transformation (Sasaki et al., 2020). Organizational legacy is suitable for investigating intergenerational change (Brinkerink et al., 2020; Jaskiewicz et al., 2015) or how actors can use histories for strategic purposes (Aeon & Lamertz, 2021). *Imprinting* is closely linked to organizational legacy and presumes that the characteristics of an organization are shaped during a sensitive period of its lifecycle, such as the founding phase or merger with another firm (Carroll & Hannan, 2004, p. 293). Despite subsequent changes in environmental conditions and new influential forces, imprinted structures, strategies, or behaviors can persist well beyond the initial period of sensitivity, shaping the character of an organization (Marquis & Tilcsik, 2013). While all three theoretical concepts are interconnected, we found imprinting theory to be the most suitable lens for our chapter. First, imprints are not just narrative devices; they can manifest in structures, behaviors, and strategic choices. As such, they are integral to integration processes during M&As and are likely to be the focus of managerial attention. Second, our focus does not primarily rest on organizational histories but on the mechanisms applied to address and influence foreign imprints persistently anchored in organizational structures.

Extant research on imprinting literature provides valuable insights into understanding how imprints change, suggesting the agentic influence of key organizational actors (Erçek & Günçavdı, 2016; Ferriani et al., 2012; Kriauciunas & Kale, 2006; Marquis & Huang, 2010; Ni Sullivan et al., 2014) such as managers involved in managing imprints by encouraging stakeholders to adopt new imprints and modify old ones (Sinha et al., 2020, p. 5). Researchers have already identified practices that actors use for this purpose: Ferriani et al. (2012) introduced the concept of reimprinting and showed how spin-off companies can retain some characteristics of their parent company while also developing new features through organizational learning initiated by new members and responses to feedback from the changing industrial environment. The transition occurs in imprinting, critical revision, and reimprinting stages, which causes a change in strategic and technological direction. Similar to the concept of foreign imprints, their conceptualization crosses organizational boundaries, yet the spin-off companies likely did not encounter imprints as "foreign." De Cuyper et al. (2020) further developed this concept, showing how imprints "sediment" after the founding phase over time. Imprints manifest through *imprint attraction* and *sharing*, resulting in a blueprint guiding organizational behavior. Reimprinting through leadership occurs through a combination of (1) *imprint reforming*, targeted activities to change original imprints, and (2) *imprint coupling*, where actors use original imprints as a resource to legitimate imprint changes (de Cuyper et al., 2020). While these studies provide important insights for managing imprints in M&As, they say little about how these processes might unfold when dealing with foreign imprints that do not derive from an organization's own history. While M&A research has provided some insights into how acquirer and acquiree merge or take over firm characteristics such as cultural patterns (Nahavandi & Malekzadeh, 1988) and make sense of such changes in the postintegration phase (Monin et al., 2013), we know surprisingly little about how they deal with each other's organizational history. As such, how organizational actors utilize foreign imprints in these processes is poorly understood, even though they likely play a crucial role. Managers need to identify and understand the imprints of the other organization to determine which imprints are linked to strategically important assets and, therefore, represent a valuable resource for the acquirer or which ones can be "easily" changed. Further, intervention in foreign imprints may face resistance from organizational members and require legitimization and sensegiving (Monin et al., 2013). As such, this chapter aims to shed light on the phenomenon of foreign imprints.

Methodology

Our study drew on a longitudinal qualitative single-case study (Langley, 1999) at Oechsle X Vinox, a merger of two traditional family firms in the wine industry. Oechsle, an international wine manufacturer that belongs to a German family-owned conglomerate, recently acquired the majority of shares of an Italian-based family-owned wine producer of approximately the same size (Vinox). Initially conceived as a joint venture, the long-term intention was full integration into a newly created holding structure. Given its long history and family ownership, Oechsle X Vinox represented a rich context for investigating the development of long-lasting imprints during an exogenous shock. This chapter emerged from a larger, long-term research project on organizational identity work mechanisms during M&A processes. During data collection, the first author noticed how managers of the acquiring company actively engaged in attending to, conserving, and ultimately transforming key characteristics and historical imprints of the acquired firm. We gathered additional data on that matter and zoomed into these dynamics in our chapter by following the specific episode postmerger integration process, in which we captured a wide variety of activities to influence the persistence or decay of foreign imprints.

Our data collection drew on multiple data sources. We based the study on extensive observation notes covering 3 years of the process, secondary data, and 30 semi-structured interviews gathered by the first author. In her previous role as assistant to the acquiree's management board, the first author was able to follow the process as an organizational insider during data collection (Laude et al., 2012), allowing for in-depth immersion to provide a thorough understanding of imprints and the various manifestations within the firm. Being multilingual offered her multiple opportunities to engage with organizational members, gain an even deeper understanding, and capture in-depth insights about the "foreign imprints" that otherwise might have been missed. The author partnered with a second independent researcher to counter the bias of the researcher's former membership in a group being studied. The second author regularly interviewed the first author about the merger, (foreign) imprints, and her role. In the follow-up, both researchers discussed surprising observations and initial patterns that emerged through those interviews. The first author returned to the data to look for supporting or disconfirming evidence, while the second author contributed theoretical and methodological framing. To ensure the anonymity of the case, we modified or adapted sensitive information such as names or industries that could reveal the identity of individuals or organizations (Jonsen et al., 2018).

The analysis was inductive and data-driven, following established protocols for coding qualitative data (Gioia et al., 2013) using MAXQDA to identify significant imprints, their transformation, and imprint mechanisms. We started the coding process with iterative rounds of first- and second-order coding. Our codes captured (1) the nature of premerger imprints inside both organizations and (2) indications of how and why these changed during postmerger integration. We utilized in vivo and open coding with labels as close to the data as possible for first-order and preliminary second-order codes to prevent imposing any pre-existing ideas onto the data. We initially focused on identifying the leading imprints the firm's patriarch introduced into the Vinox organization. To accomplish this, we analyzed the interview data, which provided consistent results and could be corroborated by secondary data such as archival documents or observation notes. We identified three dominant imprints and their manifestation within Vinox. We then started a second round of coding to identify courses of action that affected these imprints throughout postmerger integration. Again, we used in vivo and open coding with labels as close to the data as possible for first- and second-order codes. As a next step, we identified the different mechanisms related to the changes of imprints during postmerger integration by using second-order or axial coding to look for similarities and patterns between the initial codes and to convert them into higher-order categories (Strauss & Corbin, 1998).

To analyze foreign imprints, we intentionally adopted the perspective of the acquiree. This did not exclude the possibility that the acquired party also engaged in foreign imprint management. However, the acquiree had more directional power in designing and implementing changes on imprints, so we focused on this player to avoid overextending the scope of the study. This process led to six second-order themes: (1) imprint conservation, (2) imprint restoration, (3) imprint enactment, (4) imprint recombination, (5) imprint reformation, and (6) imprint substitution. In a final step, we grouped the second-order themes into aggregate dimensions to create a data structure that allowed us to theorize two overarching themes: (1) imprint stabilization and accentuation and (2) imprint transformation. This formed the basis for the development of our findings, describing the evolution and underlying mechanisms of transforming imprints during postmerger integration (Figure 6.1).

Findings

We identified three distinct foreign imprints that characterized Vinox before the merger and that Oechsle engaged with strongly: (1) *quality and innovation excellence,* (2) *the cathedral,* and (3) *our firm, our family.* They were the force behind Vinox's operations and manifested through cognitive and structural aspects. The imprints were primarily established by the former patriarch, who continued to shape the firm despite not being operationally active anymore. Our following analysis outlines how actors across Oechsle and Vinox stabilized and transformed these imprints through six mechanisms during postmerger integration (Figure 6.1).

The imprint of quality and innovation excellence. At the age of 20, the patriarch, as the founder's son, entered the family business and took over the operative lead in the late 1950s. Driven by his will to continually improve product quality, he was responsible for several innovations that imprinted the firm and was the first in the industry with many wine production innovations. Thus, most of the success stories and innovations essential for the company are attributed to the patriarch. We consider the production process, the relevance of the Italian headquarters as a production site, and being located in the local wine region as structural imprint manifestations, as organizational members always referred to these elements as what constituted quality excellence for Vinox.

> There are three common things in the history of Vinox. The first thing is internationalization. The second thing is innovation in products .... Third is process innovation: All the changes we are doing in the process, being the leaders in process and development. Process and development, innovation in products, and internationalization has always been the DNA of the Vinox family. And where this is coming from is very clear to me. There was a visioner, an entrepreneur, who was the firm's patriarch. (Head of Finance, Vinox)

In the organization, the traditional expertise in the production process was evident in technical departments such as production, quality management, and enology. The members of these departments were highly skilled and had great confidence in their abilities. Under the guidance of the knowledgeable patriarch, these departments produced numerous innovations in products and processes, resulting in high production volumes with excellent quality. However, this also led to a high level of complexity

Chapter 6 Acquiring history? — 113

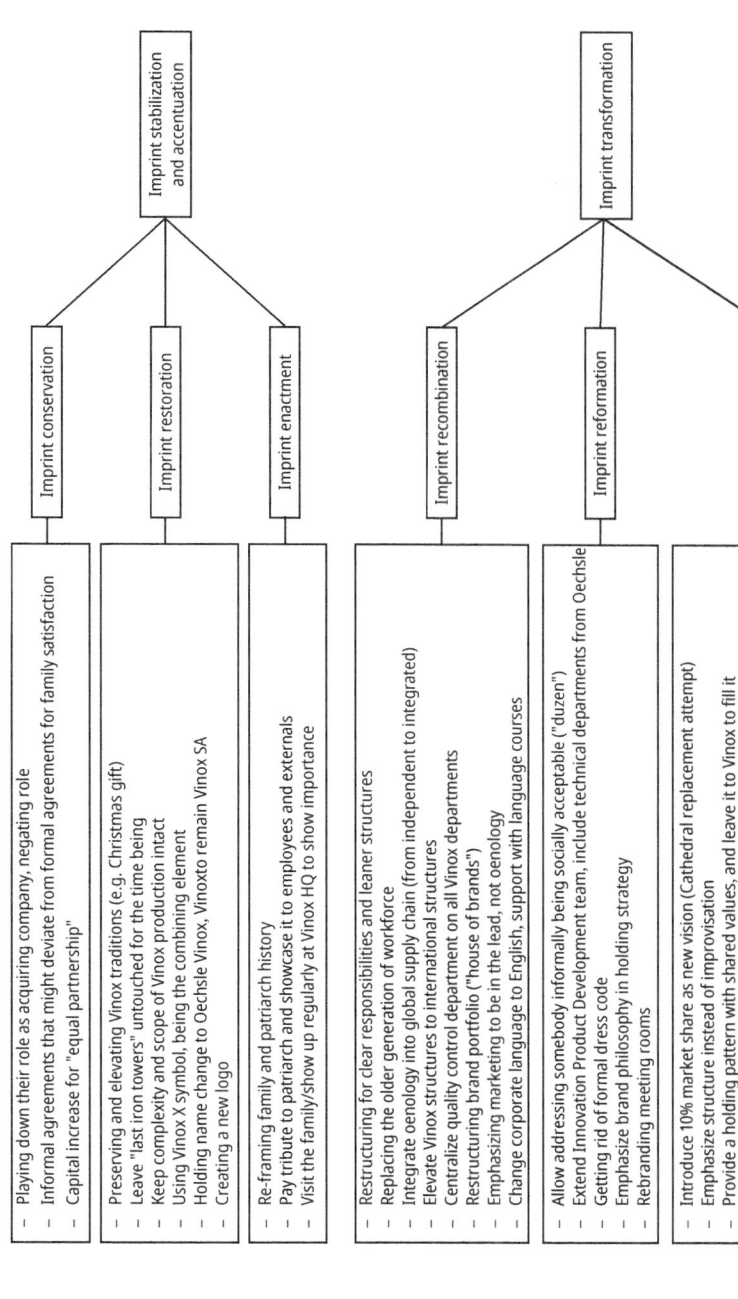

Figure 6.1: Foreign Imprint Mechanisms.

and entrenched structures, which, according to organizational members, were impossible to change and were deeply rooted in the company. For the entire organization, this imprint also manifested itself in a feeling of superiority over competitors. Innovation in products was previously nurtured, first and foremost, through the international Vinox marketing team. Many market innovations stemmed from their work and yielded expertise for creative product concept development and processes from idea to market entry execution that turned into success. Oechsle was built differently.

> Well, there were many ideas beforehand, but nothing came out of it. It [innovation projects] wasn't seriously pursued, or at some point, it was even stopped altogether .... The idea was somehow to do it in such a way that if it didn't really work out, the fall would not be so high. And then it becomes less and less innovative; then it's somehow more just a 'me too' approach. (Manager, Oechsle)

We summarized this imprint under the term *quality and innovation excellence.* This imprint had been a core reason that Oechsle, by its admission a more conservative organization, was interested in the merger with Vinox. Oechsle's management had no intention to fundamentally change the imprint, as it made no economic sense and was likely to impact Vinox negatively. Instead, both management teams agreed upon restructuring projects for cost-saving purposes that supported but did not change the traditional production processes at Vinox. While Oechsle's management stabilized the imprint at Vinox, they planned to incorporate and connect this imprint into the structures of the newly merged organization. Indeed, after realizing the importance of this imprint, projects that would bring more profound change were postponed to a later date.

In engaging with the imprint at Vinox, Oechsle had engaged in *foreign imprint conservation,* preserving and strengthening the imprints within their original context. During several interviews, Vinox employees shared the impression that a lot, but at the same time not much, had changed at Vinox. In an attempt to introduce this imprint into the new organization, Oechsle's management encouraged the extension of the acquiree's innovation product development team by including its own production, development, and quality management departments in the process. Within Oechsle, there had always been an admiration for the bold innovation at Vinox, which was in contrast to how cautiously Oechsle pursued its innovation activities:

> But this, really this complete change, to break away from asking (as in the past) in the first stages of development: What can I actually do? But rather: What do I actually want? That was a significant change, especially with the success of Vinox with new products that historically have nothing to do with Vinox. (Manager, Oechsle)

To bridge the foreign local imprint, members at Oechsle and Vinox engaged in *imprint coupling,* which refers to recombining and reinterpreting desired foreign imprint manifestations to translate them into one's own imprint manifestations. While this occurred on a structural level by integrating teams, imprint coupling unfolded particularly in everyday interactions, such as adopting a new, shared dress code. While Oechsle's conservative dress code was primarily seen as an expression of professional merchandising, Vinox's style was more relaxed and less uniform. At Oechsle, this was seen as an expression of innovation excellence—more dynamic and modern. The management implemented this through their role model function, and organizational members at Oechsle and Vinox quickly followed their example. The merger gave them the legitimacy to embody the new spark of innovation excellence through clothing choices.

Imprint reformation is a foreign imprint management mechanism with more intervention. Stabilizing the *quality and innovation excellence* imprint as a first step further allowed the new organization to engage in *imprint reformation,* which we understand as using explicit actions to change components of the original foreign imprint. To be integrated into the new global supply chain, Oechsle management transformed departments engaged in quality and innovation activities, such as production or marketing, from being independent to being integrated. They also worked on centralizing quality control departments and gaining uniform alignment on groupwide aspirations, as every production facility had its own quality control and enology department in the past. Vinox's imprint was reformed with Oechsle's imprint as a blueprint that provided more explicit responsibilities and leaner structures:

> Oechsle had much more experience dealing with bottlers; they achieved that the bottler in 1 month has the mold and produces the bottle. So I would say the operative way of thinking of Oechsle—with the technique, with culture, and very focused on methodology and doing things on time—and the creative world of Vinox has merged in this thing and has made it possible to launch many new products .... That wouldn't have happened with Vinox alone. (Manager, Vinox)

The imprint of the cathedral also stemmed from the patriarch and his vision of global success, which was the leading force behind the firm's international expansion. Under his management, Vinox became the world's leading Chianti producer and the most successful Chianti wine brand worldwide. Through his personality and engagement, the patriarch transferred his bold vision of Vinox to everyone inside the organization, fostering a strong commitment and loyalty. A shared vision that the family patriarch lived and passed on provided a common direction: 'Building the cathedral' meant spreading the Vinox brand worldwide, with associated costs less relevant.

> The whole company had one goal in mind, and that was the goal that the patriarch always represented at the time: "We want to be present all over the world. And we want the whole world to know Vinox. No matter what it costs. No matter if we only sell five bottles in Burma and 100 somewhere in Laos. It doesn't matter! We want to be present all over the world. And we don't care whether it costs a million, or five, or ten, we just do it, that's our goal." And the whole company had that attitude, you know? And everyone was pulling the rope in the same direction. (Former CMO, Vinox)

The term "cathedral" was particularly familiar to employees in the marketing and export departments. Apart from describing the patriarch's vision, it stood for internationality and brand strength, encouraging employees to make bold moves to fulfill the overall goal of global success. Hence, Vinox developed into a marketing-centered organization that constantly evolved with high marketing spending and a certain appetite in accordance with to the spirit of the times. Prior to the merger, strengthening and spreading the Vinox brand worldwide *(the cathedral)* was decisive for the strategic orientation of the Italian company (apart from family-related interests). As a multi-brand company with a broad portfolio, Oechsle subsidiaries found it more challenging to grow brands at a comparable rate, as funds had to be distributed among many brands. Their strategic focus was control-driven, concentrating more on overall company performance. The merger allowed a strategy shift towards a stronger emphasis on branding through foreign imprint stabilization and transformation mechanisms. Apart from the branding expertise and the international brand strength, the Oechsle management was particularly fond of the motivational and striving aspects that *the cathedral* entailed, fostering an entrepreneurial spirit and a strong bond among employees worldwide. At the same time, however, the less strict cost management, high degree of autonomy, and sprawling organizational structures associated with this imprint should not be encouraged. The aim was to combine the positive aspects of the two companies' imprints.

Given that the *cathedral imprint* depended strongly on the patriarch, Oechsle again engaged in *foreign imprint conservation* by accentuating prominent imprint carriers. We define imprint carriers as subtle manifestations of imprints through habits or artifacts of everyday organizational work that are intuitively associated with the superordinate imprint from within. For the acquirer, one example was the names of the meeting rooms at the headquarters. Some of these were founded historically, while others were assigned to the most important country organizations acquired in the past and were an expression of the specific history and internationality of the firm. The new focus on brands adopted by Vinox was further manifested in renaming the meeting rooms, with rooms now bearing brand names—weighted according to the importance of the brand—in line with the new global brand strategy.

An essential imprint carrier of *the cathedral* was the company and brand name Vinox, with a dominant "X," which is derived from the company's history. Instead of being incorporated solely into the Oechsle group of companies, the company name was also adopted in the holding name "Oechsle X Vinox." The "X" was prominently displayed in the logo and adopted in the internal branding. This practice is worth mentioning because although Oechsle has made many acquisitions in the past, with one exception, it has never impacted the name of the group of companies. Based on *imprint conservation* that targeted the reminiscence of *the cathedral,* imprint coupling around the aforementioned "X"—the symbol of the acquiree's brand—targeted the translation of such a symbol into the new organization. Originally used as a key brand recognition feature, the "X" was given a new strategic meaning. Among other things, it was stylized as the connecting element between the two organizations and thus occupied a prominent place in the new organization. The *imprint coupling* went beyond the symbolic recombination by including the underlying brand philosophy in a new joint corporate strategy. It was the impetus to reshape the brand portfolio strategically and consistently focus the strategy on strong brands and their growth. This adjustment led to increased prioritization of international premium brands, and the acquirer's brand in particular.

> No, we don't live from our German brands. That is an important component, but our main brands are international brands, which are also largely produced elsewhere. We are not what we were before: A German company with foreign companies that are also involved with us. (Manager, Oechsle)

Oechsle management engaged in *imprint reformation* to transform *the cathedral imprint*. The overarching goal of bringing the Vinox brand to the world and making it the most successful global Chianti brand motivated the creation of a new vision and goals. This required some departments, particularly those related to technology and production, to undergo fundamental mindset shifts to align with the new vision and goals. Instead of prioritizing technical wine expertise, the brand- and consumer-centric approach encouraged a partial rethinking of habits and processes and the introduction of new ways of working. Management emphasized that the brand's success depended on the ability to meet the customer's taste (and not that of wine experts, enologists, or product developers). While the Vinox marketing department was already internalizing and "preaching" this aspect, other departments had to adjust and refocus. The technical departments had, out of their professional expertise, ideas of how a product had to taste, while the sales department wanted to cater to clients' needs by developing niche brands and taste profiles that were missing from their portfolio. Meanwhile, the hospitality department preferred historically accurate niche products.

Imprint substitution is a process of replacing original imprints with other imprints, and it is the most intensive form of foreign imprint transformation. The chief executive officer (CEO) of Oechsle, who had met the patriarch several times and encountered the "cathedral" imprint in person during his visits, believed that it was crucial to find a new vision for Vinox. In an effort to replace the cathedral imprint in its motivational and striving aspects, the CEO took some time for thought experiments to translate "hard numbers" into a concrete, "emotionalizing" new vision for Oechsle X Vinox. The new goal was that by 2023, one out of every 10 glasses of sparkling wine would come from Oechsle X Vinox. This would equate to a 10% market share in both volume and value. At the same time, the CEO and his team also recognized the power of a strong imprint for Oechsle X Vinox:

> We need something to believe in again. We must create a vision that inspires all employees to work on this dream with all their might. Vinox was run like a missionary and had this "cathedral." We need that, too. (Top Management, Oechsle)

Even though the vision was successfully disseminated across the new organization, it could not raise the same intrinsic motivation that had previously driven performance. Nevertheless, the objective of achieving a 10% market share was understood.

At the same time, the entrepreneurial spirit to "fight" for "their" company supported the feeling of belonging to a family—the Vinox family, best described through the imprint *of our firm, our family*. The patriarch imprinted the organization in that direction through his charisma, emphasis on personal connections with all employees, and dedication to their well-being beyond work hours. He was known for his close relationships with employees and often took the time to walk around and meet them.

> Yes, I am a soldier of Mr. Vinox. He signed me, gave me all the confidence and wings to do everything I have done. He has been my champion, and I know he considers me part of his family. (Production Worker, Vinox)

Not only the workers but also the workers' families were relevant to the patriarch—a fact that many of his workers considered the core difference between a family business and a non–family business. This was also the reason for the loyalty and ties to the neighboring village, where the patriarch initially recruited a large part of his workforce, which subsequently reinforced *our firm, our family* as an imprint in the company. His paternalistic leadership style nurtured the imprint's existence in various ways. For instance, instead of performing classic feedback interviews, he gave a bonus to everyone and had a little chat with them that lasted for 5 to 10 minutes every Christmas. The daily conversations with the workforce on the shop floor served as a source of stability; his motivating vision gave them a goal and direction. Even before the merger, this imprint had suffered due to internal conflicts between the owning family lines in the years leading up to and after the patriarch's departure from operational management. This resulted in disagreements between departments and parallel working processes and structures, harming firm performance. It was a period in the organization's history when the imprint was less emphasized but still present.

Oechsle management was convinced that the virtues that could be traced back to the patriarch should remain. They saw a connection between the family business character and the employees' loyalty, commitment, and work motivation, which was considered worth preserving. Therefore, the transfer of these attributes was considered desirable.

> Before, we had a terribly divided family for various reasons. And now we have a family business culture .... Based on business principles, we see the whole thing as an organism that needs to be kept alive together. I believe the company is now much more family-run in a good sense .... So

we are now reformulating the whole thing again, in contrast to the episode in between. What do you call that? A reframing. (Top Management, Vinox)

In the past, it was primarily the owner families and the patriarch as the head of the family who shaped the preservation of family affiliation inside the firm through their presence, ownership, and leadership. As the ownership situation changed, Oechsle management used foreign imprint mechanisms to redirect focus toward the remaining patriarch-shaped imprints, the cathedral and innovation excellence, presenting them as success factors of the past that were about to be preserved and revitalized in a manner other than the *our firm, our family* way. One way the *our firm, our family* imprint was visible was through a variety of firm traditions that were established and nurtured by the former owners and often connected to the patriarch. Particularly in the first months after the merger, actors at Oechsle enacted *our firm, our family imprint* conservation by preserving such firm traditions. Despite an extensive cost-cutting program, the Oechsle management desired and welcomed the continuation of traditions at Vinox. Thus, all employees in Italy continued to receive a living turkey as a Christmas gift, a tradition that existed for several decades, previously handed over personally by the patriarch and his family. The acquirer prioritized imprint conservation and autonomy over adherence to cost-saving plans, thus fostering Vinox's uniqueness, as they did not introduce similar changes at their site.

Beyond the means of conservation, some original imprints were carefully restored and nurtured by the acquirers' management through *imprint restoration*. They downplayed their role as the acquiring company and emphasized the influence of the remaining owners, starting with complementing structural aspects that highlighted this imprint inside the firm despite the new shareholder structure. First, they financed a capital increase for "equal partnership," calling it an alliance and acting accordingly, in contrast to a takeover with a dominant position. They preferred to avoid using terms like "acquisition" or "merger" whenever possible. A collaboration agreement settled the details of that cooperation, such as shared goals, payment, and dividend arrangements. Instead of strictly adhering to the agreement in the subsequent implementation, they ensured that compliance with the agreements would not disadvantage the owning family. If necessary, they suggested "informal agreements" for the advantage and well-being of the remaining family shareholders.

> Although many people think that in the future, Oechsle would take the 100%. For them, that the family is here, it's a kind of relief…. Possibly, in 2 or 3 years, it will not be that important because many people now would be working since the merger. But for the people working before the merge, to see the CEO and the patriarch walking in the offices, to see them, to see the family faces, it is still vital, I think. Although it's clear that everyone knows that Oechsle is the one who is managing and making most of the decisions. But it gives some comfort. (Top Management, Vinox)

Building on conserving and restoring original imprints, these imprints would be even more accentuated and stabilized through *imprint enactment* or "staging" imprint interpretations to demonstrate their symbolic expressiveness and enhance manifestation. Oechsle management tried to behave in a family-like and respectful manner toward the employees, but above all, toward the remaining co-owners and the patriarch. They maintained regular contact in a trusting and respectful manner, as well as regular visits. They also continued to give the patriarch a stage when desired and encouraged these appearances. We observed how even minor activities like these were perceived by members of an organization, who then classified them based on their imprint and expectations.

> As his [the patriarch's] assistant, I have seen much respect for the patriarch. I have seen respect for the older person, for the person who created this business. This is very important, I think. But I have seen this respect; I have seen it a lot. (Employee, Vinox)

Against the background of previous familiar conflicts overshadowing Vinox, the Oechsle management performed imprint enactment by retelling the family and patriarch's history on various occasions, emphasizing the events that led to the firm's international success while omitting the period of aimlessness and uncertainty that followed, instead of events of the recent past. During official speeches in front of staff or shareholders, in online appearances, and events like management meetings and sales conferences, they framed the firm's success stories of the past as the patriarchs' and families' achievements: the patriarchs' role, the international significance of the brand, and why both organizations complement each other. The intermediate steps, such as the almost two decades of disagreement in the family, declining business performance, or the role of the previous CEO, were downplayed or even omitted. In the first weeks and months, the acquirer and acquired CEO used their inaugural visits to key subsidiaries to convey the connection between the family and the company's history of success to the workforce. While apparent during the entire postmerger integration period, these storytelling-oriented imprint restoration measures were particularly present during the first period in which employees from both companies met for the first time. This required cooperation between the two management teams. Imprint enactment targeted the family directly, primarily to gain respect and trust, as it demonstrated the intention to manifest the family's legacy within the firm instead of erasing it. It further targeted the acquirer staff itself to shape the impression and relevance of the new partner. Lastly, and most importantly, they also targeted the acquiree's workforce as an "audience" to confirm the impression of manifesting the patriarch's imprints within the newly merged organization.

Especially in the first days of the merger, *imprint conservation, restoration, and enactment* stabilized and accentuated the *our firm, our family imprint*. As the merger progressed, foreign imprint mechanisms were introduced to transform imprint manifestations, such as the practice of hiring preferably from the local village, which strengthened the sense of family belonging and its relative importance in the firm in the past. This hiring practice of the past also led to a surplus and redundancy of workers that was incompatible with new goals and restructuring plans. Hence, the management of both organizations decided on a soft restructuring approach, leading to the replacement of an older, locally rooted generation through "natural" retirement and attractive settlement agreements over the first years. While many job positions were not replaced, those responsible for hiring from the local villages no longer prioritized hiring. Workers newly added to the firm were not attached to the family anymore, and it was no longer a source of loyalty to the firm.

> The roots, you know, now we are losing a little of this. Because many people are retiring and there are so many new faces. But these faces are very young people. They don't come from the wine business. They come from the city, but they are not related to the wine industry. (Employee, Vinox)

As a result of the imprint reformation, the *our firm, our family imprint* lost its general visibility and influence on organizational structures without disappearing for good. Instead, Oechsle introduced new imprints through *imprint substitution*. Alongside integration projects, the Oechsle management was keen to introduce a shared "reporting culture," a significant Oechsle imprint. The introduction of a new strategy, goals, and budget requirements had implications for multiple departments at Vinox: The adaptation of the profit and loss presentation to the Oechsle standard, the application of the respective software solution, the obligation to prepare monthly sales and profit reports, and the associated commentary from the business units placed an unfamiliar administrative burden on employees in production, marketing, sales, and international sales offices in terms of daily routines, areas of responsibility, processes, priorities, and leadership philosophy.

> Now, we have a more aligned organization with similar responsibilities. That makes it a lot easier. (Production Manager, Vinox)

In many ways, the reporting culture substituted imprints or imprint manifestations at Vinox, emphasizing structure instead of improvisation. This new direction was less emotional than a charismatic leader providing guidance for his family, but after a period of uncertainty, this gave back the feeling of security and conveyed a sense of continuation that before was drawn from the *our firm, our family imprint*.

> Because afterward, there has been a management with determination, yes, with a lot of determination. And perhaps with less improvisation and less chaotic than with the patriarch. He was a genius. I think he is more of a head, more in the business sense. For me it is good, and as I am now of an age, this model works very well for me. (Supply Chain Manager, Vinox)

As the family's influence faded, more open, transparent communication replaced the previous communication politics. For instance, instead of continuing the patriarch's practice of office walks, they increased the workforce for internal communication and implemented regular town hall meetings to inform the staff about the current business performance, news, and updates.

> The town halls—I think the last one was a month ago, if I remember correctly. They explained things a little bit and so on: "Well, we have gone to this percentage, and now we are doing this to the people." So it helps them with fear to say: "Well, look, they explain things to me that nobody would explain to me and I would not know, so I feel like I belong to this company." (Supply Chain Manager, Vinox)

As there was no patriarch walking through the offices daily to have a chat anymore, the international Oechsle management, as well as the local Vinox management, made an effort to communicate through more and new channels, deploy an open-door policy, and try to share more information in general. Besides replacing communication patterns of the past associated with the patriarch figure, the change in communication style aimed to promote openness and transparency.

> They explained things in more detail. For example, the name change (Oechsle X Vinox). We thought, why first Oechsle and not Vinox if Vinox is the bigger brand? But the CMO explained the background of it. (Hospitality Manager, Vinox)

Discussion

This chapter sought to address how organizations deal with foreign imprints by studying a merger between two traditional wine producers. Following all three foreign imprint developments, we show a two-step process of how organizations manage and, ultimately, transform foreign imprints into integrated imprints (see Figure 6.2). Given the nature of foreign imprints as both unknown to the acquiring company and potentially endangered due to the postmerger integration, actors first accentuate imprints so they receive attention in both organizations and stabilize them to incorporate them further. Then, they engage in a transformation process that partly modernizes imprints without changing their nature or replacing elements lost during the postmerger integration. Those foreign imprint mechanisms alter imprints and their manifestations, differing in intensity and direction of change to serve the purpose of the newly merged organization. We conclude that the first stabilization stage is crucial, regardless of whether gradual imprint modifications or significant transformation efforts succeed. As such, we provide new insights into the intricate process of how organizations and their actors engage with and manage foreign imprints. In so doing, our chapter makes several contributions.

First, our chapter illuminates the issue of "foreignness" in dealing with organizational histories and imprints. Unlike firms transforming their own imprints (Ferriani et al., 2012; Snihur & Zott, 2020), the foreignness of imprints seemingly requires more preparatory work. Our findings indicate that imprint transformation starts with imprint stabilization and follows a two-step process: First, foreign imprint mechanisms like imprint conservation, restoration, and enactment stabilize and accentuate established foreign imprints. This is particularly relevant given that the acquirer firm and

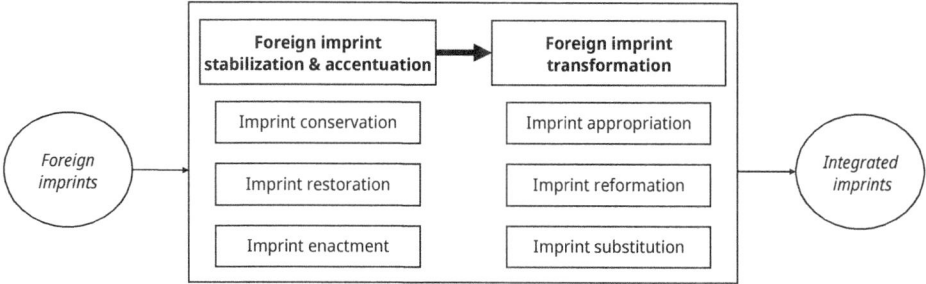

Figure 6.2: Foreign Imprint Management Process During Postmerger Integration.

its members are often unaware of the other firm's imprints, as prior assessments of acquisition targets typically focus on financial or physical asset-related information (Dao & Bauer, 2021; Weber et al., 2012). We argue that these practices can not only preserve foreign imprints but primarily enhance their visibility as a preparatory step before they can be altered and, hence, integrated into the merged organization. On the side of the acquired organization, enhancing the visibility of their imprints demonstrates the acquired organization's sensitivity and appreciation of the foreign imprints. It underlines their importance for the new organization—an important signal, especially in sensitive periods characterized by a high degree of uncertainty (Ullrich et al., 2005). Appreciating foreign imprints through these acts of highlighting, emphasizing, and preserving can be a first step in gaining "legitimization" in the eyes of the acquired organization to make subsequent changes. As such, imprint management can be valuable in acquirers' toolkits and extend legitimacy strategies during M&As (Suddaby & Greenwood, 2005) as a practice that goes beyond narrative work. Stabilization and accentuation mechanisms also give foreign imprints visibility toward the new partner, the acquiree. In doing so, they can play an important role in helping members of the organization understand the newly acquired organization, which may also ease other aspects of the postmerger integration process. We see links to other aspects that contribute to the success of M&As, such as the creation of learning opportunities (Vermeulen & Barkema, 2001), the construction of images of us vs. them (Vaara et al., 2003), and managing cultural distance (Vaara et al., 2012).

Second, we know that organizational history holds rhetorical power during strategic change (Suddaby et al., 2010) that can be used to develop organizational identity (Gioia et al., 2000), form competitive advantage (Foster et al., 2011), or establish continuity in strategy processes (van Baalen & Brunninge, 2009). Yet, such understandings of history among organizational actors are rarely uniform and often manifest as multivocal entities (Foroughi, 2020). By applying the imprinting lens, we look beyond its usage through narrative elements and point toward its integrative potential for transformation. Our findings show how organizations and their actors can manage and, to a certain degree, steer such multivocality. For instance, by making foreign imprints visible, organizations can take the first steps towards making changes to their own imprints that may require modification but are challenging to undertake due to their entrenched nature within the organization. Imprint accentuation thus may help to "soften" "traditionalizing" or "inertial" forces that are said to be responsible for imprint persistence (Hannan & Freeman, 1989; Stinchcombe, 1965, p. 169). We think that using imprints as a resource, as described by de Cuyper et al. (2020), can be useful, too. We observed how imprints can be used as a resource through practices of imprint recombination, in which foreign and own imprints are combined and thus enable the acquirer to appropriate foreign imprints in parts that otherwise would be challenging to introduce in their own organization.

Last, our findings show how organizations draw on symbolic *imprint carriers* primarily used to accentuate foreign imprints. This seems to happen above all when parts of the original imprint actually lose their substance, as with the *our firm, our family imprint* due to the change in ownership. Instead of stabilizing the imprint's core through continuing the family influence, we observe how symbols representing the logic behind the imprint, such as the feeling of belonging to a family, are strategically used and emphasized. This further helps us contribute to the discussion around tensions between the persistence and decay of imprints during sensitive periods beyond founding (Marquis & Tilcsik, 2013).

References

Aeon, B., & Lamertz, K. (2021). Those who control the past control the future: The dark side of rhetorical history. *Organization Studies*, *42*(4), 575–593. https://doi.org/10.1177/0170840619844284

Anteby, M., Molnár, V., Battilana, J., Dobbin, F., Golden-Biddle, K., Glynn, M. A., Lorsch, J., Margolis, J., Marquis, C., Neeley, T., Nohria, N., Ramarajan, L., Tushman, M., Wrzesniewski, A., & Yu, T. (2012). Collective memory meets organizational identity: remembering to forget in a firm's rhetorical history. *Academy of Management Journal*, *55*(3), 515–540. https://doi.org/10.5465/amj.2010.0245

Brinkerink, J., Rondi, E., Benedetti, C., & Arzubiaga, U. (2020). Family business or business family? Organizational identity elasticity and strategic responses to disruptive innovation. *Journal of Family Business Strategy*, *11*(4), 100360. https://doi.org/10.1016/j.jfbs.2020.100360

Coraiola, D. M., Foster, W. M., Mena, S., Foroughi, H., & Rintamäki, J. (2023). Ecologies of memories: Memory work within and between organizations and communities. *Academy of Management Annals*, *17*(1), 373–404.

Carroll, G. R., & Hannan, M. T. (2004). *The demography of corporations and industries*. Princeton University Press., https://doi.org/10.1515/9780691186795

Chatterjee, S., Lubatkin, M. H., Schweiger, D. M., & Weber, Y. (1992). Cultural differences and shareholder value in related mergers: Linking equity and human capital. *Strategic Management Journal*, *13*(5), 319–334. https://doi.org/10.1002/smj.4250130502

Coman, S., & Casey, A. (2020). *New directions in organizational and management history*. De Gruyter.

Dao, M. A., & Bauer, F. (2021). Human integration following M&A: Synthesizing different M&A research streams. *Human Resource Management Review*, *31*(3), 100746. https://doi.org/10.1016/j.hrmr.2020.100746

de Cuyper, L., Clarysse, B., & Phillips, N. (2020). Imprinting beyond the founding phase: How sedimented imprints develop over time. *Organization Science*, *31*(6), 1579–1600. https://doi.org/10.1287/orsc.2020.1372

Dias, M., Pan, S. L., Tim, Y., & Land, L. (2023). Managing historical conditions in information systems strategizing: An imprinting perspective. *The Journal of Strategic Information Systems*, *32*(3), 101794. https://doi.org/10.1016/j.jsis.2023.101794

Ellis, S., Aharonson, B. S., Drori, I., & Shapira, Z. (2016). Imprinting through inheritance: A multi-genealogical study of entrepreneurial proclivity. *Academy of Management Journal*, *60*(2), 500–522. https://doi.org/10.5465/amj.2014.0150

Erçek, M., & Günçavdı, Ö. (2016). Imprints of an entrepreneur and evolution of a business group, 1948–2010. *Business History*, *58*(1), 89–110. https://doi.org/10.1080/00076791.2015.1044522

Ferriani, S., Garnsey, E., & Lorenzoni, G. (2012). Continuity and change in a spin-off venture: The process of reimprinting. *Industrial and Corporate Change*, *21*(4), 1011–1048. https://doi.org/10.1093/icc/dts001

Foroughi, H. (2020). Collective memories as a vehicle of fantasy and identification: Founding stories retold. *Organization Studies*, *41*(10), 1347–1367. https://doi.org/10.1177/0170840619844286

Foroughi, H., & Al-Amoudi, I. (2020). Collective forgetting in a changing organization: When memories become unusable and uprooted. *Organization Studies*, *41*(4), 449–470. https://doi.org/10.1177/0170840619830130

Foster, W. M., Suddaby, R., Minkus, A., & Wiebe, E. (2011). History as social memory assets: The example of Tim Hortons. *Management & Organizational History*, *6*(1), 101–120. https://doi.org/10.1177/1744935910387027

Gioia, D. A., Corley, K. G., & Hamilton, A. L. (2013). Seeking qualitative rigor in inductive research: Notes on the Gioia methodology. *Organizational Research Methods*, *16*(1), 15–31. https://doi.org/10.1177/1094428112452151

Gioia, D. A., Schultz, M., & Corley, K. G. (2000). Organizational identity, image, and adaptive instability. *Academy of Management Review*, *25*(1), 63–81. https://doi.org/10.2307/259263

Hannan, M. T., & Freeman, J. (1989). *Organizational ecology*. Harvard University Press. https://doi.org/10.4159/9780674038288

Jaskiewicz, P., Combs, J. G., & Rau, S. B. (2015). Entrepreneurial legacy: Toward a theory of how some family firms nurture transgenerational entrepreneurship. *Journal of Business Venturing*, *30*(1), 29–49. https://doi.org/10.1016/j.jbusvent.2014.07.001

Jenkins, K. (2003). *Re-thinking history*. Routledge Classics. https://doi.org/10.4324/9780203426869

Johnson, V. (2007). What is organizational imprinting? Cultural entrepreneurship in the founding of the Paris opera. *American Journal of Sociology*, *113*(1), 97–127. https://doi.org/10.1086/517899

Jonsen, K., Fendt, J., & Bastien Point, S. (2018). Convincing qualitative research: What constitutes persuasive writing? *Organizational Research Methods*, *21*(1), 30–67. https://doi.org/10.1177/1094428117706533

Kriauciunas, A., & Kale, P. (2006). The impact of socialist imprinting and search on resource change: A study of firms in Lithuania. *Strategic Management Journal*, *27*(7), 659–679. https://doi.org/10.1002/smj.537

Langley, A. (1999). Strategies for theorizing from process data. *Academy of Management Review*, *24*(4), 691–710. https://doi.org/10.2307/259349

Laude, L., Vignon, C., & Waelli, M. (2012). Observer les organisations de l'interieur. *Revue Internationale de Psychosociologie et de Gestion Des Comportements Organisationnels*, *XVIII*(45), 55–76. https://doi.org/10.3917/rips1.045.0055

Marquis, C. (2003). The pressure of the past: Network imprinting in intercorporate communities. *Administrative Science Quarterly*, *48*(4), 655–689. https://doi.org/10.2307/3556640

Marquis, C., & Huang, Z. (2010). Acquisitions as exaptation: The legacy of founding institutions in the U.S. commercial banking industry. *Academy of Management Journal, 53*(6), 1441–1473. https://doi.org/10.5465/amj.2010.57318393

Marquis, C., & Tilcsik, A. (2013). Imprinting: Toward a multilevel theory. *The Academy of Management Annals, 7*(1), 195–245. https://doi.org/10.5465/19416520.2013.766076

Monin, P., Noorderhaven, N., Vaara, E., & Kroon, D. (2013). Giving sense to and making sense of justice in postmerger integration. *Academy of Management Journal, 56*(1), 256–284. https://doi.org/10.5465/amj.2010.0727

Nahavandi, A., & Malekzadeh, A. R. (1988). Acculturation in mergers and acquisitions. *Academy of Management Review, 13*(1), 79–90. https://doi.org/10.2307/258356

Ni Sullivan, B., Tang, Y., & Marquis, C. (2014). Persistently learning: How small-world network imprints affect subsequent firm learning. *Strategic Organization, 12*(3), 180–199. https://doi.org/10.1177/1476127014543772

Sasaki, I., Kotlar, J., Ravasi, D., & Vaara, E. (2020). Dealing with revered past: Historical identity statements and strategic change in Japanese family firms. *Strategic Management Journal, 41*(3), 590–623. https://doi.org/10.1002/smj.3065

Simsek, Z., Fox, B. C., & Heavey, C. (2015). "What's past is prologue": A framework, review, and future directions for organizational research on imprinting. *Journal of Management, 41*(1), 288–317. https://doi.org/10.1177/0149206314553276

Sinha, P. N., Jaskiewicz, P., Gibb, J., & Combs, J. G. (2020). Managing history: How New Zealand's Gallagher Group used rhetorical narratives to reprioritize and modify imprinted strategic guideposts. *Strategic Management Journal, 41*(3), 557–589. https://doi.org/10.1002/smj.3037

Snihur, Y., & Zott, C. (2020). The genesis and metamorphosis of novelty imprints: How business model innovation emerges in young ventures. *Academy of Management Journal, 63*(2), 554–583. https://doi.org/10.5465/amj.2017.0706

Stinchcombe, A. (1965). Social structure and organizations. In J. G. March (Ed.), *Handbook of organizations* (pp. 142–193). Rand McNally.

Strauss, A. L., & Corbin, J. M. (1998). *Basics of qualitative research: Techniques and procedures for developing grounded theory* (Vol. 2). Sage.

Suddaby, R., & Foster, W. M. (2016). History and organizational change. *Journal of Management, 43*(1), 19–38. https://doi.org/10.1177/0149206316675031

Suddaby, R., Foster, W. M., & Trank, C. Q. (2010). Rhetorical history as a source of competitive advantage. *Advances in Strategic Management, 27*, 147–173. https://doi.org/10.1108/S0742-3322(2010)0000027009

Suddaby, R., & Greenwood, R. (2005). Rhetorical strategies of legitimacy. *Administrative Science Quarterly, 50*(1), 35–67. https://doi.org/10.2189/asqu.2005.50.1.35

Suddaby, R., & Jaskiewicz, P. (2020). Managing traditions: A critical capability for family business success. *Family Business Review, 33*(3), 234–243. https://doi.org/10.1177/0894486520942611

Ullrich, J., Wieseke, J., & Van Dick, R. (2005). Continuity and change in mergers and acquisitions: A social identity case study of a German industrial merger. *Journal of Management Studies, 42*(8), 1549–1569. https://doi.org/10.1111/j.1467-6486.2005.00556.x

Vaara, E., Sarala, R., Stahl, G. K., & Björkman, I. (2012). The impact of organizational and national cultural differences on social conflict and knowledge transfer in international acquisitions. *Journal of Management Studies, 49*(1), 1–27. https://doi.org/10.1111/j.1467-6486.2010.00975.x

Vaara, E., Tienari, J., & Säntti, R. (2003). The international match: Metaphors as vehicles of social identity-building in cross-border mergers. *Human Relations, 56*(4), 419–451. https://doi.org/10.1177/0018726703056004002

van Baalen, P., & Brunninge, O. (2009). Using history in organizations: How managers make purposeful reference to history in strategy processes. *Journal of Organizational Change Management, 22*(1), 8–26. https://doi.org/10.1108/09534810910933889

Vermeulen, F., & Barkema, H. (2001). Learning through acquisitions. *Academy of Management Journal*, *44*(3), 457–476. https://doi.org/10.2307/3069364

Weber, Y., Rachman-Moore, D., & Tarba, S. Y. (2012). HR practices during post-merger conflict and merger performance. *International Journal of Cross Cultural Management*, *12*(1), 73–99. https://doi.org/10.1177/1470595811413111

White, H. (1984). The question of narrative in contemporary historical theory. *History and Theory*, *23*(1), 1–33. http://www.jstor.org/stable/2504969 https://doi.org/10.2307/2504969

Peter K. Spink, Mary Jane P. Spink, José Hercílio P. de Oliveira, and Roberth M. Tavanti

Chapter 7
Legacy and collective action: Learning from faith-based communities and parishes

Introduction

This chapter is about ordinary, everyday organizations and the legacies of knowledge and skills that are used in getting things done. Ordinary everyday organizations are those that are present as we go about our daily lives (De Certeau et al., 1998). Some are more visible as we move around, while others have so few obvious organizational attributes that we hardly recognize them as such (Ahrne & Brunsson, 2011). There are those in which we are active participants, those we go to for supplies, leisure, or information, and those we walk past. In the same way that they are part of our day-to-day lives, we in turn by participating, going in and out, or walking by become constitutive of somebody else's everyday (Barker & Wright, 1954).

Everyday organizations are usually local and place based, and their ways of organizing are somewhat flexible, even when hierarchy is present. They can include sports clubs, local associations, community forums, cooperatives, social work organizations and support groups, advice centers, food banks, charity shops, libraries, local businesses, places to eat and drink, parishes, and other religious organizations. Mostly they get on with doing what they normally do, but they can become sources for change, supporting short-term grassroots movements on local issues or even more widely (Almeida, 2019). They are underrepresented in the organizational and management studies literature, which as Vandenventer, Lloveras, and Warnaby (2024) suggested in their study of everyday organizing in a housing estate, tends to privilege formal sites and workplaces. It is not therefore surprising that the same applies to their presence in the area of organizational history. Yet they too have histories and can contribute to the discussion of legacy.

The stimulus for this chapter was a number of events involving Roman Catholic parishes in the southwestern working-class periphery of São Paulo, Brazil. The region underwent wide-scale growth from internal migration in the 1960s and 1970s, characterized, in the absence of any public-sector response, by piecemeal self-help construction on informal lots. At this time, 92% of Brazil's population considered themselves Catholic, and the activities of its churches and parishes were, especially in the case of the new arrivals, very much part of everyday life.

The chapter is divided into five parts, including this introduction, which will discuss legacy and illustrate our approach with examples from other studies in which modes of religious organization have played a role. The second part looks at methodological and theoretical issues at the junction of organizational research and history, especially in relation to the study of collective memory in everyday organizing. It also includes a brief introduction to parishes and popular Catholicism in Brazil.

In the third section, we describe the setting in which the question of legacy and the role of parishes as mnemonic communities of organizing skills initially emerged. This was a request to help a faith-based social organization register its 25 years of active engagement in service development. In facing the question of where to start, we were led, through successive iterations, to the period of Brazilian military government (1964–1985), when from the mid 1970s on, bottom-up community-based social movements—or new social actors as later described in the civil society literature—emerged to make their presence felt in the public sphere.

In the fourth part, we present the results of our interviews and documentary analysis, which suggested that much of the success of these issue-based movements was related to the fusion of a new intellectual Catholic organizing vocabulary with an older mnemonical and social legacy of everyday religious organizing; brought by the migrants along with their bags on the buses and lorries from the interior of Brazil and linked to the yearly cycle of religious events. In the final part, we discuss the relevance of the results for further studies.

Legacy as an expression in use

Bequest, heritage, inheritance, and legacy form a diffuse set of interlinked words with overlapping meanings and varying nuances that are all active in the public domain. The terms are used by lawyers, by international organizations in different fields, analytically when discussing organizational history, and informally in everyday talk. They all relate to the notion of a relationship, of something being handed down from a predecessor to a person, persons, or collective. But the significance of the action and the manner in which it obliges the latter to the former is open.

For example, a bequest can come with clear conditions that tie future actions formally to the past. Or in the middle ground between past and present, rather than being treated as an asset to be freely disposed of, the inheritance of a property or estate may be seen as a moral requirement for continuity. Here there is no legal requirement for conditions to be met, but a sense of obligation, co-constructed within an intergenerational frame. Or, again, moving from the present to the past, heritage can be found in the cultural and environmental fields as the way in which the present constructs a past that requires preservation.

Legacy is part of this elastic set of expressions that link the past and the present, with their different versions of causality, from essentialist to constructionist. However, more recently, it has gathered academic significance in a number of fields, as a focus for the implications of the different processes whereby past and present both intersect and are used. For example, Robinson (2022), working in the field of postcolonial transitional justice education, distinguished between dealing with injustice as "truth telling" about the past and understanding how the past impacts the present. She made a distinction between legacies as an essentialized causal relationship between the past and the present, and legacies that refer to how people construct causal relationships between the past and present—which is key in postcolonial justice.

Given the variety of ways in which legacy and its companion terms are used in everyday speech and in professional speech in different fields, definitions will inevitably vary. Here we follow the focused approach for the organizational arena adopted by Eisenman and Casey (2023 and this volume). They see legacy as a "collective understanding of a past event or individual that is significant in the present. Based on this significance, it becomes a force that affects present choices. This collective understanding is both cognitive and emotional, and its meaning is transmitted through stories." They continued: "This definition requires us to elaborate several ideas: What is an event? Who is the collective that understands it as significant, how is this significance determined, and how does the significance evolve? And what are the organizational implications of such significance?" These questions are similar to those developed by Wittenberg (2015) in his analyses of "legacy arguments."

While this definition serves well for the majority of organizational history studies, in which a founder or founding event is identifiable, including those that involve a variety of identifiable social and organizational actors (Coman & Casey, 2021), it may need adjusting when dealing with everyday organizing and organizations, where settings are less bounded, often plural, and loosely coupled. Similar processes may apply, but in a more scattered form. There will be significant events and stories, some more shared and others less so, which can contribute to or restrict the present. But also present are the taken-for-granted activities, which happen without any special consideration. Mutch (2018, 2021) distinguished between 'practise' as a verb and practices as nouns: how things are done. He viewed practices as emergent from human activity but later solidified into rituals and routines that are open to the investigation of their historical development and their antecedents. Practices in this sense can be seen as companions to stories, both contributing to and consolidating ways of doing things. Mutch developed his ideas in the field of everyday religious organization in Presbyterian Scotland, going behind the scenes of the familiar church services to look at the bundles of practices that were key to continuity. Putting stories and practices together is to connect them, in a similar way that Law and Mol (1995) discussed the intersection of sociality and materiality, or Latour (2005) referred to shifting networks of human and nonhuman actors.

Religious organization in the everyday

Religion usually appears in organizational history studies in its institutional form along with the family, the economy, or the system of government. Until recently, little attention was given to its daily presence in society. There are various reasons for this, including the domination of secular societies in the West. Religious studies are a separate field from organizational studies, both on campus and in journals. There are also a large variety of religions, and with organizational studies increasingly concerned with management, few have learned how to think about them in an organizational frame (Cadge & Wuthnow, 2015). Even in the more obvious areas of nongovernmental, nonprofit, third sector, or voluntary research, or in development studies, religion and faith-based organizations continue to be significantly underrepresented in the academic literature.

The field of organizational history and memory is no exception and, consequently, if studying the everyday itself is difficult, looking for the everyday contributions of religious organizations becomes harder still. The following examples, drawn from different disciplines, including organizational history and legacy, demonstrate some of the potential, but also serve as an alert to difficulties and limits.

The first example is that of the Southern Christian Leadership Conference, set up in 1957 under the founding leadership of Martin Luther King Jr. This organization continues today as a "nonprofit, non-sectarian, inter-faith, advocacy organization." Every social history of the human rights movement in the United States will have a special place for the Southern Christian Leadership Conference, but few will mention that a major part of its early success, in extremely hostile circumstances, came from it being an organization "literally built on the institutional infrastructure of black churches, which catalyzed the civil rights movement" (King & Haveman, 2008, p. 500). However, as the authors commented, while all churches have resources that can potentially be deployed by social movement organizers, not all churches support social movements. Independently of denomination, there are those that are theologically "this-worldly," that embrace participation in the secular world, and those that are "other-worldly" and do not.

Mutch (2021) provided numerous examples of the role of organizational solutions migrating from the back office of religious practices to other areas of action in his detailed studies of Scottish Presbyterianism, including early notions of governance, financial organization, and accountability. Among these was his discussion of possible influences behind the introduction of salaried managers in a Liverpool public house chain, nearly a hundred years before this became a nationwide practice (Mutch, 2006).

The final example comes from Basque and Langley's (2018) study of the Canadian Desjardins Group, a Quebec-based cooperative financial institution founded by Alphonse Desjardins in 1900:

> Alphonse was raised in a poor family and grew up to become a journalist. During his life, he became concerned by the problem of loansharking, which in his view contributed to maintaining his fellow French Canadians in poverty. He discovered the cooperative movement developing in Europe while working in the Canadian Parliament as a stenographer and began encouraging the foundation of small savings and loans cooperatives (called "caisses populaires"). He began in his hometown of Lévis, and subsequently extended his work from Quebec to Ontario. He founded

163 caisses during his lifetime. . . . . Each cooperative was associated with a parish, and the Catholic clergy were deeply involved in managing the caisses, seen as non-profit community organizations dedicated to the economic emancipation of working-class French Canadians in a society dominated by Anglo-Saxon economic interests. . . . According to its website, in 2016, Desjardins had $258.4 billion in assets, over 7 million members and clients, 47,655 employees, and 4,571 elected officers. (pp. 4–5)

Basque and Langley's study justifiably focused on the growth of the Desjardins Group and the way in which the legacy founder figure was invoked in the ongoing dynamics of organizational identity. But the study left aside a question: What led Alphonse to the Catholic parishes? Was it their territorial organization, their mainly French origin, or their literate and numerically skilled clergy? What was this more subtle legacy of skills and resources, stories and practices on which Alphonse was able to build? What were the antecedents?

Theoretical and methodological challenges in studying the history of ordinary everyday organizations and their collective memories

The main challenge that faces scholars of everyday life is that it is mundane, ordinary, composed of all sorts and bits of organization, and taken for granted. As De Certeau (1984) commented, everyday practices have been traditionally seen as the obscure background of social activity instead of recognizing that they "depend on a vast ensemble which is difficult to delimit but which we may passionately designate as *an ensemble of procedures*" (p. 43). In a similar way, Geertz (1983, p. 75) proposed to treat "common sense as a relatively organized body of considered thought." Implicit in both is a performative notion of collective memory, of something learned and passed on to be drawn on as practice, "a generative constitutive enacted process that produces various types of cultural and material consequences constantly manifesting in the present through performance" (Foroughi et al., 2020, p. 1731).

The everyday is also present when Halbwachs (1950) discussed the subtle way in which continuous flows of thought hold on to and retain from the past that which is still alive in the consciousness of a specific group or bounded setting. But his contribution to the everyday went much further and is often forgotten. As the everyday is unbounded, collective memory is inevitably polyphonic, the product of many collective memories that may overlap in parts but are located within specific sociocultural settings. Foroughi (2020) showed the importance of applying these notions to organizational settings, and we sought to do the same for the everyday, where space and place take on broader dimensions. In Halbwachs' discussion of the role of space and collective memory, place or "location" (his term) grounds social relationships, creating routines and practices, expectations and memories. Even those forms of association that may seem to be without an obvious spatial base, such as the legal, economic, and religious spheres, are, he argued, also located in different ways. Collective memory, as he saw it, unfolds within a spatial framework, which we suggest is both social and technical in the mediated sense proposed by Wertsch (2002).

Events are important for Halbwachs, and they are central to religious groups. These are, almost by definition, mnemonic. Take, for example, the rosary in the Catholic Church. The rosary is a reminder of a sequence of prayers that should be said regularly, either individually or in a group. It doesn't require the presence of a priest (the significance of which will be discussed in the case study). There are also buildings shaped in a particular way; images and banners to remind people of key figures. Time is both linear and cyclical. Key days in the yearly calendar serve to remember religious events and figures, some of which are quite real in terms of their historical presence. Each special day will be different and require collective action by priests and parishioners; children will learn from their mothers and fathers and the elderly will tell their tales. There will be serious moments on these special days but also many opportunities to get together, share news, and enjoy each other's presence. The year goes forward but also comes around again. For example, in the Roman Catholic calendar, there will be Christmas, the arrival of the Kings, Easter, Corpus Christi, All Souls, and the days of the different patron saints and remembrance ceremonies. They may be seen as communities of memory (Bellah et al., 1996) or mnemonic communities (Coraiola et al., 2023), but the memories serve many purposes.

However, the yearly cycle only happens if the special day as practice happens, and each event is different. In the Catholic Church, the priest may have a role, but it is often that of a supporter rather than conductor of a collective enterprise where there is much to be done. Decorations have to be made, processions have to be organized, and participants have to be fed. There will be differences from parish to parish, from region to region, and from country to country, but in all of the settings the learning passes from one to the other. Stories are told, skills revived, activities remembered, and new ones developed. Parishioners and other participants will learn and gain confidence in their capacity to act, not just in these special events, but elsewhere. Other religions will have their events, but they will serve similar functions.

Methodologically, studying the day-to-day requires finding the day-to-day. In what has become the customary organizational and management studies approach to investigation, there is a preferred sequence that leads to an empirical study: "question, literature, sample, study." Even where this is based on case methods, the case, to use Stake's typology (2003), is more likely to be justified for instrumental reasons, directly or as part of a collection of similar cases. Both are valid approaches to advancing knowledge about management, organizations, and their history and memory, but they depend on assumptions of visibility. It is necessary to know they exist as an empirical possibility from which to draw a sample, before they can be chosen.

We didn't set out to study the role of the parishes in everyday life; our concern was with questions of urban and institutional vulnerability. Contacts in the peripheral southwest of the city had led to the suggestion that we should take part in a longstanding human rights forum (the Forum in Defense of Life and Against Violence), which in turn led to other discussions with forum members. These varied from activist residents, community leaders, and social and health service professionals to public-sector managers, local government officials, and the occasional academic or research student.

How we got involved with parishes is described in the next part. Methodologically, it was an example of Stake's third type of case, the intrinsic case study that happens "because first and last, the researcher wants better understanding of this particular case. Here it is not undertaken primarily because the case represents other cases or because it illustrates a particular trait or problem, but because, in all its particularity and ordinariness, the case itself is of interest" (Stake, 2003, p. 136). Intrinsic case studies are usually also examples of grounded research (Strauss & Corbin, 1990), because researchers are not sure what they might lead to, and those of the everyday can be quite chaotic.

Parishes and popular Catholicism

What is this "parish" which became the territorial basis for Catholic Christian organization and whose echoes can be found in secular Louisiana, USA, and in the French and UK local government structure? First and foremost, it is a contiguous territorial unit. Where one parish ends, another starts; hence their historical importance as record keepers. In France, there were some 60,000 *paroisse* at the time of the revolution, all of which held the records of births, marriages, and deaths. In 1789, the National Assembly created the commune as the lowest level of administration and used the village-centered *paroisse* as its basis. There were adjustments, especially in large towns, but there are still some 35,000 communes today, many with similar territorial limits. In England the move from papal to regal control of the Christian church had very little effect on the parishes, which continued to combine religious and civic responsibilities until 1895, when they became civil parishes with a council elected by public vote. Today more than a third of the population of England has a town or parish council (in Scotland and Wales there were variations).

The French *paroisse* came from the Latin *paroecia,* a version of the Greek *paroikia* which means to "sojourn" or a place to sojourn; to be from elsewhere and to stay temporarily in a dwelling. Its sense of territoriality is derived from this practice, as Edwin Hatch (1881), a 19th century theologian and historian, remarked:

> Driven from city to city by persecution, or wandering from country to country an outcast or a refugee, a Christian found, wherever he went, in the community of his fellow Christians a wel-

come and hospitality. The practice of hospitality was enjoined as the common virtue of all Christians: in the New Testament itself stress is laid upon it by St. Paul, St. Peter, and St. John. (p. 44)

Over time these "safe places" would formalize their internal structures, but the practices remained, and the name gradually migrated from a description of these practices to the territory in which they took place and, from the third to fifth century, to a description of religious administrative arrangements.

In each country where Catholicism became established, there would be differences. The Catholic Portuguese arrived in Brazil around the time that the Catholic Spanish were arriving in other parts of what would later be called "Latin America." But accompanying the explorers was not the church in its hierarchical form but the monastic orders, especially the Franciscans and Jesuits. Brazil has a seaboard of nearly 7,500 kilometers, and the early explorers built their settlements along the coast. In time they moved inland, but the centers of influence and the capital cities of the early provinces remained close to the coast, creating the distinction between "capital" and "interior." The early churches were built by the religious orders in these coastal centers, each with its own following. Large landowners in the interior would build chapels, as would residents of rural hamlets and villages. From time to time, a priest would go out from one of the major centers to baptize, hold first communions, marry, pray for the dead, and say mass. For the rest of the time, the local communities would meet together to pray with the rosary, discuss daily affairs, and plan their processions and religious festivities. While religious in origin, these activities were also important moments of social gathering and leisure, opportunities to meet friends and relatives and enjoy life.

The result, as described in a key reference document published by the National Conference of Brazilian Bishops (CNBB), was a Catholicism "characterized by the intense participation of the lay population in associations, where there was a lot of prayer and few masses. The lay community was particularly active in the chapels, where they would pray together with the rosary and start their processions" (CNBB, 2014, p. 25). The later relation between the chapels, associations, and the increasingly present church-based parish with its priest was not easy. Attempts in the 19th century to include the chapels as a formal part of the parish were only partly successful:

> The lay communities remained attached to their feasts, processions, their devotion to their saints and prayers. The clergy insisted on the moral and dogmatic education in the faith. The parish became identified as the exclusive place of the priest. Popular catholicism survived without really aligning itself within parochial life. (CNBB, 2014, p. 25)

These were the memories, the stories, and the practices that the migrants of the 1960s and 1970s brought with them in the converted lorries and buses that transported them to São Paulo.

> You know, they talk about our parishes here as being parishes of the periphery—but I don't think they are. They are made up of lots of people from the interiors, from Minas Gerais, the

Northeast. . . . They are people with a sense of profound and collective devotion. It doesn't matter which priest will come to take care of the parish; they have their processions, their special events that keep going because of their traditions. (H. B. O., Parish Priest in Southwest São Paulo, 2018)

The empirical setting and its questions

The Forum for the Defense of Life and Against Violence began in 1997 as a reaction to a wave of violence in the region. It went on to become a key civil society gathering point for mobilization on social issues—what Haug (2013) described as a meeting arena. It took place in the parish hall of one of the more active Catholic churches which, shortly after the parish was formed in 1988, had founded an independent social service organization (the Martyred Saints Society) that grew to become a leading and innovative social services provider.

One day, the parish priest, who was an important force in the forum and also the society's president, asked us if we could help him and his colleagues register the story of the society's 25 years. We have a "research in action" approach to fieldwork, which means being prepared to help and be useful. It also seemed a very good way of getting to learn more about this densely packed region of the city.

Our initial idea was to start with the founding of the society. In 1988, one of the available strategies for supporting much-needed and absent public services was a self-help approach that could later apply for municipal support. Individual parishes have very limited economic and legal independence within the diocese, and in order to manage municipal service contracts, the more active parishes had started to create their own social nonprofit organizations.

> The daycare center was our first activity in the parish. In the 1980s there was a lot of unemployment, and the women went out to work in daily domestic service and cleaning jobs—which did have a positive effect in terms of liberation—but where to leave the children? The church had these spaces and chapels that were little used during the week. I remember that we charged a symbolic fee so there was a sense of contribution, but it didn't cover costs. We added in all the donations from the baptisms, and we also had parties, dances, and other festivities. This was 1988—it would take 2 years before we got the contract with the municipality. (J. C., parish priest and president of the society, 2013)

Another starting point would be to go back to the time when, in 1988, the parish was created as part of the reorganization of a previous much larger parish. The two priests from the Irish St. Patrick's Missionary Society had been working in a neighboring municipality where they had also created a nonprofit association:

> Interviewer: You arrived with a lot of experience from the previous parish where a lot of social organizing took place with the help of social movements. What were your first thoughts?

> To do nothing, at least for 6 months or more. To be present and listen, let the parish decide where we should live, let the communities define the priorities. (E. J. M., Parish Priest, 2013)

Who were these communities and the parishioners? We started to talk with small groups over coffee and cake, mainly women parishioners and activists, and these conversations suggested that we should go further back to the 1960s and 1970s when the São Paulo metropolitan region, with its new industrial opportunities, became a major attraction for internal migration but without a corresponding housing supply.

> We fought for the land, for people to have their own piece, not those shacks. . . . We fought for water, electricity, asphalt for the roads, day nurseries, everything. We had to dig wells, and not everybody had wells, so we shared them. My well was about 30 to 32 meters deep. (Helena, in group discussion with women residents, 2013)

The result was two lines of investigation. The first continued with the history of the Martyred Saints Society (named after the parish) and its many innovative responses to issues raised by parishioners and later from the late 1990s by the meetings of the forum. We used an oral history approach with recorded discussions that were later transcribed and collated into thematic sections, corroborating where possible by documents. The idea was to let those involved in the society tell its story; we acted as curators (Spink et al., 2019).

The second investigation, the focus of this chapter, followed the suggestions to look backwards. It took place over the following years with conversations, field notes, archival material about the region, academic reports and unpublished dissertations about the 1970s, and community documents registering oral history. In terms of method, following Stake's third type of case through day-to-day events is certainly chaotic, as each step opens up new material and questions. Documents and comments pointed not only to the importance of this earlier period, but to the different ways in which the arrival of the migrants and the role of the Catholic Church were interpreted. In a number of academic texts and professional church documents, there was an underlying image of rural workers, without experience and competence in urban life, living in vulnerable and impoverished circumstances and needing organizing. Then there were the former migrants' own descriptions of their activities, events, and movements, which showed a different and collective capacity for getting things done.

Faith, coffee, cake, and action in M'Boi Mirim and Vila Remo

In the M'Boi administrative district where the Santos Mártires church and society were located, the population grew from 30,000 in 1970 to 271,000 in 1980, 484,000 in 1991, and some 600,000 currently. During most of the early part of this period, which included the military dictatorship from 1964 to 1985, there were no effective social housing programs. The land available for the newly arrived workforce was made up of former small market garden farms. The process of dividing the land into plots was piecemeal, with no land use planning or regulation. As a result, there were few fully documented plots and no basic services, and the newcomers built very simple wooden structures that the municipal administration would knock down.

> But, 2 or 3 days later, in the middle of the night, others would be put up and the community began to grow and grow, from where Gloria's shop is down to the other road. Then we began to build with bricks and the municipality stopped bothering. Then the owners of the fields started to divide them up into plots and sell them. Then we bought a half plot and built two rooms and a kitchen. The well was in the middle of the kitchen. We bought a pump, installed it, and closed the top of the well. But before that I hauled a lot of water by hand, with the bucket. It was difficult, very difficult, but nice in its own way. My husband worked at night, and during the day, he would do the housework for me. At night, after I arrived from my work, right in the middle of town, I would wash the clothes, the nappies . . . .. The buses were full, they ran only hourly. (Helena, group discussion with women residents, 2013)

Families built their own houses, room by room, aided by neighbors who worked as laborers on building sites in richer areas of the city and who shared the new architectural techniques they were learning for filled-in concrete frames (Lara, 2009). On weekends, they would take turns helping each other, mixing concrete and raising walls.

> Interviewer: Gloria, you said that the women here are strong.
> Because if you don't have faith in prayer, nothing will happen and you won't get there. For example, when I met Maria Felipe [a key community figure along with her husband in the housing movement], it was because of praying; things were very bad and I got on my knees and prayed to St. Joseph, asking him, "Help me, because this fight has been going on for 30 days and I can't stand it anymore; I don't know where it's going to go." (Gloria, group discussion, 2013)

In the region of the southwest periphery, as elsewhere, the Catholic Church spread out as the migrants arrived. At this time, with nearly 90% of the Brazilian population declaring themselves Catholic, religion was part of everyday life. Groups of people would get together to pray in spaces that were available, such as kitchens and garages, encouraged by the local priest. These small groups would grow, with support, and become incorporated as "communities" into the wider parish structure where a more central "community" would take the role of parish church. Each community would choose a religious figure and in time build a small meeting room that would become a chapel. Each community would have a council, as would the parish, and together they would organize the yearly cycle of significant events, feast days, and processions. In 1967, the 70 square kilometers of the current M'Boi administrative district in the southwest had only one parish. By 2015, there were 18, together with some 48 parish-based communities, usually between three and five per parish.

It was here, in the mid 1970s, now with two parishes and their various communities spread across this area of the periphery with its population from the different interiors, that the older traditions of community-based popular Catholicism, with its processions, pilgrimages to local shrines, and small local chapels, merged with a new movement within the Catholic Church. This was influenced by the Second Vatican Council (1962–1965), critical liberation theology, and the Conference of Latin American Bishops in Medellín, Colombia (1968), which emphasized working to reduce poverty through supporting and developing parish communities, referred to as ecclesiastical base communities (CEBs). In São Paulo, this would become "Operation Periphery" (Oliveira, 2008).

A progressive Franciscan was made archbishop of São Paulo in 1970. Following Medellín, he spoke of the importance of joining with the new generations of migrants to lead the discussion about poverty reduction and develop community leaders. It would become known as "the preferential option for the poor." In 1972, the archdiocese sold its elegant official palace and with the funds, plus other donations received, purchased small plots of land on the periphery to help build more community centers for religious and nonreligious activities. Overall, some 506 centers were built (Monteiro, 2017, p. 61).

> I have a lot of good memories about our parties and events of special feast days. We got everybody together by word of mouth. We didn't have money and we didn't know how to do the decorations, but we would go asking house by house. Everybody brought a little and we made our own dresses and danced. . . . Everything we earned went to help the building of our little chapel. (Helena, group discussion with women residents, 2013)

> These small meeting halls that were being built in each neighborhood served for mass and also for spaces to cooperate and show solidarity. There the women met in the mother's clubs, the children in the preschool playgroups, the young people, the singers, and others to study and organize the very real fight for water, nurseries, schools, land registration, improvements to the favelas, public transport, lighting in the streets, local health services, amongst others. (Dalila, a former religious social worker, 2021)

The second parish, *Nossa Senhora das Graças*, was formed out of the first as the population expanded outward over the southern area. By the time part of it was separated along with six communities and their councils to form the Martyred Saints Parish, it had 18 constituent communities. It was popularly known as the parish of Vila Remo after the neighborhood where its principal church was located and would become a reference point in the mid and late 1970s for the "mothers' club movement."

There had always been activities for women, especially mothers, in the low-income housing areas, supported by middle- and upper-class philanthropic organizations teaching skills such as needlework and discussing good health practices. Following a movement in the church towards recognizing and strengthening its communities, many of these became self-organizing, some maintaining support, others not, and as "new" mothers' clubs, the focus switched to living conditions and social demands.

By the mid 1970s, there were some 30 clubs meeting weekly in different parts of Vila Remo with a monthly coordination group of one representative from each club to "bring" the problems raised by each group and "take back" suggestions for action. Jointly, the "Mothers Clubs of the Vila Remo Parish" wrote an open letter to the municipal and state governments, complaining about the high increase in living costs. The letter was published in the press and discussed in the election of 1974. In 1975, they carried out a quantitative survey showing how low salaries were forcing other family members to enter the labor market. "Members of 70 mothers' clubs distributed 2.000 questionnaires house to house" (Singer, 1980, p. 97). The movement spread, and the "Zona Sul Mothers' Clubs" and the "Cost of Living Movement" would start a process that would take on the military regime (Monteiro, 2017; Sader, 1988).

"Operation Periphery" had considerable impact and would go on to influence, among other groups and movements, the renovation of trade unions and the rise of the Brazilian Workers' Party. Much of what has been written about this period emphasizes the work of the church's leaders and professional activists in the area of popular education, who were very involved in discussing the practice of the CEBs with the local priests. Without a doubt, the church hierarchy played an essential role, not only in providing support for buying land, but also in being very active in everyday meetings and, in a difficult political period, providing legitimacy for the issues being raised. However, in most formal documents, there is little mention of the part played by the migrants themselves, especially the women who took care of the day-to-day.

Seen in the practice of everyday life, there are clearly different action languages present (Spink, 2019). The mysticism of popular Catholicism from the interiors may have seemed strange to those whose action vocabularies were more academic and urban. Both contributed, but in the discussions and meetings, the protests and marches, much of the success was due to the way that those who came in the buses and lorries from the interiors—a journey that could take some 2,000 kilometers—were able to use and adapt the skills of meetings, processions, and collective faith to these new settings.

> Then we began to discover and understand what was community, people getting together through their faith, to build their lives together. There was great spirituality, a very strong mystique amongst people. The most popular of events were directed towards their saints with processions; bit by bit we began to bring in the Bible, for reflection. We helped to make faith more logical and practical. If we were wrong in taking a little bit of the emotion out of the devotion to the saints, we rebuilt it in a different way, giving value to their popular beliefs. In the CEBs there was a lot of solidarity. Everybody would get together at the weekends to help build houses with friends and neighbors and the community centers. The difficulties with the lack of water, nurseries, schools, and other things motivated the union in a cause that was everybody's. (J. C., Martyred Saints parish priest, 2018)

> At the beginning we had very little to offer because everything was so different, but we had a present and listening ear. This, I think, helped to release latent organizational skills in the people that were part of their baggage; when they had a name and a function in their local community

> where the Church was very central to their lives. (E. J. M., former priest of Martyred Saints Parish, 2024)

It is important here to avoid the impression that the church's actions in the city were the result of pastoral and theological unanimity. There were, returning to King and Haveman (2008), "this-worldly" priests and parishes and also "other-worldly" priests and parishes. Tensions between communities and parishes would continue, and analyses of church documents from the period show that among priests, there were those highly engaged with "Operation Periphery," those less active yet supportive, and those who didn't want to know (CNBB, 2014; Oliveira, 2008).

Many years later, in the 1990s when this region was the focus of gang-based violence and vigilante groups, a number of social organizations and parishes, including Santos Mártires, decided it was time to make a statement, which continues to be part of the calendar and which had echoes of those earlier processions—this time directed towards social change.

> At that time [mid 1990s] the region was marked by killings. The UN had declared Jardim Angela the most violent place in the world, even worse than Cali, Colombia, which had been the previous year's spotlight. What could we do—as priests? We got together with other active priests in the region, including the Center for Human Rights and Popular Education in Campo Limpo, which was supported by the diocese, and slowly we realized that the more we retreated from violence, the more crime and organized crime would take over. So, we decided to have a march on All Souls Day [November 2, 1996], starting from the different parishes and meeting up in the main cemetery of the region, where all the victims of violence are buried. Many were in doubt whether it would work or whether as priests we should be involved, but we found a car with a loudspeaker and at 7.30 in the morning the two of us stood in the street outside the church. We thought nobody would come, but at 7.50, people started pouring in and we set off with a thousand followers. Along the way the other parishes were joining in, and we were 5,000 when we reached the cemetery. . . . But after this, what would be the next steps. That is when the Forum in Defense of Life and Against Violence began [February 1997]. The forum is really a space for the articulation of organized civil society in the region; it has a lot of participation from the different social organizations, schools, communities, and associations. (J. C., Martyred Saints parish priest, 2013)

Discussion and conclusions

We are trained as social and organizational scholars to base our research on clear questions that have a theoretical and empirical base. Sometimes the reverse happens and ordinary events and everyday organizations themselves, as it were, ask the questions. Methodologically, the result is a type of case study in which, intrinsically, the case is in charge and not the researcher. This was the starting point for the chapter, which led us in turn to the literature on organizational history and, more precisely, to the theme of legacy. Here we took the definition of Eisenman and Casey (2023) as a starting point while suggesting that in the less bounded settings of the everyday, the definition might need to be extended to include practice (as a noun) as well as stories, giving more attention to antecedents as more subtle elements of legacy. We also used examples from the literature to show how antecedents and practice may help expand comprehension of organizational history and legacy as a performative process.

This theoretical position, including practices and antecedents, was demonstrated in the case study itself, which also showed the importance of learning the historians' art of looking for descriptive material that may have been produced at the time certain events happened, as well as oral or written recollections.

Learning how to extend the historical study of the more explicit type of organizational setting normally found in organizational history and memory studies to the mundane and taken-for-granted everyday is a major challenge. There are few, if any, temporal markers and key events to start from that might lead to stories. It may be that in these looser, polyphonic settings, practices rather than stories offer an alternative starting point in studying the dynamics of legacy.

Studying everyday organizing and organizations can make a useful contribution to the area of organizational history and memory and, more importantly, the role of legacy in relation to change. Our research may have focused on "this-worldly" parishes, but there are many other "this-worldly" organizations and associations in daily life. There are a number of settings where everyday organizing takes place and where skills and resources can be key in confronting social issues and arguing for change.

Hopefully, with themes such as community-based activism, social movements, and major issue mobilization—such as climate change—finding their way into the organizational studies agenda, concern will also grow about the need to understand the legacies on which these key organizations, networks, forums, and other bits and pieces of organizing can draw and, in doing so, help them be more effective. Perhaps the next time we walk down our local streets, we might pay more attention to the different meeting spaces that have spanned and provided support for different generations, including religious spaces.

References

Ahrne, G., & Brunsson, N. (2011). Organization outside organizations: The significance of partial organization. *Organization, 18*(1), 83–104. https://doi.org/10.1177/1350508410376256

Almeida, P. (2019). *Social movements: The structure of collective mobilization*. University of California Press.

Barker, R. G., & Wright, H. F. (1954). *Midwest and its children: The psychological ecology of an American town*. Row Peterson. https://doi.org/10.1037/10027-000

Basque, J., & Langley, A. (2018). Invoking Alphonse: The founder figure as a historical resource for organizational identity work. *Organization Studies, 39*(12), 1685–1708. https://doi.org/10.1177/0170840618789211

Bellah, R. N., Madsen, R., Sullivan, W. S., Swidler, A., & Tipton, S. M. (1996). *Habits of the heart: Individualism and commitment in American life*. University of California Press.

Cadge, W., & Wuthnow, R. (2015). Religion and the nonprofit sector. In W. W. Powell & R. Steinberg (Eds.), *The nonprofit sector: A research handbook* (2nd ed., pp. 485–505). Yale University Press.

CNBB (National Conference of Brazilian Bishops). (2014). *Comunidade de Comunidades: Uma nova paroquia —a conversão pastoral da paróquia.* 52ª Assembleia Geral Aparecida – SP, 30 de abril a 9 de maio de 2014.

Coman, S., & Casey, A. (2021). The enduring presence of the founder: A historical and interdisciplinary perspective on the organizational identity of collection museums. In M. Maclean, S. R. Clegg, R. Suddaby, & C. Harvey (Eds.), *Historical organizational studies: Theory and applications* (pp. 131–148). Routledge.

Coraiola, D. M., Foster, W. M., Mena, S., Foroughi, H., & Rintamaki, J. (2023). Ecologies of memories: Memory work within and between organizations and communities. *The Academy of Management Annals, 17*(1), 373–404. https://doi.org/10.5465/annals.2021.0088

De Certeau, M. (1984). *The practice of everyday life.* University of California Press.

De Certeau, M., Giard, L., & Mayol, P. (1998). *The practice of everyday life vol 2: Living and cooking.* University of Minnesota Press.

Eisenman, M., & Casey, A. (2023). *Theorizing events toward constructing legacy: A research agenda.* Presented at the 39th EGOS Colloquium, July 6–8, 2023, Cagliari.

Foroughi, H. (2020). Collective memories as a vehicle of fantasy and identification: Founding stories retold. *Organization Studies, 41*(10), 1347–1367. https://doi.org/10.1177/0170840619844286

Foroughi, H., Coraiola, D. M., Rintamäki, J., Mena, S., & Foster, W. M. (2020). Organizational memory studies. *Organization Studies, 41*(12), 1725–1748. https://doi.org/10.1177/0170840620974338

Geertz, C. (1983). *Local knowledge: Further essays in interpretive anthropology.* Basic Books.

Halbwachs, M. (1950). *The collective memory.* Harper and Row.

Hatch, E. (1881). *The organization of the early Christian churches. Eight lectures, 1880.* Rivingtons.

Haug, C. (2013). Organizing spaces: Meeting arenas as a social movement infrastructure between organization, network and institution. *Organization Studies, 34*, 5–6, 405–732. https://doi.org/10.1177/0170840613479232

King, M. D., & Haveman, H. A. (2008). Antislavery in America: The press, the pulpit and the rise of antislavery societies. *Administrative Science Quarterly, 53*, 492–528. https://doi.org/10.2189/asqu.53.3.492

Lara, F. L. (2009). The form of the informal, investigating Brazilian self-built housing solutions. In F. Hernandez (Ed.), *Rethinking the informal cities: Critical perspectives from Latin America* (pp. 23–38). Berghahn Books.

Latour, B. (2005). *Reassembling the social.* Oxford University Press. https://doi.org/10.1093/oso/9780199256044.001.0001

Law, J., & Mol, A. (1995). Notes on materiality and sociality. *The Sociological Review, 43*(2), 274–294. https://doi.org/10.1111/j.1467-954X.1995.tb00604.x

Monteiro, T. N. (2017). *Como pode um povo vivo viver nesta carestia: O movimento de custo de vida em São Paulo (1973–1982).* Editora Humanitas/FAPESP.

Mutch, A. (2006). Public houses as multiple retailing: Peter Walker & Son, 1846–1914. *Business History, 48*(1), 1–19. https://doi.org/10.1080/00076790500204677

Mutch, A. (2018). Practice, substance and history: Reframing institutional logics. *Academy of Management Review, 43*(2), 242–258. https://doi.org/10.5465/amr.2015.0303

Mutch, A. (2021). Writing the history of practices. In M. Maclean, S. R. Clegg, R. Suddaby, & C. Harvey (Eds.), *Historical organizational studies: Theory and applications* (pp. 25–38). Routledge.

Oliveira, C. (2008). *Operação periferia: Um estudo sobre a Operação Periferia na Arquidiocese de SP (1970–1980), perspectivas para a missão na cidade.* Dissertação de Mestrado em Teologia, Pontifícia Faculdade de Teologia Nossa Senhora da Assunção (UNIFAI).

Robinson, N. (2022). Conceptualising historical legacies for transitional justice history education in postcolonial societies. *History Education Research Journal, 19*(1), 10. https://doi.org/10.14324/HERJ.19.1.10

Sader, E. (1988). *Quando novos personagens entraram em cena: Experiências, falas e lutas dos trabalhadores de grande São Paulo (1970–1980)*. Editora Paz e Terra.

Singer, P. (1980). Movimentos de bairro. In P. Singer & V. C. Brant (Eds.), *São Paulo: O povo em movimento* (pp. 83–107). Editora Vozes/CEBRAP.

Spink, M. J., Spink, P. K., & Tavanti, R. M. (Eds.). (2019). *Sociedade Santos Mártires de Jardim Ângela: Uma chama de esperança*. Programa Gestão Pública e Cidadania/Terceiro Nome.

Spink, P. K. (2019). *Beyond public policy: A public action languages approach*. Edward Elgar. https://doi.org/10.4337/9781788118750

Stake, R. E. (2003). Case studies. In N. K. Denzin & Y. S. Lincoln (Eds.), *Strategies of qualitative enquiry* (2nd ed., pp. 134–164). Sage.

Strauss, A. L., & Corbin, J. (1990). *Basics of qualitative research: Grounded theory procedures and techniques*. Sage.

Vandenventer, J. S., Lloveras, J., & Warnaby, G. (2024). Seeking organizational geographies: A multi-dimensional spatial analysis of everyday organizing. *Organization Studies*, *45*(8), 1133–1160. https://doi.org/10.1177/01708406241248983

Wertsch, J. W. (2002). *Voices of collective remembering*. Cambridge University Press. https://doi.org/10.1017/CBO9780511613715

Wittenberg, J. (2015). Conceptualizing historical legacies. *Eastern European Politics and Societies*, *29*(2), 366–378. https://doi.org/10.1177/0888325415577864

Part III: **The role of legacy in organizational change and imagined futures**

Viviane Sergi, Joëlle Basque, Ann Langley, and Nora Meziani
Chapter 8
The power of the mundane: Small stories as ambivalent carriers of legacy

Consider the following two anecdotes, found in a feature story published on digital media publication CNET, presenting the preserved Silicon Valley offices of Bill Hewlett and Dave Packard, the founders of Hewlett-Packard (HP), located in the HP headquarters in Palo Alto, California (Figures 8.1 and 8.2) (Martin, 2016).

Bill Hewlett once left a penny on his desk, quipping that eventually someone would take it.

His secretary replied that no, everyone was in such awe of him, no one would ever take it.

No one ever picked it up, the penny stayed. Soon, visitors began leaving money as an homage to Bill which continues to this day.

Figure 8.1: Paying homage to Bill Hewlett.

What are such small stories? Are these simply charming anecdotes evoking a distant past, reminding us of the particularities of founders, or could there be more than meets the eye? In this chapter, we propose viewing such anecdotes, which we define as 'small stories,' both as cultural artifacts and as important, but ambivalent, carriers of legacy. By small story, we designate material in which a deceased founder is seen

Both Bill Hewlett and Dave Packard were known to have an "open door" policy towards HP employees, welcoming anyone in to discuss the company.

Just how extreme the "open door" policy was is evident in the discoloration of the floor -- dark color hidden behind the door resisted years of fading.

Figure 8.2: Materializing an open-door policy.

as acting in his or her daily life, doing or saying something that may appear ordinary, in contrast to acting in exceptional circumstances. Such small stories can be found in various forms and in a variety of locations, such as companies' websites, annual reports, or promotional material. That such small stories are not only preserved in archives but are told or used in present times identifies them as historical material that matters.

We argue in this chapter that such small stories can be useful resources in anchoring elements from the past in present times. Yet, at the same time, the messages they carry are subject to multiple and shifting interpretations, depending on when, where, and how they are evoked. As time passes, stories that once seemed to reflect the deepest values of the organization can appear quaint or even ridiculous. Elements that once signaled positive traits can take on a darker meaning. Finally, some small stories may carry forward elements of legacy that can inhibit rather than inspire future leaders and employees. In this chapter, we explore some of these implications, drawing on three detailed illustrative vignettes as well as other examples, like those that introduce the chapter.

Organizational history, legacy, and narrative

As studies of history and memory in organizations have shown, an organization's past can be a rich reservoir of material that can become resources for present circumstances (Casey & Olivera, 2011; Coraiola et al., 2023; Foroughi et al., 2020; Ravasi et al., 2019). Generally speaking, studies have demonstrated how elements from the past can help in sustaining the current organizational culture or can be useful in negotiating strategic change (Hatch & Schultz, 2017; Sasaki et al., 2020). In specific situations, material from the past—elements that otherwise no longer exist concretely in the present, like a discontinued product line, an earlier building, or a deceased founder—can move from historical trace and distant memory to become assets, useful for current issues (Basque & Langley, 2018; Hatch & Schultz, 2017; Ravasi et al., 2019; Schultz & Hernes, 2013). Our chapter hence begins with the recognition that an organization's past may be more alive than we usually think, and that it might even be quite relevant and useful to make it and keep it present, at specific times, in the life of organizations. Although this idea is not new, research around this topic has rarely built on the theoretical inspirations we combine and has tended to focus on grander, less mundane material than small stories. Our analysis building on these inspirations leads us to recognize that what is related to the past, especially the legacy of significant organizational actors, does not need to be grand to make a difference in present circumstances.

Hunter and Rowles (2005, p. 328) defined legacy as a "mechanism for transmitting a resilient and enduring image of what we stood for." This implies that legacy is somehow substantial, solid, and enduring. However, more recent work on legacy (e.g., Radu-Lefebvre et al., 2024) has nuanced this view, noting that legacy is a dynamic concept that requires coconstruction and remains open to interpretation. Radu-Lefebvre et al. (2024) thus defined legacy as "a psychological, relational, and historical concept whose nature is immaterial and only comes into life through direct interaction with senders belonging to a prior generation or through artifact mediated interaction with senders located in the past" (p. 23).

A founder's legacy, especially in the form of a vision, has been recognized as impacting the firm's strategy (Harris & Ogbonna, 1999). However, how is this vision communicated? Is making a legacy endure necessarily a question of continuity, or could it also encompass change? This is where the potential contribution of narratives has been recognized. Hammond, Pearson, and Holt (2016) highlighted that family stories can be considered legacy artifacts, i.e., a medium for coding legacy, and they recognized that storytelling can transmit legacy. Similarly, in the context of family firms, Labaki, Bernhard, and Cailluet (2019) argued that "narratives [understood as family stories] are constructed to make sense of what was done in the past and its relation to the present, in a way they can be appropriated, mobilized, and used by different audiences to achieve different goals" (p. 531). Indeed, Barbera, Stamm, and De Witt's (2018) narrative analysis of a three-generation family firm showed that while the stories told may be similar, they are used in varied ways, depending on the needs of current leaders. The authors thus suggested that from a narrative perspective, legacy can be seen as both stable and fluid at the same time.

We take inspiration from this narrative perspective on organizational phenomena and extend it with insights from the communicative constitution of organization (hereafter, CCO) stream of scholarship, more specifically the Montreal school of CCO, which puts forward a performative view of communication. The Montreal school argues that organization—and hence, organizational phenomena like legacy—happens and is constituted in communication. Compared to other schools of CCO (i.e., the four-flows and the Luhmannian schools), the Montreal school decenters the most agency from human actors, paying specific attention to how nonhuman actors make a difference in ongoing action (Putnam, 2022). The Montreal school is known for its conceptual developments, introducing original constructs such as presentification (Benoit-Barné & Cooren, 2009) and ventriloquism (Cooren, 2010) to account for elements (such as a rule, a previous agreement, a value, a principle, and so on) that can make a difference when brought up and *made to speak* in a conversation. Through recurring invocations within conversations, these elements crystallize into *texts* that serve as the basis for collective action, a process that illustrates the importance of communicative acts for the constitution of organizations (Taylor & Van Every, 2000). This *text-conversation* dynamic, a core idea of the Montreal school, serves to establish continuity and persistence through time, but also to introduce variations, as every conversation may either consolidate or modify the significations that are attached to these *texts*. Building on the Montreal school allows us to attend to the organizing properties of texts, conversations, and narratives and to reveal elements (human and nonhuman alike) that play a part and make a difference in organizing.

Nelson (2003) suggested that a founder can continue to exert influence through a variety of mechanisms, such as imprinting and ownership control. We suggest that this influence can also be maintained through storytelling, including the telling of small stories, because these small stories are communicative acts that make elements from the past present in current circumstances. This is what the process of *presentification* (Benoit-Barné & Cooren, 2009) implies, proposing that making elements present in text and stories is not a purely linguistic exercise, but also has concrete organizing effects. Influenced by these ideas, we explore the form that such small stories can take, and what roles they may play in organizing where founders (notably those who have passed away) nevertheless remain important figures.

Connected to a key figure like a founder, the concept of legacy may, at first glance, evoke a rather grandiose heritage, such as Steve Jobs' commitment to product innovation. It is a rather more banal phenomenon that we investigate in this chapter: how legacy can be kept alive and transmitted through the use of small stories. We highlight the possible implications of these stories for sustaining legacy, but also for leadership and organizational identity. We argue that while such small stories may appear mundane, viewing them from a narrative and CCO perspective reveals how they can play a part in maintaining or modifying a legacy, while sometimes creating unintended effects.

We start with the recognition of the crucial role of language and communicative activities in keeping present elements that otherwise would be confined to an organization's past and thus may disappear. Furthermore, we recognize that retaining elements from the past may be useful in the present and even for the future of an organization, contributing to maintaining a form of continuity. This continuity requires active work to be established, as the *text-conversation* dynamic described above illustrates. Hence, we engage with the idea that an organization's continuity cannot be taken for granted and needs to be produced, reproduced, and maintained over time, a dynamic in which the presence, through communicative acts, of deceased founders and their legacy may play a role. We show how the use of small stories may not only encapsulate this legacy, but embed a paradox between continuity and change. Drawing on vignettes of deceased founders from different organizations, we describe and illustrate the manifestations of this paradox and discuss some of its possible consequences. This leads us to expose the inherent ambivalence and fragility of small stories.

'Seeing' small stories: A methodological note

The ideas we develop in this chapter are inspired by a larger research project that explores how deceased founders remain important figures in their organizations even after their demise. The initial impetus for this project came from a historical exploration of the case of one organization, the Desjardins Group, a financial services cooperative in which the founder, Alphonse Desjardins, remained a key identity marker in organizational communications over a period of 80 years (Basque & Langley, 2018). This led us to search for other organizations, mainly corporations but also family businesses, that appeared to make significant use of founder figures in their corporate communications. As we searched for publicly available data in which organizational founders appeared, we became intrigued by the ubiquity of what we later identified as 'small stories.' These small stories, often vivid, intrigued us, given their apparent anecdotal nature, and we continued to accumulate them alongside our main project. We found small stories in internal bulletins, journalistic interviews, public speeches, books, and company websites. We also paid special attention to related visual material such as photographs of deceased founders or traces of them in material artifacts (representing them or connected to them, as a key product). This open exploration allowed us to collect small stories from several organizational settings including Apple, Delta Airlines, Desjardins, Hewlett-Packard, and McIlhenny Company, which served as inspiration for the ideas we propose in this chapter.

Founders, small stories, narratives, and legacy: A proposal

Important figures such as deceased founders may be kept present within their organizations and beyond in a variety of ways: the presence of their name in the company name or in its products; visual representations like photos, videos, artworks, etc.; references to the values they embodied or professed throughout their lives, to what was important for them; and also stories featuring decisions they made, key moments in their lives, or moments pertaining to important organizational events. These examples represent the three categories of legacy that Hunter and Rowles (2005) identified, namely, biological, material, and values. Schultz and Hernes (2013), for their part, referred to textual, oral, and material carriers of memory. In particular, what deceased founders have done for their organizations, big and small, is often preserved via stories, either recounted by people who have encountered them personally (oral memory) or told through various documentary traces (textual memory). In fact, stories are a key means by which collective organizational memory and legacy are preserved and transmitted over time (Coraiola et al., 2023; Hamilton et al., 2017; Hammond et al., 2016).

While references to the name of a founder or visual representations of them may appear more static, stories that feature them are much more dynamic, open to multiple interpretations and often appealing to the imagination and the senses (Foroughi, 2020). Given the role of narratives in connecting the past and the present (Rantakari & Vaara, 2017), stories featuring deceased founders may play an important role in sustaining their memory, including what they embodied and what was important to them within the everyday life of their organization—hence constituting their legacy. Following researchers who have put forward dynamic views of legacy (e.g., Barbera et al., 2018; Hammond et al., 2016), we propose that legacy is not a fixed repository of elements that would be produced once and for all after a key organizational actor has left his or her organization and that would generate effects by itself. Rather, building on ideas from CCO, we argue that a legacy needs to not only be remembered, but also made and remade present in current circumstances. In other words, legacy does not exist and persist by itself, but needs to be actively maintained over time. Efforts to sustain legacy may be deliberately and consciously pursued for instrumental reasons, or alternatively, they may occur more organically and naturally when organization members retain an ongoing attachment to the past. We suggest that stories that are told and retold contribute to this work of enabling a legacy to endure. Our proposal derives from a combination of theoretical influences, which we now present briefly.

Narratives

The term *narrative* covers the concept of story and that of narration (Rantakari & Vaara, 2017) and rests on a temporal organization of its elements (Czarniawska, 2004). In organization studies, narrative can refer to a theoretical lens, a methodological approach, and/or a type of data; narratives have proven instrumental in understanding identity and identification, processes of sensemaking and sensegiving, and also in connection to change (Rhodes & Brown, 2005). Importantly for our proposal, studies of organizational culture have shown that stories have collective effects and are associated with preserving organizational memory and communicating beliefs (Coraiola et al., 2023; Rhodes & Brown, 2005, p. 172). Hence stories are the means through which important organizational facets, like values, can be communicated and legitimized. We adopt the definition proposed by Rantakari and Vaara (2017) of narrative "as a temporal discursive construction that provides means for individual, social, and organizational sensemaking" (p. 271). Based on the different perspectives they identify in the vast literature on narratives, we combine two traditions on narratives: one that acknowledges that narratives are social constructions of reality (what they call the narrative construction perspective) and another that recognizes that narratives have organizing properties (the narrative agency perspective) that can influence action. Together, these two traditions conceptualize narratives as participating in organizational phenomena in an active way.

A communication-centered perspective

Beyond recognizing the place and roles of narratives in organizational life, our proposal is broadly inspired by the CCO stream of scholarship (Putnam & Nicotera, 2009), which proposes that communication processes have organizing properties and that organizational phenomena of all kinds emerge from these organizing properties. This perspective rests on an active view of communicative action as playing a key part in constituting phenomena. It proposes that it is through communication that organizational phenomena emerge and are sustained. The conceptual apparatus of CCO thus offers us tools to theorize how organizational phenomena are created, maintained, and transformed in time and over time. Applied to our inquiry, it suggests that the past (represented here by deceased founders) can continue to be made present and even influence future organizational action *through* communication, suggesting that this presence of the past in present issues is achieved through discursive and material communicational processes.

Applied to the issue of legacy, a CCO perspective amounts to attributing organizing properties to small stories featuring deceased founders, highlighting that, once they circulate, they may play a role in making their legacy endure over time and hence *matter* for their organization. The verb *mattering* here is of particular importance. Reflecting on the tendency to separate what seems to belong to the discursive from what appears as material, Cooren, Fairhurst, and Huët (2012) reminded us that we can question this binary and "rather focus on the multiple ways by which various forms of reality (more or less material) come to *do things* and even *express themselves* in a given interaction" (p. 296, italics in original). Hence, "what matters or does not matter has to do with what materializes (or does not materialize) in an interaction, whether through the form, for instance, of preoccupations, discussions, or activities" (Cooren et al., 2012, pp. 298–299). In this sense, a CCO perspective makes playful use of the two meanings ascribed to the verb *mattering*, highlighting that it refers at the same time to what materializes and what is important or relevant (Cooren, 2020; Cooren et al., 2012).

While Cooren et al. (2012), and more generally CCO studies, focus specifically on interactions, we extend their insights to postulate that using small stories of deceased founders in various contexts (e.g., on a company website or in important documents) plays a role in materializing in the present a person who is no longer there, hence making the person and their legacy still matter for their organization. As we suggest, this materialization happens in the form of narratives, both big and small. "Grander" narratives (e.g., the story of how a company was founded or how it went through a profound change) may tend to attract more attention from researchers and organizational actors alike and may be an obvious illustration of this materialization and its potential importance for organizations, yet the same ideas can apply to stories that seem more mundane or peripheral to the founding story.

Small stories and their characteristics

Small stories[1] can be distinguished from other forms of narrative based on at least five characteristics. First, small stories have an anecdotal and mundane character: they feature the deceased founder saying or doing something that "says something" about the organization, exemplifying or illustrating something that could be interpreted as important for the organization but not necessarily in connection with grand events, significant transformations, or key turning points. However, the notion of small and mundane does not mean limited in potential to transmit what characterizes or is important for an organization. In fact, a key part of the impact of small stories derives from their very nature: anchored in daily life, depicting in a lively manner what is important from the history of an organization, attaching it/exemplifying it through a key person and thus generating "bite-sized" lessons that can easily be told

---

[1] It should be noted that we use the term *small stories* in a manner that is slightly different from how it has been developed in a stream of research located in narrative inquiry, where researchers pay attention to stories as they occur in natural interactions between people (Bamberg & Georgakopoulou, 2008).

and used in a variety of contexts (e.g., expressing values and culture, in socialization efforts, in branding/marketing, for decision making).

Second, small stories have a realistic dimension, in the sense that they rest on situations or events that have a certain historical verisimilitude. They are not invented situations (at least, not deliberately so). Small stories make use of recounted or observed events expressed in a narrative form. They tell of situations that may have been directly experienced by the storyteller (as in the case where someone witnesses a deceased founder doing what is at the heart of the story) or not (as in the case of a founder whose death belongs to a past that no one still alive has experienced firsthand), but they are *brought into* present times in a lively manner that embodies the founder who is no longer present.

This highlights a third key characteristic of small stories: their evocative nature. Small stories go beyond simple quotations of the deceased founder. While they can involve what a deceased founder may have had the habit of saying—like, for example, a famous expression or saying repeated often by this person—they also include other elements that make them into stories. Because these anecdotes take on the form of stories, they can exert a form of narrative power on people, such as catching their attention, providing striking images, and generating emotions and reactions (Crawford et al., 2022; Foroughi, 2020). The evocative power derives both from their status as stories and from the fact that they bring back into present times someone whose behaviors, actions, and characteristic ways of being belong to the past. These elements from the past have to be re-presented, in the sense of being made present another time, and stories, given their features, are especially well-suited vehicles to accomplish this temporal articulation between the past and the present (Coraiola et al., 2023; Rowlinson et al., 2014). However, this 're-presentation,' while resting on events that may have occurred, is not purely factual like a biography would be: it re-embodies the deceased founder, reanimates him or her, evoking through a small story something larger than the anecdote itself.

Fourth, small stories are mobile. They can be told, printed, tweeted; they can be shared in a myriad of ways, both internally and externally; and they can circulate from one context to another, constituting elements of 'collective memory' that may spread within and beyond a particular organizational community (Coraiola et al., 2023). If we use the example of Bill Hewlett and Dave Packard's office presented in the opening of the chapter, we can imagine that the two small stories shared are part of the preserved office, which is part of a building that HP still occupies and uses. However, these stories are not limited to internal members, as the article illustrates: the stories can circulate by being told in different settings. This echoes a characteristic Cooren (2004) associated with texts and documents in contrast to more ephemeral conversations that may evaporate and be forgotten once uttered.

Yet, contrary to textual elements that may be fixed, small stories are more plastic and adaptable—their final characteristic. The same story can be told in different ways and can be used in different ways in different contexts (Barbera et al., 2018;

Hoon et al., 2023). As material from the past, small stories always trigger an appreciation in present times—either when they are extracted from archives, presented, and explicitly interpreted, or when an audience comes into contact with them. This appreciation is needed because the interpretation of small stories is always performed by current actors in present circumstances. Changes—both social and organizational—may thus affect how current actors understand a small story and also a deceased founder's legacy (Rowlinson & Hassard, 1993). This plasticity of small stories is connected to their evocative power, as we suggest that it is partially through what they evoke (values, principles, feelings) that they will come to mean different things for audiences. But these characteristics may make small stories prone to reinterpretations that may distract audiences from what tellers intended. This highlights the unstable nature of small stories: their meaning is never fully fixed, mirroring literature (e.g., Radu-Lefebvre et al., 2024) that argues for a dynamic view of legacy.

We now illustrate these ideas by presenting three vignettes, each revolving around a deceased founder and elements that can be interpreted as part of their legacy, articulated in the form of a small story (or collection of stories). The vignettes include a presentation of the company's background, its founder and some of the small stories we identified, as well as the context in which they are mobilized. We draw on the vignettes to reflect on what these small stories can produce for their organizations, notably in contexts of continuity and change.

Small Stories in Action

Vignette 1: Collett E. Woolman and Delta Airlines

Background: Reaching to the past to revive the fortunes of Delta Airlines. Delta Airlines was founded in 1925 by Collett E. Woolman, who died in 1966. The period following September 11, 2001, was fraught with difficulties for U.S. airlines, and in 2004, Delta Airlines was literally near bankruptcy. In an article posted on the company's News Hub in 2015, Ed Bastian (2018), the chief executive officer (CEO) from 2016 to the present, attributed its revival and current success in part to an initiative of the leadership team who mobilized employees by revisiting the writings of the founder. In 2007, they created a document called *Rules of the Road* (Delta Airlines, n.d.), which outlined a set of basic principles and reminded employees of the founder's philosophy of taking care of the customer by always putting themselves in their shoes. (One of the famous quotes from C. E. Woolman was to "put yourself on the other side of the counter.") This document has been distributed to all employees since 2007. In parallel, the company began sharing profits with employees and enacting the founder's vision of being an "employee-driven enterprise." We see here how Woolman's legacy was taken up by his successors, relying on his past words. The legacy also manifests itself and is transmitted in small stories.

Small stories as carriers of legacy. Ed Bastian has frequently cited C. E. Woolman in his communications, including in *Sky Magazine* (offered to all travelers on the airline[2]), in employee communications, and in public speeches. Speaking about a person who died when he was only 9 years old and whom he almost certainly never met, Bastian noted: "I still stop every day to consider the lessons of Mr. Woolman as I work to serve Delta's customers and employees" (Delta Sky magazine, August 2017, p. 12). Notably, this column includes this passage:

> Mr. Woolman had a passion for growing orchids, and he personally pinned one on the lapel of every new flight attendant who joined the company. He was so beloved by Delta employees that on his 25th anniversary with Delta, they presented him with a new Cadillac, which he kept until his death.
>
> Has Delta still evolved since his time? Certainly. Mr. Woolman would be amazed to experience Delta today, with our newest generation of aircraft, . . . amenities like lie-flat seats . . . and technological advances such as the Fly Delta App . . . that make traveling more convenient than ever before. But I suspect he would also see a lot that is familiar—a company that is built on a foundation of its employees, knowing that if they are happy and satisfied, they will take great care of its customers, who will reward us with their business and loyalty. Mr. Woolman pioneered that concept and it is integral to Delta's success today as it ever was. (Delta Sky magazine, 2017, p. 12)

This passage includes two small (micro) stories in the first paragraph: one about growing orchids and pinning them on the lapels of flight attendants, and a second one about being gifted with a car. Both small stories can be seen as reminders of C. E. Woolman's personality, as a warm human being who cared for his employees and was much loved by them in return. A similar story to the second one in the Delta Flight Museum reinforces the message: "A painting of Woolman, now at the Delta Flight Museum, was presented to him 'on behalf of the pilots of Delta Air Lines, our wives and children, in appreciation for what you have done for us and permitted us to do for ourselves'" (Delta Flight Museum, n.d.).

But beyond the amusing aspect of these stories, we see from the passage above that they need to be contextualized, and their connection to the founder's legacy needs to be explicitly articulated. This contextualization is needed, in part, because the stories on their own could be seen as odd or even disturbing by the standards of present times: pinning the orchids evokes a different era, exemplified in a different way women were treated in workplaces[3]; the CEO being gifted a Cadillac by his employees may have been touching in the 1950s but might be seen as troubling in the

---

[2] His monthly column that was fully devoted to Woolman's legacy can also be found on Bastian's LinkedIn page: https://www.linkedin.com/pulse/lasting-legacy-ed-bastian.
[3] Flight attendants at Delta were all women until 1973. See Delta Flight Museum's online presence: https://www.deltamuseum.org/delta-history/delta-brand/uniforms/the-jet-age.

21st century. Following CCO terms, with this contextualization, these stories are made to speak in a certain way to guide their interpretation and to avoid materializing ideas that might generate criticism or controversies. After the telling of the stories, Bastian signals what these small stories are intended to illustrate: Woolman's preoccupation with employee satisfaction, which for him was inherent to good customer service. In so doing, he makes them matter in connection to what remains the core of Delta's mission. Bastian goes on to appropriate Woolman's dedication to customer service as a distinctive feature of Delta in the present time as well,[4] claiming it explicitly as a legacy. This interpretation is reinforced by two direct quotes from Woolman in the same article: "It is never sufficient to just transport people. We must transport people with the highest respect and safety" and "The airline industry is keenly competitive. All of us have good planes. The only way in which we can excel is in the quality of service."

When one digs into publicly available archival material about Delta, other small stories can be found. Consider this story told by Barbara Woolman Preston, daughter of C. E. Woolman, shared on the Delta Flight Museum website:

> All of a sudden, he [C. E. Woolman] would call Mother and have four people he was bringing home for lunch because they'd had a mechanical [delay with the aircraft], and they were on the flight and he just brought them home for lunch. . . . And sometimes I'd wake up on a cot in the hall, and there would be a passenger that had gotten put off overnight, that Daddy had brought home and put in my bed.

We again get a glimpse of who C. E. Woolman was in daily life, both as a CEO and as a man, through this small story. Revealing the mobility of small stories, this same story is quoted word for word in an article on the difficulties of receiving and offering good customer service (Smith, 2016). Using the legacy of the founder may play a part in nurturing a culture of employee satisfaction and good customer service. The repetition, lamination, and circulation of small stories like these, which all seem to convey a similar kind of message of humanity and attention to others but do so in slightly different ways, can contribute to sustaining a coherent collective memory of the founder even among those who never knew him (Coraiola et al., 2023; Hoon et al., 2023). Yet, using these small stories could become trickier if this culture centered on employees and customer satisfaction were to change: they could make the difference between the present and the past starker, and could generate more ambivalent reactions (along the lines of what "Delta used to be known for . . ."). This highlights the ambivalence of small stories whose meaning is not stable but is always reinterpreted in light of the present. In turn, this underlines the importance of making the stories matter in connection with present challenges.

---

[4] See, for example, this extensive list of awards received by the company (https://news.delta.com/delta-americas-most-awarded-airline), which makes it the most awarded American airline.

Vignette 2: Edmund McIlhenny and the McIlhenny Company

Background: Edmund McIlhenny and the origins of Tabasco. The McIlhenny Company is known for its hot sauce, Tabasco®, created by Edmund McIlhenny in 1868 on Avery Island (then Petite Anse Island), Louisiana. The company founding narrative, which can be found on the company's website (Tabasco, n.d.) and in newspaper articles, tells us that McIlhenny's father owned a plantation, and his family was wealthy, but after the Civil War, he returned to the plantation to find it in ruins (Ringle, 1993). He decided to plant pepper seeds he had received as a gift from a Mexican guest before the war. The diet in the Reconstruction South was dull and repetitive, particularly by Louisiana standards. To add flavor, Edmund decided to create a sauce from his peppers. After some experimentation, he found the perfect recipe for his sauce in 1868, packaged it in used cologne bottles, and named it "Petite Anse sauce" after the original name of the island (Vinoski, 2022). Soon after, he would name his sauce "Tabasco," the name of the Mexican state from which the peppers were thought to have come. He patented the recipe in 1870, and by 1901, Tabasco had gained international fame, primarily due to the marketing prowess of John and Edward, Edmund's sons. The company has been producing and selling the famous sauce since then, using the same recipe, the same ingredients, and a quite similar process. The company is still family owned and located on Avery Island, and it remains committed to the founder's values of simplicity, quality, family, and attachment to the islands and to Louisiana. The current CEO is Harold Osborn, a fifth-generation heir of the founder.

Small stories as carriers of legacy. Given their size, small stories can be embedded in grander narratives, like founding stories. In the McIlhenny Company, a key small story is embedded in the founding narrative summarized above: the mysterious gifted seeds and their growth. Tabasco's website only mentions that the seeds were given to Edmund McIlhenny without identifying who gifted them. What is emphasized is the origins of the seeds and the little red stick that the company still uses today to assess the peppers' ripeness:

> A food lover and avid gardener, Edmund McIlhenny was given seeds of Capsicum frutescens peppers that had come from Mexico or Central America. On Avery Island in South Louisiana, he sowed the seeds, nurtured the plants and delighted in the spicy flavor of the peppers they bore. Many years later field hands used a little red stick, or 'le petit bâton rouge,' to measure the ripeness of the peppers. Staying true to history of TABASCO® Brand, we still use it today to ensure the quality of our harvest. (Company website)

In this substory of the founding story, the seeds and their product, the peppers, are presented to create a continuity with the past through the use of the little red stick that materializes the same gesture, the same practice that is used to harvest the peppers. What is made to matter is the care that goes into harvesting the peppers, which is still present today. However, an article written by a descendant of the McIlhenny family explained that the seeds were a gift from a "prewar guest" and that the peppers were the only produce still growing in the garden of the ruined plantation (Ringle, 1993). This version differs from the official version, as it negates the initiative of the founder in sowing the seeds, implying that the harvest was the result of his talent as a gardener.

The seeds are used narratively by family members to show continuity in the legacy, even though all the peppers can no longer be cultivated solely on Avery Island because of the growth of the company. This allows them to demonstrate their direct involvement as guardians of the sauce's quality and their fidelity to the original recipe. John Simmons, senior manager of agriculture and sixth-generation member of the family, and Harold Osborn, a fifth-generation member of the McIlhenny family and newly appointed CEO, talk about this in a Louisiana local newspaper article:

> "Tabasco is sold in 197 countries and territories, so we have to send seeds from Avery Island to farms we've worked with for generations where they can be grown year-round," said John Simmons, senior manager of agriculture and sixth-generation McIlhenny family member. "Our CEO and the family select the seeds to be sent to the farms so [the McIlhenny family] still has a hand in almost every part of making Tabasco.
>
> Osborn said he believes the company's founder, Edmund McIlhenny, would be proud of what's been done with his hot sauce. "I think he'd be proud of what we're doing and that we've maintained the tradition and standards he put in place," Osborn said. "He loved food and was very meticulous in the way he made the cause [sic], and we've changed that very little. We're still sticking to his recipe. (Boudreaux, 2019)

Yet, a controversy surrounds the mysterious seeds. Another version of this small story suggests that the seeds and even the idea of the sauce might have been filched from another man, Maunsel White, from New Orleans, who had used the same peppers to create a hot sauce and had named his sauce Tabasco 15 years prior to Mr. McIlhenny. This story is evidenced by a newspaper article dating back to 1850 (Rattray, 2019). In spite of this controversy, which remains unsettled, the small story of the seeds remains a powerful evocative device to keep the deceased founder's legacy present, both materially (the sauce itself) and in terms of values (being committed to quality and to the original recipe), thus creating a reminder of the company's mission. However, the fact that the family's version of the story could be disputed points to the fragility of small stories, a characteristic that they share with any narrative.

Vignette 3: Alphonse Desjardins and the Desjardins Group

Background: Alphonse Desjardins and the *caisses populaires*. The Desjardins Group is a cooperative bank founded in 1900 in Lévis, Québec, by Alphonse Desjardins. Troubled by the problem of usury that plagued the rural population, Desjardins wanted to give access to small loans to farmers and working-class people living outside the large metropolitan centers. He opened the first savings and loans cooperative called a *caisse populaire* in his hometown with the help of his wife and a group of neighbors. Then, with the support of the Catholic Church, he founded 163 *caisses populaires* mostly in the province of Quebec. Today, Desjardins is a major financial institution in Canada, with 7.7 million clients and members and $422.9 billion in total assets.

Small stories as carriers of legacy. Alphonse Desjardins, who died in 1920, remained through time a key figure in the organization he founded (Basque & Langley, 2018), and small stories about him and his life abound, many of them collected in a comic book about his life published in 1990 (Prouche, 1990), 70 years after his death. Other stories were recounted in an employee magazine, the *Revue Desjardins*, published regularly between 1935 and 2015. Alphonse Desjardins was a deeply religious man who relied importantly on the Catholic Church to support his original project of creating savings and loans cooperatives in local communities attached to the parishes. One small story that captured his religious devotion is recounted by his successor, Cyrille Vaillancourt, in the *Revue Desjardins* in 1941. We see how this story supported an understanding of the *caisses populaires* as a noble enterprise of divine inspiration, whose survival through the Great Depression of the 1930s was supported by God himself—a message that may seem unusual today, but that might have resonated deeply at this time and place.

> As someone asked recently, how can you explain the prodigious, if not miraculous development of the Caisses Populaires? How were they able to traverse the great financial crisis we have experienced in recent years? In the last ten years, haven't we seen several large financial businesses collapse?
> The reason is simple but at the same time great, great in the power of God. Mr. Desjardins, a man from the disinherited class counted for the success of his enterprise only on God himself. . . . Thus, on 6th December 1900, in his parish church, before the meeting that would establish the basis of his future organization, Mr. Desjardins knelt before the altar and recited the following prayer that he had himself composed. (Vaillancourt, 1941, p. 3)

The prayer mentioned in this quotation and dedicated to the Sacred Heart of Jesus was reproduced in the text. It expresses the wish that if the development of the *caisses populaires* was not destined to succeed, that Alphonse Desjardins would be struck with a disgust that would prevent him from continuing his work.

The story and the prayer were reproduced multiple times in articles in the *Revue Desjardins*, especially in the 1930s to the early 1960s. In these occurrences, the small story can be read as connecting Alphonse Desjardins' impetus to create the cooperative bank with his faith. This might have been an important connection to make at a time when the Catholic Church occupied a central place in most of Quebec's institutions. Yet, this story was told with variations and made to matter at different times for different purposes.

Indeed, a second version of the same story exists, where the prayer was not composed for the foundation of the first cooperative bank, but rather in the face of threats of bankruptcy in 1905. This alternative version appears in 1967, suggesting that prior accounts were erroneous. Other stories surrounding the founding of the cooperative bank showcase Alphonse Desjardins' piousness but omit the Sacred Heart prayer. Over time, we see that the small story of the prayer disappears from internal publications. The prayer remains mentioned today, notably on Alphonse Desjardins' French Wikipedia page (Wikipedia, n.d.), but it is only loosely connected to his motivation to create the cooperative bank. Interestingly, we found a recent reference to this prayer in an academic article (Kaell, 2023) that sheds a different light on the connections between Catholic faith and capitalism. Combining historical and anthropological analysis, this article suggests that Alphonse Desjardins succeeded in blending religion and economy, which recasts his actions not as solely motivated by his faith, but rather as finding a way to merge Catholicism and early 20th century capitalism. From occupying a key place in the founding narrative of the Caisses Desjardins, the Sacred Heart small story has now transformed into a historical relic that no longer serves the organization, but that may be useful for other endeavors, such as historical analysis. Thus, we see that the need for this story to matter has varied over time through different communicative acts—from a close connection between Desjardins and the Catholic Church, to a marker of Quebec's religious heritage, to being part of Quebec's history and (outdated) religious identity. Within the company itself, the story has virtually disappeared, revealing the fragility of small stories as carriers of collective memory: Forgetting occurs naturally when these stories are not continually rehearsed and repeated (Anteby & Molnar, 2012; Casey & Olivera, 2011).

Discussion: Reflecting on the power of small stories

An organization's past can be viewed as a deposit of potential resources and as a source of assets that can contribute to affirming or reiterating what is important for an organization (Coraiola et al., 2023). In this sense, the past may be past, but it can remain present and valuable for embodying an organization's culture ("what characterizes us, what matters to us") or for expressing its collective identity ("who we are"). While we may tend to focus on elements from the past that are striking, major, or exceptional, we have argued in this chapter that more modest elements, such as small stories as we have defined them, can become useful in a variety of circumstances or contexts. In this discussion, we draw on the illustrations introduced above to reflect on three aspects of small stories: their power as carriers of legacy, their ambivalence, and their ultimate fragility.

The power of small stories as carriers of legacy

Building on CCO's insights, we suggest that small stories about founders have organizing properties and exert their power in at least four ways: articulating the *raison d'être* of the organization (the what and why), acting as carriers of organizational culture (the how), humanizing founders and creating empathy for them by their very mundanity and by ricochet potentially for the organization, and serving as resources to promote continuity or change.

Following Cooren et al.'s (2012) ideas on materialization and mattering, one of the powers of small stories centering on deceased founders may be to manifest and materialize the *raison d'être* of the organization, and to make sense of it, by referring to the founder's supposed thoughts and values via a mundane situation that features the founder. In this sense, telling small stories may be an invitation to reflect collectively on this *raison d'être*, with the aim of making the organization endure by keeping links with the past while projecting it into the future. As mundane means not only means "ordinary" but also "transitory" (Merriam-Webster, n.d.), small stories may therefore construct a sense of guidance at a certain point in time, which may point either to continuation or to transformation, depending on the circumstances in which a small story is evoked, or *made to speak* (Benoit-Barné & Cooren, 2009), how it is contextualized and how it is interpreted (both by the person telling the story and the people hearing it). As Hernes and Schultz (2017) noted, pieces of history can be "rediscovered" and used by different actors on different occasions to inspire and provide guidance, with more or less centrality to the company's core identity and *raison d'être*. Small stories are a good example of this phenomenon, with their own particularities.

In addition to the vignettes cited above, a widely known example is that of Steve Jobs, who is the focal point of grand narratives at Apple (concerning its foundation and its revitalization in the 1990s) but who also features in many small stories that symbolize Apple's commitment to innovation. Notably, Apple (n.d.) maintains a page on its website named "Remembering Steve," where people can still share their thoughts on him, whether or not they knew him; furthermore, small—and positive— stories about Steve Jobs have been used by Tim Cook as he has reflected on Jobs' legacy on the anniversary of his death (shared through emails that are publicly available, or on social media[5]). In this case, telling small stories about Steve Jobs in this way may keep the best of him alive. Such a positive portrayal may help in inspiring innovation, fostering engagement and passion for the company. His figure also serves as a socializing mechanism (employees are invited to become 'carriers' of his legacy, hence serving a 'higher' purpose) that is deeply connected to organizational identity (Basque & Langley, 2018; Foster et al., 2011; Hatch & Schultz, 2017).

More broadly, small stories are also carriers of culture—i.e., 'how we do things around here.' As Kuhn (2008) explained with reference to CCO/Montreal School ideas, *texts* can become authoritative when they are used repetitively in conversations, leading actors to prioritize the collective good over personal interests and serving as a reference point to guide action. We suggest applying this idea to small stories. For ex-

---

[5] See, for example, his tweets on October 5, the day on which Steve Jobs passed away, such as https://x.com/tim_cook/status/1577662907218677761 and https://x.com/tim_cook/status/915921335993344001.

ample, at Delta, small stories of Woolman contribute to motivating employees and socializing them into the customer-oriented culture of the company as well as inspiring the confidence of travelers in the solidity, safety, and service orientation of the airline. The stories of Hewlett-Packard that introduced this paper serve a similar role. For example, the story about the open-door policy and its traces in the very marks on the floor of Dave Packard's office reminds today's managers and employees about this foundational principle inscribed in the HP Way (Packard, 1995), creating expectations that would be difficult to violate. Interestingly, in this case, it is not just the small story itself, but the connection to material memory traces—the marks on the floor (Hatch & Schultz, 2017; Schultz & Hernes, 2013)—that reinforce the story, confirm its authenticity, and preserve it into the future.

Small stories also serve to materialize past leaders (Auvinen, 2012), recapturing their humanity through evocative personal details. Reaching beyond abstract or grandiose expressions of values, mundane stories like those told about Collett Woolman (the orchids and the Cadillac) and the first story in the introduction about Bill Hewlett (leaving a penny on his desk) contribute to this materialization by presenting a more human and personal side of the individual who has passed away, bringing them and their values down to earth as real people. Such stories invite a certain nostalgia, conveying the message that this is someone that it would have been good to know. We invite researchers interested in legacy not to neglect the more mundane aspects of small stories that cumulatively express this humanity, sometimes quite profoundly.

Finally, small stories can be used both to sustain the continuity with a certain past of the organization and to serve as prompts to catalyze or justify organizational transformation. Small stories centering on deceased founders are not restricted to a specific temporality (that of the past) or tonality (that of nostalgia). They can embody both continuity and change; they can therefore offer a form of flexibility, at least in some cases. Thus, in 2007, executives at Delta Airlines appear to have resurrected the ideas of C. E. Woolman as a foundation for renewal of the company, subsequently drawing on his words and on small stories to reorient the future. Similarly, Schultz and Hernes (2013) described how executives at Lego Corporation drew on stories told by employees with long tenure in their effort to renew the organization's identity in 2005 to 2007. They referred in particular to a 'duck story' from the 1930s which was used to underline the company's commitment to quality. Notably the 'small story' recounts how the founder chastised his son for trying to save money by using only two coats of paint on wooden ducks sent to Sweden, instead of the normal three (Schultz & Hernes, 2013, p. 14). Our proposal to focus more deeply and systematically on small stories in future research, and to see that telling them can help in materializing a legacy in the present and hence matters for an organization, builds on and extends work on memory like that cited above, especially in relation to organizational identity, its maintenance, and its possible transformation.

The ambivalence of small stories

While small stories may be usefully mobilized by successors for the purposes indicated above, they are not without their downsides, as some of our vignettes illustrate. For example, stories from the past may become dated and problematic as contexts change. The vignette of the Desjardins Group shows how a small story expressing the founder's deep religious convictions was originally interpreted as central to the organization's mission and *raison d'être*. However, the story was gradually suppressed as profound societal changes undermined its resonance, requiring leaders to rethink the ways in which they framed the founder's ideas. As this story disappeared and other links to the founder's original words and beliefs became less easy to sustain in the present, representations of the founder became more abstract, theoretical, and iconic (Basque & Langley, 2018), potentially losing some of the intimate and human connection still seen with other leaders like C. E. Woolman. Yet even here, as mentioned earlier, the small stories told about him often seem rather dated and potentially anachronous. To remain meaningful over the years, these stories need to be carefully interpreted and contextualized. Indeed, Anteby and Molnar (2012) revealed how important historical events may be deliberately ignored or "forgotten" when they do not fit with desired organizational identities. There is room for more research on the processes by which previously iconic small stories (like that of Desjardins' prayer to the Sacred Heart) may be subject to reinterpretation or deliberate 'forgetting,' reshaping collective memory and shifting understandings of organizational culture and identity over time (Mariano et al., 2020b).

Small stories about founders may also be seen as ambivalent because they are subject to challenge (as in the case of Tabasco and McIlhenny), or because they lay out standards of behavior that today's organizations ultimately find it impossible to meet. For example, in reading the stories about C. E. Woolman, one might wonder whether Delta Airlines has become so big and impersonal that it has inevitably lost the closeness that Woolman stood for. Nostalgia about a wonderful past is not necessarily conducive to optimism about the future (Suddaby et al., 2023). Indeed, some 'small stories' may be inherently ambivalent about their subjects, placing them in a questionable light. Again, Steve Jobs at Apple is a well-known case in point. Websites offer not only uplifting stories about his inspiring qualities, but also many stories about his dark side involving insensitive or bullying treatment of others, including colleagues and his own family. While raising questions and debate, however, it is far from clear whether these stories actually detract from or add to the mystique of his legacy at Apple (Austen, 2012).

Overall, our exploration reveals the paradoxical nature of small stories in enabling continuity and change. On the one hand, they may laud deceased founders for their visionary capabilities oriented towards the future, projecting openness to change. On the other, they may serve to reproduce the past, limiting possibilities for change.

The fragility of small stories

While our chapter has led us to outline that the mundane, in the form of small stories revolving around deceased founders, can be consequential for organizations that preserve and make use of them, we underline that this power is also fragile and limited. Because of their nature, small stories may be particularly prone to natural or inadvertent forgetting. Thus, for small stories to play a role in embodying a deceased founder's legacy, preservation mechanisms are needed to include such mundane material in organizational archives (Coraiola et al., 2023; Mariano et al., 2020a, 2020b). Furthermore, as with any archival material, small stories need to keep circulating, which in turn requires that these stories are known and used. Compared to other elements that can be part of a legacy, like biological elements (e.g., a genetic connection) or material elements (e.g., objects) (Hunter & Rowles, 2005), small stories appear flimsy. Yet, as our vignettes have shown, their nature does not prevent them from actively contributing to keeping a deceased founder's legacy visible, present, and ultimately alive. Moreover, the linking of small stories to material elements (e.g., as in the Hewlett-Packard stories we opened with) or the use of small stories in relation to the presentation of corporate museum exhibits (Nissley & Casey, 2002; Ravasi et al., 2019) can serve to sustain both the cultural and identity-related meanings of the stories themselves as well as the meanings of the particular artifacts they are connected to.

While small stories can be viewed as vectors of a deceased founder's legacy, the characteristics we have presented also highlight that they can be part of an organization's tradition. Building on Shils's (1981) definition of tradition, Suddaby and Jaskiewicz (2020) defined this concept as "patterns of belief, customs, and symbolic practices that are transmitted from generation to generation" (p. 234). They put forward a "hybrid structure of traditions as both structure (what gets transmitted across generations) and agency (the process of transmission) [that] creates the opportunity to view traditions both as essentialist constructs that endure through time and as subjective constructs that are constantly being reinterpreted in an ever moving present" (Suddaby & Jaskiewicz, 2020, p. 234). Small stories can be part of what constitutes an organization's tradition, as telling stories is a symbolic practice. More significantly, small stories also present the dual structure that Suddaby and Jaskiewicz attributed to tradition, which echoes that of legacy, as suggested by Radu-Lefebvre et al. (2024). This dual structure may help shed light on small stories' ambivalence.

Indeed, small stories of founders may open up a web of complex issues, where legacy, memories, and legitimacy are entangled. When the issue at stake is change, those who choose to use these stories may be caught between resisting change in order to preserve the founder's legacy and spirit and embracing change to honor the visionary character of the founder. The overall effects of these small stories may vary among different audiences, based on the perceived legitimacy of the person who used the small story. Thus, if small stories can be seen as a double-edged sword (preserving something from the past, but in doing so, possibly impeding change), they remain fully open to interpretation and reinterpretation in current circumstances, which may make their message also about inspiration and transformation. The ambivalence regarding continuity and change we have discussed is tightly connected to their narrative form that renders them plastic and open to multiple interpretations.

In this chapter, we have focused on deceased founders, as these individuals represent, in many organizations, important figures whose presence is maintained after their demise. However, the concept of small stories, and the roles they can play in an organization, can also be extended to other important actors, including actors who have retired or departed. The key characteristics that we have delineated for small stories do not restrict them to founders or deceased persons. The study of small stories, as linked to legacy and change, may thus be expanded to include other key organizational actors and events. Further exploration of small stories of all kinds could specifically address how they contribute to memory work: what place they occupy within it, how they are used, and how and why they emerge, evolve, and disappear.

References

Anteby, M., & Molnar, V. (2012). Collective memory meets organizational identity: Remembering to forget in a firm's rhetorical history. *Academy of Management Journal*, *55*(3), 515–540. https://doi.org/10.5465/amj.2010.0245

Apple. (n.d.). Remembering Steve. Retrieved January 29, 2025, from https://www.apple.com/ca/stevejobs/

Austen, B. (2012). The story of Steve Jobs: An inspiration or a cautionary tale? *Wired*. https://www.wired.com/2012/2007/ff_stevejobs/

Auvinen, T. (2012). The ghost leader: An empirical study on narrative leadership. *EJBO: Electronic Journal of Business Ethics and Organizational Studies*, *17*(1), 4–15. http://ejbo.jyu.fi/pdf/ejbo_vol17_no1_pages_4-15.pdf

Bamberg, M., & Georgakopoulou, A. (2008). Small stories as a new perspective in narrative and identity analysis. *Text & Talk*, *28*(3), 377–396. https://doi.org/10.1515/TEXT.2008.018

Barbera, F., Stamm, I., & DeWitt, R.-L. (2018). The development of an entrepreneurial legacy: Exploring the role of anticipated futures in transgenerational entrepreneurship. *Family Business Review*, *31*(3), 352–378. https://doi.org/10.1177/0894486518780795

Basque, J., & Langley, A. (2018). Invoking Alphonse: The founder figure as a historical resource for organizational identity work. *Organization Studies*, *39*(12), 1685–1708. https://doi.org/10.1177/0170840618789211

Bastian, E. (2017, August). A lasting legacy. *Delta Sky Magazine*, p. 12.

Bastian, E. (2018). Delta's heritage sets it apart. *Delta News Hub*. http://news.delta.com/bastian-deltas-heritage-sets-it-apart

Benoit-Barné, C., & Cooren, F. (2009). The accomplishment of authority through presentification: How authority is distributed among and negotiated by organizational members. *Management Communication Quarterly*, *23*(1), 5–31. https://doi.org/10.1177/0893318909335414

Boudreaux, D. (2019, June 29). The Tabasco life: Incoming CEO Harold Osborn embraces his early start with the McIlhenny Co. *Acadiana Advocate*. https://www.theadvocate.com/acadiana/news/business/the-tabasco-life-incoming-ceo-harold-osborn-embraces-his-early-start-with-the-mcilhenny-co/article_c83922e2-9686-11e9-808d-5b9559567c85.html

Casey, A. J., & Olivera, F. (2011). Reflections on organizational memory and forgetting. *Journal of Management Inquiry*, *20*(3), 305–310. https://doi.org/10.1177/1056492611408264

Cooren, F. (2004). Textual agency: How texts do things in organizational settings. *Organization*, *11*(3), 373–393. https://doi.org/10.1177/1350508404041998

Cooren, F. (2010). *Action and agency in dialogue: Passion, incarnation and ventriloquism*. John Benjamins Publishing. https://doi.org/10.1075/ds.6

Cooren, F. (2020). Beyond entanglement: (Socio-)materiality and organization studies. *Organization Theory*, *1*(3). https://doi.org/10.1177/2631787720954444

Cooren, F., Fairhurst, G., & Huët, R. (2012). Why matter always matters in (organizational) communication. In P. M. Leonardi, B. A. Nardi, & J. Kallinikos (Eds.), *Materiality and organizing: Social interaction in a technological world* (pp. 296–314). Oxford University Press. https://doi.org/10.1093/acprof:oso/9780199664054.003.0015

Coraiola, D. M., Foster, W. M., Mena, S., Foroughi, H., & Rintamäki, J. (2023). Ecologies of memories: Memory work within and between organizations and communities. *The Academy of Management Annals*, *17*(1), 373–404. https://doi.org/10.5465/annals.2021.0088

Crawford, B., Coraiola, D. M., & Dacin, M. T. (2022). Painful memories as mnemonic resources: Grand Canyon Dories and the protection of place. *Strategic Organization*, *20*(1), 51–79. https://doi.org/10.1177/1476127020981353

Czarniawska, B. (2004). *Narratives in social science research*. Sage. https://doi.org/10.4135/9781849209502

Delta Airlines. (n.d.). *Delta rules of the road*. Retrieved January 29, 2025, from https://content.delta.com/content/dam/delta-www/pdfs/policy/delta-rules-of-the-road.pdf

Delta Flight Museum. (n.d.). Delta leaders: C. E. Woolman. Retrieved January 29, 2025, from https://www.deltamuseum.org/delta-history/leaders/c-e-woolman

Foroughi, H. (2020). Collective memories as a vehicle of fantasy and identification: Founding stories retold. *Organization Studies*, *41*(10), 1347–1367. https://doi.org/10.1177/0170840619844286

Foroughi, H., Coraiola, D. M., Rintamaki, J., Mena, S., & Foster, W. M. (2020). Organizational memory studies. *Organization Studies*, *41*(12), 1725–1748. https://doi.org/10.1177/0170840620974338

Foster, W. M., Suddaby, R., Minkus, A., & Wiebe, E. (2011). History as social memory assets: The example of Tim Hortons. *Management & Organizational History*, *6*(1), 101–120. https://doi.org/10.1177/1744935910387027

Hamilton, E., Cruz, A. D., & Jack, S. (2017). Re-framing the status of narrative in family business research: Towards an understanding of families in business. *Journal of Family Business Strategy*, *8*(1), 3–12. https://doi.org/10.1016/j.jfbs.2016.11.001

Hammond, N. L., Pearson, A. W., & Holt, D. T. (2016). The quagmire of legacy in family firms: Definition and implications of family and family firm legacy orientations. *Entrepreneurship Theory and Practice*, *40*(6), 1209–1231. https://doi.org/10.1111/etap.12241

Harris, L. C., & Ogbonna, E. (1999). The strategic legacy of company founders. *Long Range Planning*, *32*(3), 333–343. https://doi.org/10.1016/S0024-6301(99)00037-0

Hatch, M. J., & Schultz, M. (2017). Toward a theory of using history authentically: Historicizing in the Carlsberg Group. *Administrative Science Quarterly*, *62*(4), 657–697. https://doi.org/10.1177/0001839217692535

Hernes, T., & Schultz, M. (2017). A temporal understanding of the connections between organizational culture and identity. In A. Langley & H. Tsoukas (Eds.), *The Sage handbook of process organization studies* (pp. 356–371). Sage.

Hoon, C., Brinkmann, J., & Baluch, A. M. (2023). Narrative memory work of employees in family businesses: How founding stories shape organizational identification. *Family Business Review*, *36*(1), 37–62. https://doi.org/10.1177/08944865231159475

Hunter, E. G., & Rowles, G. D. (2005). Leaving a legacy: Toward a typology. *Journal of Aging Studies*, *19*(3), 327–347. https://doi.org/10.1016/j.jaging.2004.08.002

Kaell, H. (2023). A perfected bank: Catholic capitalism in early twentieth-century Quebec. *History and Anthropology*, *35*(4), 848–870. https://doi.org/10.1080/02757206.2023.2172722

Kuhn, T. (2008). A communicative theory of the firm: Developing an alternative perspective on intra-organizational power and stakeholder relationships. *Organization Studies*, *29*(8–9), 1227–1254. https://doi.org/10.1177/0170840608094778

Labaki, R., Bernhard, F., & Cailluet, L. (2019). The strategic use of historical narratives in the family business. In E. Memili & C. Dibrell (Eds.), *The Palgrave handbook of heterogeneity among family firms* (pp. 531–553). Palgrave Macmillan.

Mariano, S., Casey, A., & Olivera, F. (2020a). Organizational forgetting part I: A review of the literature and future research directions. *The Learning Organization*, *27*(3), 185–209. https://doi.org/10.1108/TLO-12-2019-0182

Mariano, S., Casey, A., & Olivera, F. (2020b). Organizational forgetting part II: A review of the literature and future research directions. *The Learning Organization*, *27*(5), 417–427. https://doi.org/10.1108/TLO-01-2020-0003

Martin, J. (2016, September 28). Hewlett-Packard's history frozen in time. *CNET*. https://www.cnet.com/pictures/hewlett-packards-history-frozen-in-time/

Merriam-Webster. (n.d.). Mundane. Retrieved January 29, 2025, from https://www.merriam-webster.com/dictionary/mundane

Nelson, T. (2003). The persistence of founder influence: Management, ownership, and performance effects at initial public offering. *Strategic Management Journal*, *24*(8), 707–724. https://doi.org/10.1002/smj.328

Nissley, N., & Casey, A. (2002). The politics of the exhibition: Viewing corporate museums through the paradigmatic lens of organizational memory. *British Journal of Management*, *13*(S2), S35–S45. https://doi.org/10.1111/1467-8551.13.s2.4

Packard, D. (1995). *HP way: How Bill Hewlett and I built our company*. Harper Business.

Prouche. (1990). *La grande aventure d'Alphonse Desjardins*. Confédération des Caisses Populaires et d'Economie Desjardins du Québec.

Putnam, L. L. (2022). Foreword. The emerging paradigm of communication constitutes organization. In J. Basque, N. Bencherki, & T. R. Kuhn (Eds.), *The Routledge handbook of the communicative constitution of organization* (pp. xxvi–xliv). Routledge.

Putnam, L. L., & Nicotera, A. M. (Eds.). (2009). *Building theories of organization: The constitutive role of communication*. Routledge. https://doi.org/10.4324/9780203891025

Radu-Lefebvre, M., Davis, J. H., & Gartner, W. B. (2024). Legacy in family business: A systematic literature review and future research agenda. *Family Business Review*, *37*(1), 18–59. https://doi.org/10.1177/08944865231224506

Rantakari, A., & Vaara, E. (2017). Narratives and processuality. In A. Langley & H. Tsoukas (Eds.), *The Sage handbook of process organization studies* (pp. 271–285). Sage.

Rattray, D. (2019). Tabasco Sauce history and lore. The ubiquitous little hot sauce we couldn't do without. *The Spruce Eats*. https://www.thespruceeats.com/tabasco-sauce-history-and-lore-3050514

Ravasi, D., Rindova, V., & Stigliani, I. (2019). The stuff of legend: History, memory and the temporality of organizational identity construction. *Academy of Management Journal*, *62*(5), 1523–1555. https://doi.org/10.5465/amj.2016.0505

Rhodes, C., & Brown, A. D. (2005). Narrative, organizations and research. *International Journal of Management Reviews*, *7*(3), 167–188. https://doi.org/10.1111/j.1468-2370.2005.00112.x

Ringle, K. (1993). Blowing the lid off Tabasco. Cousin Ken's spicy tale of the family business. *Washington Post*. https://www.washingtonpost.com/archive/lifestyle/food/1993/04/21/blowing-the-lid-off-tabasco/2ad6643b-025f-484e-b895-23ad82ecdcc8/

Rowlinson, M., Casey, A., Hansen, P. H., & Mills, A. J. (2014). *Narratives and memory in organizations* (Vol. 21). Sage.

Rowlinson, M., & Hassard, J. (1993). The invention of corporate culture: A history of the histories of Cadbury. *Human Relations*, *46*(3), 299–326. https://doi.org/10.1177/001872679304600301

Sasaki, I., Kotlar, J., Ravasi, D., & Vaara, E. (2020). Dealing with revered past: Historical identity statements and strategic change in Japanese family firms. *Strategic Management Journal*, *41*(3), 590–623. https://doi.org/10.1002/smj.3065

Schultz, M., & Hernes, T. (2013). A temporal perspective on organizational identity. *Organization Science*, *24*(1), 1–21. https://doi.org/10.1287/orsc.1110.0731

Shils, E. (1981). *Tradition*. University of Chicago Press.

Smith, E. (2016). The history of the call center explains how customer service got so annoying. Vice. https://www.vice.com/en/article/the-history-of-the-call-center-explains-how-customer-service-got-so-annoying/

Suddaby, R., Israelsen, T., & Mitchell, R. (2023). Entrepreneurial visions as rhetorical history: A diegetic narrative model of stakeholder enrollment. *Academy of Management Review*, *48*(2), 220–243. https://doi.org/10.5465/amr.2020.0010

Suddaby, R., & Jaskiewicz, P. (2020). *Managing traditions: A critical capability for family business success* (Vol. 33). Sage.

Tabasco. (n.d.). The history of TABASCO® brand. Retrieved January 29, 2025, from https://www.tabasco.com/tabasco-history/

Taylor, J. R., & Van Every, E. J. (2000). *The emergent organization: Communication as its site and surface*. Routledge.

Vaillancourt, C. (1941). Quarante ans! *Revue Desjardins*, *7*(1), 3.

Vinoski, J. (2022). McIlhenny Company is the most popular condiment company you've never heard of. *Forbes*. https://www.forbes.com/sites/jimvinoski/2022/10/05/mcilhenny-company-is-the-most-popular-condiment-company-youve-never-heard-of/

Wikipedia. (n.d.). Alphonse Desjardins. Retrieved January 29, 2025, from https://fr.wikipedia.org/wiki/Alphonse_Desjardins

Ian G. Jones
Chapter 9
Rhetorical history as history: Legacies of a rhetorical history strategy

Since the 'historic turn' (Booth & Rowlinson, 2006; Clark & Rowlinson, 2004) in organization studies, researchers have increasingly incorporated the past and differing interpretations of history into their research. Various scholars have shown how organizations can use their pasts as a resource in pursuit of their contemporary strategic objectives (Rowlinson & Hassard, 1993; Suddaby et al., 2010; Wadhwani et al., 2018), to link themselves to national or regional symbols and stories (Foster et al., 2011; Oertel & Thommes, 2018; Poor et al., 2016), to create continuity or legitimize change in strategy (Maclean et al., 2014, 2018, 2020; Ybema, 2014), and to create an organizational identity that forefronts the values they claim to stand for (Basque & Langley, 2018; Booth et al., 2007; Rowlinson & Hassard, 1993). These narratives often have similar structural elements and focuses, with many highlighting the importance of those who founded the company, using periodization from national history to embed themselves into that national historical narrative, and focusing on the successes of the company while ignoring the failures (Delahaye et al., 2009).

While many studies have examined the agency of managers when it comes to using history as a resource, relatively few have looked at the constraints that this decision creates for future managers. This chapter examines how the legacy of using the past as a strategy can affect future managers of the organization, focusing on Barclays Bank PLC. Between 2012 and 2015, Barclays used its past as part of the Transform Programme, a project that aimed to overhaul the bank's activities and organizational culture. However, in 2015, the chief executive officer (CEO) responsible for the Transform Programme, Antony Jenkins, was fired, and a new CEO, Jes Staley, was recruited. Jenkins' removal was in part due to his continuing focus on the cultural change that he had implemented, along with disputes over the strategic direction of the bank, its investment banking activities, and perceived poor share price performance (Ahmed, 2015; Brinded, 2015). While Staley did not immediately abandon his predecessor's use of the past strategy, the removal of Jenkins, who had become personally associated with it, suggested to outsiders that Barclays was abandoning its focus on corporate culture (Jenkins & Arnold, 2015b). Staley ceased mentioning changing Barclays' corporate culture in 2016 and officially changed Barclays' corporate purpose in 2018.

Despite Staley's decision to end the bank's focus on changing its corporate culture, the Transform Programme had been aimed both internally and externally. Hence, internal and external stakeholders, including members of the press, had an acute awareness of the Transform Programme's aims and the content of the historical narrative underpinning it, which was the official version of Barclays' history. Staley's

https://doi.org/10.1515/9783111631462-010

decision to move away from it was seen in the context of a different historical narrative—one where Barclays had been unable to change its corporate culture and live up to the values of its Quaker founders. The Transform Programme, which had been met with hopeful skepticism (Greenham & Lewis, 2014), became just another example of Barclays' inability to change (Augar, 2018a), while at the same time introducing onlookers to a more noble history that the firm could be compared against. In effect, the rhetorical history that was used to try to change Barclays became part of a historical narrative that interpreted the firm as unable to change.

Rhetorical history

How organizations use their pasts as a resource has been a subject of study for some time, with some of the earliest work focusing on how organizations use their pasts to shape internal and external perceptions of their corporate culture (Rowlinson & Hassard, 1993). Indeed, constructing a new, or changing an existing, corporate culture or identity appears to be one of the main tasks for which managers find history useful. Work by Holt (2006) and Poor et al. (2016) has shown how U.S. companies Jack Daniels and Colt, respectively, connected themselves to prevailing U.S. national historical narratives. While Jack Daniels used these prevailing narratives to change its brand identity—moving from a prestigious bourbon brand to one associated with the common man, the cowboy, and the American frontier—Colt used similar imagery from the outset but instead connected itself to the military to produce a competitive advantage over other gun makers. For Jack Daniels, this was not a short-term effort, as later work has shown how the firm continues to draw on its legacy as a form of nostalgia as it reconstructs its corporate identity (Seifried et al., 2023). Likewise, Foster et al. (2011) showed how Tim Hortons, a Canadian coffee chain, connected itself to prevailing Canadian cultural icons such as ice hockey and the military. Building a corporate identity or culture need not only connect to national narratives, with Oertel and Thommes (2018) showing how relatively recently formed German watchmaking firms use regional reputations for high-quality craftsmanship to construct an identity associated with that level of quality.

The past can be a useful resource for managers when constructing a corporate culture or identity, as it can provide them with multiple ways to manage change. Managers can use historical narratives to show a clean break with the past (Ybema, 2014) or emphasize their continuity with what came before while making changes (Hampel & Dalpiaz, 2023; Maclean et al., 2014, 2018), use founding ideals and individuals to support organizational changes they are planning to make (Basque & Langley, 2018), or use the past as a means of maintaining organizational identity in the face of ambiguity, challenge, or changing organizational contexts (Foroughi, 2020; Lyle et al., 2022). While these uses of the past can be aimed internally, a well-constructed identity based on a historical narrative can be deployed externally and allow firms to "outpast" (Lubinski, 2018) their competitors to achieve a competitive advantage.

While managers have used historical narratives to enact change within organizations, the past is not completely malleable and can also constrain managers. Indeed, factual accuracy acts as a constraint on managers when constructing historical narratives, lest the later discovery of discrepancies between historical records and the organizational narrative embarrass the firm (Booth et al., 2007). Indeed, when the historical record is incongruous with the managers' preferred version of the company's history, organizations have been shown to engage in "organizational forgetting" to manage the firm's history in pursuit of their strategic goals (Anteby & Molnár, 2012; Mena et al., 2016; Nissley & Casey, 2002). Such forgetting can be more challenging when the history is well known due to a preeminent founder (Cailluet et al., 2018) or when professional historians are involved in the creation of the narrative (Coller et al., 2016).

The multiple voices within firms that contribute to the creation of historical narratives can also create problems when attempting to construct a single historical narrative that a firm can base its corporate culture or identity on (Smith & Russell, 2016). While having multiple historical narratives within a firm can enable employees to reaffirm their commitment to their perceived organizational purpose (Foroughi, 2020), it can also lead to internal conflict when diverging historical narratives support different beliefs about what a firm's future strategy should be (Parker, 2002). Such problems can be more acute in family firms, as the history is both organizational and familial (Davis & Harveston, 1999), although, ironically, rhetorical history strategies can also be used to overcome these problems (Ferri & Takahashi, 2022; Hoon et al., 2023; Lubinski & Gartner, 2023; Manelli et al., 2023). Regardless, it is clear that managers cannot take for granted that they will be the sole arbiters of what an organization's history will be seen to be by multiple audiences.

Efforts to curate an organization's historical record can create a disconnect between what is expected of a factual historical narrative and what the organization produces (Smith & Simeone, 2017). Indeed, efforts to curate a firm's history can lead to ethical issues where managers intentionally or unintentionally construct historical narratives that obscure immoral business activities (Booth et al., 2007; Coraiola & Derry, 2020). Connecting audience expectations with the historical narrative is important, as a narrative that appears authentic to the past and accurate according to established historical records can make it a more useful resource for the organization (Hatch & Schultz, 2017; Zundel et al., 2016). Indeed, brash attempts to construct organizational narratives by managers can lead to employee resistance, resistance from those tasked with creating the narrative, and even the construction of counternarratives (Aeon & Lamertz, 2021; Kivijärvi et al., 2019).

Despite the extensive research on how firms construct rhetorical history narratives and what they are used for, there is little on how these narratives continue to affect organizations after their initial strategic purpose has been achieved, abandoned, or changed. Indeed, there appears to be an underlying assumption in the rhetorical history literature that skillful managers can reconstitute the firm's historical resources as needed to pursue their contemporary organizational goals (Suddaby et al., 2010; Wadhwani et al., 2018). Hence, when the goals change, skillful managers will be able to construct new, or alter the existing, historical narrative to fit the new aims. However, as mentioned above, there are clear constraints on a manager's ability to use history at will (Aeon & Lamertz, 2021; Booth et al., 2007). Organizational pasts can act to constrain the options that a firm has for reimagining the past, as shown in Hatch and Schultz's (2017) study of Carlsberg, where managers at subsidiaries with their own historical narratives resisted the imposition of an overarching Carlsberg narrative that threatened to subsume theirs.

It is also unclear whether rhetorical history narratives can act to constrain future managers, in effect acting as a form of path dependency (David, 1985) that pressures managers to act in a particular way or face censure and resistance. Indeed, in the case of constructing a new corporate culture or identity, it stands to reason that the more successful the rhetorical history strategy employed, the more likely it would be to act as a constraint on future managers (Dobusch & Schüßler, 2013). Furthermore, once managers have utilized a rhetorical history strategy to construct a corporate culture or identity, abandoning it or committing resources to radically alter it can be seen as a waste to stakeholders, thereby leading to organizational "lock-in" (Sydow et al., 2009). While these pressures could be endogenous as they relate to corporate culture, exogenous pressures may exist for the firm to conform to an identity that it itself has argued is historical and "authentic" (Hatch & Schultz, 2017). However, how these pressures manifest and how managers respond to them is, as yet, understudied.

Methodology

The data for this study consisted of interviews conducted with Barclays employees, internal documents created at Barclays, and publicly available sources produced by news organizations in the UK. While the analysis for these data types has similarities (discussed below), they were used for different parts of the chapter. The interviews and internal documents created by Barclays relate to the creation and purpose of the historical narrative that was a key part of the Transform Programme. However, they are not relevant for the period after the Transform Programme was abandoned, as the documents predate it and the interviewees were not asked about this. Instead, secondary sources from the British press between 2012 and 2021 were used to examine the media's response to the Transform Programme, the historical narrative produced as part of it, and the response following Barclays' decision to abandon the strategy.

The author conducted a total of 21 interviews with 22 interviewees as part of his doctoral research; 16 of these were done face-to-face, with the remaining five conducted via phone. Face-to-face was preferred as it can potentially deliver richer qualitative data than phone interviews (Irvine et al., 2013; Rubin & Rubin, 2005). Additionally, one of these interviews was a group call between the researcher and two interviewees, at their request. The interviews were semi-structured, with a general interview schedule that was adapted depending on the interviewee's role at Barclays and experiences with Barclays Group Archives (BGA). The interviews were also recorded and transcribed by the researcher.

Internal documents were initially targeted due to their relevance to the planning and creation of the historical narrative, as well as the importance of such documents in the planning of events to disseminate the narrative. These events included annual general meetings, training material that was created to teach the new values, historical anniversaries, and documents related to the creation of the narrative itself and the Transform Programme. Further documents were collected based on the interviewees' responses, in particular documents that were hosted on Barclays' intranet that propagated Barclays' historical narrative but were not held in the archives. Additionally, newspaper and media articles were collated through keyword searches using the Nexis database. This search was limited to publications within Britain, since that is the site of Barclays' headquarters, is the market in which it is most dominant, is arguably where its scandals that were the catalyst for the Transform Programme were most widely reported, and is the country with which its identity is most associated.

Searches on the Nexis database for "Barclays" and "history" between 2012 and March 2024 with the subject of "Barclays PLC" and limited to major British newspapers such as *The Times, The Guardian*, and the *Financial Times*, as well as their associated websites resulted in 609 matches. These results were reviewed, and duplicates were removed, leaving 371 articles. These articles were read and coded for whether they referred to Barclays' history and, if so, how; if and how they referred to the Transform Programme; and whether the articles used Barclays' history, as presented by the firm in the Transform Programme, to praise or criticize the bank's current actions when they conformed to or deviated from what the article argued is Barclays' historical continuity.

Barclays' rhetorical history strategies

2008, Payment Protection Insurance, London Interbank Offered Rate, and the Transform Programme

By 2012, Barclays had been involved with several high-profile scandals that had damaged its reputation with customers, shareholders, employees, and regulators. One of the earliest was Barclays' attempt to purchase Lehman Brothers in 2008 before its collapse, a deal that damaged relations with British regulators and the Chancellor of the

Exchequer, Alistair Darling, due to the potential danger of Lehman Brothers' debts bringing down Barclays (Augar, 2018b; Tooze, 2018). Barclays further earned the ire of the British government by taking the private option to raise capital to fulfill the Financial Services Authority's (FSA) new capital requirements rather than accept government funds and a public stake in the business (Augar, 2018b).

In 2009, Barclays became embroiled in the Payment Protection Insurance (PPI) scandal, suffering heavy fines for its role in the mis-selling of PPI products—products that were responsible for between 32% and 42% of Barclays PLC's UK retail and business pretax profits between 2001 and 2005 (Salz & Collins, 2013). Finally, in 2012, Barclays was fined £59 million by the FSA (2012) ($92 million in 2012 values) and $200 million by the U.S. Commodity Futures Trading Commission (2012) for its part in rigging the London Interbank Offered Rate (LIBOR). The fallout from the LIBOR scandal led to the resignation of both Barclays's chairman, Marcus Agius, and its CEO, Bob Diamond, within the space of one 24-hour period.

Barclays' new CEO, Jenkins, responded to this crisis of legitimacy in two ways: through an independent review led by solicitor and executive vice chairman at Rothschild Bank, Anthony Salz (Jenkins, 2012; Salz & Collins, 2013), and by launching the Transform Programme to overhaul the operations and organizational culture of the bank (Diamond, 2013; Greenham & Lewis, 2014). In December 2012, Barclays held an internal event where Jenkins announced the Transform Programme. Attendees at the event were presented with brochures featuring a timeline of Barclays' development, photos of historical artifacts, and a video titled *Made by Barclays* (Huntley, 2012) that explained the bank's historical narrative and would be a key resource for educating internal and external stakeholders about the narrative.

Using the past to build a new corporate culture

Barclays was not the only bank trying to create a new set of corporate values in 2012, nor was it the only bank to use its history in this strategy, with Goldman Sachs and Deutsche Bank engaging in similar programs (Hill, 2013). While commentators welcomed the commitment to cultural change, they were skeptical as to whether it reflected real change or merely a public relations exercise and whether such commitments to putting ethics before maximizing profits were possible considering the profit-maximizing logic of the sector they operated in (Greenham & Lewis, 2014; Jenkins & Massoudi, 2013). However, for the most part, commentators were willing to see what Barclays did to live up to the claims it was making regarding its new set of corporate values, in part due to the new management that was introducing it. Indeed, Jenkins would become personally associated with the Transform Programme, being dubbed St. Antony, viewed not only as the person responsible for introducing it but also as genuinely committed to delivering the cultural change promised (Arnold, 2015a; Duke, 2014; Jenkins, 2014).

The Transform Programme utilized two main sets of data to produce the values that would form the core of Barclays' new corporate culture: over 2,000 interviews with employees, and research into the bank's history conducted at BGA, the bank's internal archives department. According to Jenkins, the choice to rely on Barclays' past was partially a desire to "anchor [the values] back to the institution's [Barclays'] place in British history and British society" so that they could counter beliefs that "the bank had become incredibly self-serving, [as] for most of its history that was not the case."

Another reason for using Barclays' past was that its Quaker founders could be used as a resource. Quakers are commonly seen as moral people in Britain (DVL Smith Ltd, 2010; Walvin, 1997), credited with being an integral part of abolishing the slave trade (Carey & Plank, 2014; Walvin, 2014), and responsible for the creation of various well-known firms in the UK that have a reputation for having treated their workers well, such as Cadbury's (da Silva Lopes, 2016; Rowlinson & Hassard, 1993) and Rowntree's (Fitzgerald, 2006). According to the former managing director of corporate communications, being able to "look back to the start of this organization, what people were doing then, what they thought the purpose of this was, what it was for, that is what we are *still* [my emphasis] for." These ideas could be linked, with one of BGA's archivists stating that they were asked to find stories that showed that "Barclays have funded good things in the economy, in terms of inventions, manufacturers," as well as "its charitable work going back to the early days of the Quakers, philanthropic work, charitable work, . . . a lot of what we now call corporate responsibility."

The narrative presented in *Made by Barclays* is the most succinct version of the history produced and was shown to all 140,000 Barclays employees as part of their training on the new corporate values. The video presents Barclays as an organization set up by "men of integrity" who "wanted to do right by their customers, clients and community" (Huntley, 2012). *Made by Barclays* links the bank to various British historic events, such as funding the first industrial railroad; highlights some of Barclays' contributions to the banking sector that moved it forward socially or technologically, such as the introduction of the ATM to Britain or promoting the first female branch manager; and links the bank to the iconic British brand Morris Minor by revealing that it was Barclays that helped fund the company in its early days.

While Barclays did attract skepticism for its efforts to change its culture, including from the Reverend Julian Welby, the Archbishop of Canterbury (Costello, 2013), few doubted Jenkins' commitment to implementing a cultural change at Barclays, even if they doubted his ability to do so ("Barclays and the Entitlement Culture," 2013; Greenham & Lewis, 2014). Indeed, parts of the financial press were even optimistic that Jenkins' focus on restoring ethical practice at the bank could improve its performance and help rally the bank's share back to its pre-2011 value ("Barclays: There's a Hole in my Bucket," 2013).

Despite this optimism, the Transform Programme and the historical narrative it was based on—Quaker morals and contributing to Britain—had opened the bank up to attack for making decisions that commentators felt were not in line with these claims of a moral heritage. Citing Barclays' commitment to the memory of its Quaker founders and pride in the actions of David Barclay, an early owner who freed slaves from a Jamaican plantation he had become owner of, members of the press attacked Barclays for its continued investment in coal, asking, "Given its recent history, is it fair for Jenkins to call forth these ghosts of its moral past?" (Confino, 2015). While arguments like this were rare, it is clear that even only 3 years into the Transform Programme, divergence between the values espoused as Barclays' historical values and the behavior the bank exhibited led to censure and pressure on the bank's managers to act in continuity with this historical narrative.

The end of the Transform Programme

In 2015, Jenkins was removed from his position as CEO, something that was seen by the press as part of a trend of banks moving away from their commitments to act more ethically following the 2008 Global Financial Crisis (Ryan-Collins, 2015). The sacking of Jenkins, along with the hiring of the new chairman, John McFarlane, who made the decision, was interpreted by the press as a sign that Barclays was abandoning its cultural change (Arnold, 2015b; Jenkins & Arnold, 2015a). Indeed, there were even fears internally that Jenkins and his efforts would be "expunged from corporate history" (Jenkins & Arnold, 2015b). While the new CEO, Staley, stated that he was committed to "complet[ing] the cultural transformation of the group" ("Jes Staley's Memo to Barclays Staff," 2015), commentators were skeptical of this commitment, fearing that he would signal a return to Diamond's style of management (Griffiths, 2015) as Jenkins' "hair shirt strategy" had become unpopular with Barclays' top management (Jenkins & Arnold, 2015b). While Barclays has never officially announced the end of the Transform Programme, the removal of Jenkins was seen by the press as a desire by the board to shift strategy and reduce emphasis on cultural change ("After Barclays Sacks Antony Jenkins," 2015; Jenkins & Arnold, 2015b). Whether Jenkins had been successful in changing Barclays' corporate culture is unclear, but there are signs that the historical narrative and internal messaging had begun to have an effect on top management, with the former managing director of corporate communications stating that "people are conscious of not doing anything that is dissonant with our history. I have heard the phrase used 'I'm not sure our Quaker founders would do this and therefore should we?'"

In March 2016, early in Staley's tenure, he was attacked for deciding to sell the bank's African operations—a historical market for Barclays (Parris, 2016)—with this episode seen as another example of how "the bank's restless soul has flip-flopped" and how its "transformation from profitable retail bank to swashbuckling, capital destroying investment bank [was] almost complete" (Davidson, 2016). Again, Barclays' history—"steeped in Quaker roots and stewarded through the 20th century by family insiders [leading] the Barclays brand to become one of the most trusted in retail banking" (Davidson, 2016)—was used to chastise decisions that were perceived as out of character for the bank based on its history.

While the decision to pull out of Africa was seen as a tragic break with a historic market, Staley would become embroiled in his own scandal that was linked to Barclays' recent past. In April 2017, it emerged that he was being investigated by the FSA and the Bank of England for attempting to uncover the identity of a whistleblower who had claimed that a recent hire, a friend of Staley's, had personal issues that affected their ability to do their job ("Barclays' Clean-up Is Set Back," 2017; Shubber, 2017). By the time the news was announced, Barclays had concluded that Staley had acted "honestly but mistakenly" and cut his pay but had decided against further action. In addition, Staley published a memo he had sent to staff apologizing for getting "too personally involved in the matter" ("Staley Email to Barclays Staff," 2017).

At the same time as the whistle-blowing scandal was reaching its conclusion, the performance of Barclays' share price and the resources given to the investment bank came under criticism from shareholders and the press. Both these issues—questions over corporate ethics and questions over the investment bank—were described as "historic dilemma[s]," dilemmas that the Transform Programme was supposed to have solved (Arnold, 2017). While the FCA's investigation into Staley ended in April 2018, with Staley receiving heavy fines (Jenkins, 2018), an ongoing court case related to how Barclays raised its private financing in 2008 rumbled on, acting as a reminder of the various scandals the bank had suffered over the years (Augar, 2018a).

To the press, these incidents were "throwback[s] to the bullish leadership of Bob Diamond" and an obstacle in completing the cultural change started by Jenkins (Dunkley, 2017). Indeed, Staley's scandal was portrayed as part of a continuity of short-lived, scandal-ridden CEOs that, despite Jenkins' best efforts, seemed to stem from Barclays' corporate culture problems (Wilson, 2017). While the Transform Programme had constructed a historical narrative that connected Barclays founders' Quaker values to the bank's contributions to the British economy and society, members of the press were constructing a narrative of Quaker values lost among a series of scandals linked to a corporate culture that the bank could not change. Indeed, it was the historical narrative that had been presented in the Transform Programme that had provided the facts and the core historical interpretation for the press's narrative, and it was Barclays' apparent inability to act in accordance with it, according to the press, that opened it up to attack.

In 2018, Barclays claimed that the goal of changing the firm's culture had been achieved and that it would pursue a new purpose of "creating opportunities to rise" while retaining the corporate values that "have been part of our DNA for over 328 years" (Barclays, 2018, p. 10). Alongside this change in purpose, McFarlane argued that the bank had moved on from the historical PPI scandal (Megaw, 2019). Despite McFarlane's claims, Barclays' attempt to move on from its past suffered another blow following revelations about Staley's relationship with disgraced financier and criminal Jeffrey Epstein. While Staley's connection to Epstein could be argued to be a personal issue linked to his previous roles at JPMorgan and therefore not reflective of Barclays, the investigations focused on how Staley had characterized his relationship with Epstein to Barclays, the FCA, and the Prudential Regulation Authority (Makortoff, 2020). Barclays supported Staley again, but in November 2021 Staley resigned following the results of the FCA and Prudential Regulation Authority investigations that found he had mischaracterized his relationship with Epstein and suggested that he may not be found fit and proper to run the bank (Griffiths, 2021; Makortoff, 2021). This instance was seen as yet another scandal in a history of scandals at the top level of Barclays, with Philip Augar describing Barclays as "just the kind of bank that attracts regulators' attention" (Morris, 2021).

Staley's resignation and Barclays' support for him until the end seemed to confirm the press's historical narrative that stood opposed to, but was highlighted by, the official narrative of the Transform Programme: that Barclays could not reform itself and did not reflect the Quaker values it claimed were a key part of its history (Augar, 2020). Ironically, Barclays' historical narrative that was produced as part of an attempt to change the corporate values of the bank had, at this point, become part of a different narrative, a narrative that the bank was unable to change.

The legacies of a rhetorical history strategy

Rhetorical history strategies have often focused on the agency of managers to construct historical narratives to pursue their strategic objectives (Suddaby et al., 2010; Wadhwani et al., 2018). However, the example of Barclays shows the limitations of managers' ability to control the historical narrative they have created once external actors are aware of it and once managers cease actively managing it. Under Jenkins, Barclays skillfully crafted a historical narrative that it could use to try to construct a new corporate culture at the bank, although how successful these efforts were is unclear. However, following Jenkins' departure, Barclays moved away from actively managing its past, and a new narrative emerged among the press that used the bank's official narrative to attack Barclays' managers' actions. Indeed, Barclays' official history of a bank founded on Quaker values and contributing to the British economy and society was used as proof that the bank had fallen from these ideals over the previous 20 years and that reversion to them was seemingly impossible.

While rhetorical history literature has begun to examine the multiple actors that are involved in creating a historical narrative and the varying interpretations they may have (Foroughi, 2020; Hatch & Schultz, 2017; Smith & Russell, 2016), relatively little has been discussed about how an organization's rhetorical history narrative can be used by other stakeholders to hold the organization accountable. Indeed, external stakeholders are generally seen as recipients of the historical narrative and are somewhat passive in how they respond (Holt, 2006; Poor et al., 2016). Barclays' example shows that this is not the case. While it is impossible to know whether Barclays' history would have been used to attack the bank regardless of the Transform Programme—as one of Britain's oldest and largest banks, certain facets of its history were already well known—Barclays' managers' choice to use its history provided an opening for its narrative to be used against them. By providing an official version of the bank's past and linking it to its corporate values and corporate culture, the narrative became a yardstick with which the media could judge the bank's contemporary actions using Barclays' own words. Hence, the Transform Programme provided an official historical narrative depicting a continuity of previous moral management that members of the press could juxtapose against the bank's contemporary actions.

A limitation of this chapter is the lack of internal documents that discussed decision-making and the pressures that managers felt they were under due to the historical narratives they had unleashed. Further research could look at how rhetorical history narratives can be used by external stakeholders to encourage or coerce particular behaviors and how managers respond to these pressures internally, especially when the narrative being used is one constructed by the firm itself. Such research would enrich our understanding of what managers can and cannot do with a rhetorical history narrative.

Connected to Barclays' managers' inability to control the historical narrative once it had been created is how the narrative had a legacy of its own. Various scholars have shown how history can be a tool for change in a firm (Hampel & Dalpiaz, 2023; Maclean et al., 2014, 2018), but Barclays' historical narrative had the potential to reduce the options that future managers had to act. While Maclean et al. (2018) showed how managers skillfully adapted themes from previous histories into new circumstances, the ways that previous choices to emphasize certain aspects of a firm's history and diminish others may constrain the options of future managers have been overlooked. The example of Barclays shows that the choice to emphasize the bank's Quaker past could act to limit the scope for action of future managers who were seen to be acting out of step with these values.

The legacy of Barclays' rhetorical history strategy had the potential to act as a form of path dependence, with internal and external stakeholders acting as checks on what is and is not acceptable behavior and strategy. Indeed, the decision to use Barclays' past to construct a new set of company values and a corporate culture suggests that the intent was to limit the scope for action of future employees and managers via a corporate culture that would encourage certain types of behavior. Although rhetorical history strategies may be tools that give managers agency, with history being a resource they can use to achieve their strategic objectives, these choices leave a legacy that becomes part of a firm's history. These choices can constrain the agency of future managers, push firms towards a particular path, and be something managers must contend with if they wish to also employ a rhetorical history strategy.

References

Aeon, B., & Lamertz, K. (2021). Those who control the past control the future: The dark side of rhetorical history. *Organization Studies, 42*(4), 575–593. https://doi.org/10.1177/0170840619844284

After Barclays sacks Antony Jenkins, it's back to gung-ho banking. (2015, July 12). The Guardian. https://www.theguardian.com/business/2015/jul/12/barclays-sacks-antony-jenkins-back-gung-ho-banking

Ahmed, K. (2015, December 3). Jenkins: My regret over Barclays' sacking. *BBC*. https://www.bbc.com/news/business-34989844

Anteby, M., & Molnár, V. (2012). Collective memory meets organizational identity: Remembering to forget in a firm's rhetorical history. *Academy of Management Journal, 55*(3), 515–540. https://doi.org/10.5465/amj.2010.0245

Arnold, M. (2015a, July 8). Barclays fires Jenkins after clash over investment banking unit. *Financial Times*. https://www.ft.com/content/74fed7c6-2537-11e5-9c4e-a775d2b173ca

Arnold, M. (2015b, July 10). Mack the Knife steps in to call the tune at Barclays. *Financial Times*. https://www.ft.com/content/133fddb6-271f-11e5-bd83-71cb60e8f08c

Arnold, M. (2017, October 9). Staley scrutinised as Barclays faces historic dilemma. *Financial Times*. https://www.ft.com/content/4f9d14d6-aac1-11e7-ab55-27219df83c97

Augar, P. (2018a, February 13). As a legal case looms, the past returns to haunt Barclays. *Financial Times*. https://advance.lexis.com/api/document?collection=news&id=urn:contentItem:5RMR-BG11-DY9P-N32Y-00000-00&context=1519360

Augar, P. (2018b). *The bank that lived a little: Barclays in the age of the very free market.* Penguin.

Augar, P. (2020, February 14). Jes Staley's Jeffrey Epstein issue is just the latest Barclays tangle. *Financial Times*. https://www.ft.com/content/3ee8bcfa-4e7d-11ea-95a0-43d18ec715f5

Barclays and the entitlement culture: Salz proposals are not sufficient to promote change. (2013, April 4). *Financial Times*. https://advance.lexis.com/api/document?collection=news&id=urn:contentItem:5841-6571-JBFS-D0PG-00000-00&context=1519360.

Barclays. (2018). *Barclays PLC strategic report 2018.* https://home.barclays/content/dam/home-barclays/documents/investor-relations/reports-and-events/annual-reports/2018/barclays-plc-strategic-report-2018.pdf

Barclays: There's a hole in my bucket. (2013, October 30). Financial Times. https://advance.lexis.com/api/document?collection=news&id=urn:contentItem:59PN-MP31-JCM7-G1TK-00000-00&context=1519360.

Barclays' clean-up is set back by new controversy. (2017, April 11). Financial Times. https://www.ft.com/content/683fd0ba-1ebb-11e7-b7d3-163f5a7f229c

Basque, J., & Langley, A. (2018). Invoking Alphonse: The founder figure as a historical resource for organizational identity work. *Organization Studies, 39*(12), 1685–1708. https://doi.org/10.1177/0170840618789211

Booth, C., Clark, P., Delahaye, A., Procter, S., & Rowlinson, M. (2007). Accounting for the dark side of corporate history: Organizational culture perspectives and the Bertelsmann case. *Critical Perspectives on Accounting, 18*(6), 625–644. https://doi.org/10.1016/j.cpa.2007.03.012

Booth, C., & Rowlinson, M. (2006). Management and organizational history: Prospects. *Management & Organizational History, 1*(1), 5–30. https://doi.org/10.1177/1744935906060627

Brinded, L. (2015, July 8). The fired Barclays CEO had two nicknames inside the bank that tell you why he was forced out. *Business Insider*. https://www.businessinsider.com/barclays-ceo-antony-jenkins-left-because-of-his-lack-of-investment-banking-understanding-2015-7

Cailluet, L., Gorge, H., & Özçağlar-Toulouse, N. (2018). 'Do not expect me to stay quiet': Challenges in managing a historical strategic resource. *Organization Studies*, *39*(12), 1811–1835. https://doi.org/10.1177/0170840618800111

Carey, B., & Plank, G. G. (2014). *Quakers and abolition*. University of Illinois Press. https://doi.org/10.5406/illinois/9780252038266.001.0001

Clark, P., & Rowlinson, M. (2004). The treatment of history in organisation studies: Towards an 'historic turn'? *Business History*, *46*(3), 331–352. https://doi.org/10.1080/0007679042000219175

Coller, K. E., Helms Mills, J., & Mills, A. J. (2016). The British Airways heritage collection: An ethnographic 'history.' *Business History*, *58*(4), 547–570. https://doi.org/10.1080/00076791.2015.1105218

Confino, J. (2015, June 2). Why Barclays must quit bankrolling coal industry: Barclays CEO Antony Jenkins talks of courage, values and purpose, so why is he a lead financier of coal, a major contributor to climate change? *The Guardian*. https://advance.lexis.com/api/document?collection=news&id=urn:contentItem:5F7R-CNP1-F021-614C-00000-00&context=1519360

Coraiola, D. M., & Derry, R. (2020). Remembering to forget: The historic irresponsibility of U.S. Big Tobacco. *Journal of Business Ethics*, *166*(2), 233–252. https://doi.org/10.1007/s10551-019-04323-4

Costello, M. (2013, December 30). Archbishop tackles bank boss on Today programme. *The Times*. https://advance.lexis.com/api/document?collection=news&id=urn:contentItem:5B5M-1431-JBVM-Y3N7-00000-00&context=1519360

da Silva Lopes, T. (2016). Building brand reputation through third-party endorsement: Fair trade in British chocolate. *Business History Review*, *90*(3), 457–482. https://doi.org/10.1017/S0007680516000738

David, P. A. (1985). Clio and the economics of QWERTY. *The American Economic Review*, *75*(2), 332–337.

Davidson, D. (2016, March 21). It's déjà vu all over again as Barclays sells short in Africa. *The Times*. https://advance.lexis.com/api/document?collection=news&id=urn:contentItem:5JBS-9WC1-DY9P-N1VK-00000-00&context=1519360

Davis, P. S., & Harveston, P. D. (1999). In the founder's shadow: Conflict in the family firm. *Family Business Review*, *12*(4), 311–323. https://doi.org/10.1111/j.1741-6248.1999.00311.x

Delahaye, A., Booth, C., Clark, P., Proctor, S., & Rowlinson, M. (2009). The genre of corporate history. *Journal of Organizational Change Management*, *22*(1), 27–48. https://doi.org/10.1108/09534810910933898

Diamond, B. (2013, February 12). Jenkins sets out Barclays reinvention. *Financial Times*. https://www.ft.com/content/470553ce-7542-11e2-b8ad-00144feabdc0

Dobusch, L., & Schüßler, E. (2013). Theorizing path dependence: A review of positive feedback mechanisms in technology markets, regional clusters, and organizations. *Industrial and Corporate Change*, *22*(3), 617–647. https://doi.org/10.1093/icc/dts029

Duke, S. (2014, March 9). ST Antony's fall from grace. *The Sunday Times*, *5*, 5.

Dunkley, E. (2017, April 10). Jes Staley hits roadblock in clean-up of Barclays. *Financial Times*. https://www.ft.com/content/5bdbac24-1df6-11e7-b7d3-163f5a7f229c

DVL Smith Ltd. (2010). People's perceptions of the Quakers. *Quaker Studies*, *15*(1), 98–107. https://doi.org/10.3828/quaker.15.1.98

Ferri, P., & Takahashi, A. R. W. (2022). Standing the test of time: Understanding how long-living family firms make use of the past to preserve organizational identity. *Management & Organizational History*, *17*, 76–96. https://doi.org/10.1080/17449359.2022.2078372

Fitzgerald, R. (2006). *Rowntree and the marketing revolution, 1862–1969*. Cambridge University Press.

Foroughi, H. (2020). Collective memories as a vehicle of fantasy and identification: Founding stories retold. *Organization Studies*, *41*(10), 1347–1367. https://doi.org/10.1177/0170840619844286

Foster, W. M., Suddaby, R., Minkus, A., & Wiebe, E. (2011). History as social memory assets: The example of Tim Hortons. *Management & Organizational History*, *6*(1), 101–120. https://doi.org/10.1177/1744935910387027

FSA. (2012, June 27). *Barclays fined £59.5 million for significant failings in relation to LIBOR and EURIBOR*. The Financial Services Authority. https://webarchive.nationalarchives.gov.uk/20120628104925/http://www.fsa.gov.uk/library/communication/pr/2012/070.shtml

Greenham, T., & Lewis, B. (2014, August 4). Barclays' Transform programme: Culture change or window dressing? *The Guardian*. http://www.theguardian.com/sustainable-business/barclays-transform-programme-culture-change-window-dressing

Griffiths, K. (2015, October 14). Barclays boss set to sail out of obscurity. *The Times*. https://advance.lexis.com/api/document?collection=news&id=urn:contentItem:5H4V-M1X1-JCJY-G3TV-00000-00&context=1519360

Griffiths, K. (2021, February 11). At centre of a storm Staley leaves Barclays: The bank has defended its departed chief, but questions remain over his transparency. *The Times*. https://advance.lexis.com/api/document?collection=news&id=urn:contentItem:640B-GR51-DYTY-C307-00000-00&context=1519360

Hampel, C. E., & Dalpiaz, E. (2023). Confronting the contested past: Sensemaking and rhetorical history in the reconstruction of organizational identity. *Academy of Management Journal*, *66*(6), 1711–1740. https://doi.org/10.5465/amj.2020.1132

Hatch, M. J., & Schultz, M. (2017). Toward a theory of using history authentically: Historicizing in the Carlsberg Group. *Administrative Science Quarterly*, *62*(4), 1–41. https://doi.org/10.1177/0001839217692535

Hill, A. (2013, October 16). Bankers back in the classroom. *Financial Times*. https://www.ft.com/content/57debbc2-302c-11e3-9eec-00144feab7de

Holt, D. B. (2006). Jack Daniel's America: Iconic brands as ideological parasites and proselytizers. *Journal of Consumer Culture*, *6*(3), 355–377. https://doi.org/10.1177/1469540506068683

Hoon, C., Brinkmann, J., & Baluch, A. M. (2023). Narrative memory work of employees in family businesses: How founding stories shape organizational identification. *Family Business Review*, *36*(1), 37–62. https://doi.org/10.1177/08944865231159475

Huntley, M. (2012, December 4). *Barclays—Made by Barclays*. Vimeo. https://vimeo.com/83306108

Irvine, A., Drew, P., & Sainsbury, R. (2013). 'Am I not answering your questions properly?' Clarification, adequacy and responsiveness in semi-structured telephone and face-to-face interviews. *Qualitative Research*, *13*(1), 87–106. https://doi.org/10.1177/1468794112439086

Jenkins, P. (2012, July 25). Salz to lead probe of Barclays business methods. *Financial Times*, *15*, 15.

Jenkins, P. (2014, March 6). Saint Antony's fall from grace. *Financial Times*, *23*, 23.

Jenkins, P. (2018, April 20). Axe removed from neck of Barclays' Jes Staley after FCA verdict. *Financial Times*. https://advance.lexis.com/api/document?collection=news&id=urn:contentItem:5S4X-1T61-JCM7-G49F-00000-00&context=1519360

Jenkins, P., & Arnold, M. (2015a, October 13). Choice of Jenkins' successor sends mixed signals. *Financial Times*. https://advance.lexis.com/api/document?collection=news&id=urn:contentItem:5H4V-8P11-DXXV-4018-00000-00&context=1519360

Jenkins, P., & Arnold, M. (2015b, October 16). Barclays: Captain credible. *Financial Times*. https://www.ft.com/content/22ce28a8-73ed-11e5-bdb1-e6e4767162cc

Jenkins, P., & Massoudi, A. (2013, February 10). Barclays plans £2bn cost-cutting. *Financial Times*. https://www.ft.com/content/d49db49a-7229-11e2-896a-00144feab49a

Jes Staley's memo to Barclays staff. (2015, October 28). *Financial Times*. https://www.ft.com/content/404b0d38-7d4d-11e5-a1fe-567b37f80b64

Kivijärvi, M., Mills, A. J., & Helms Mills, J. (2019). Performing Pan American Airways through coloniality: An ANTi-History approach to narratives and business history. *Management & Organizational History*, *14*(1), 33–54. https://doi.org/10.1080/17449359.2018.1465825

Lubinski, C. (2018). From 'history as told' to 'history as experienced': Contextualizing the uses of the past. *Organization Studies*, *39*(12), 1785–1809. https://doi.org/10.1177/0170840618800116

Lubinski, C., & Gartner, W. B. (2023). Talking about (my) generation: The use of generation as rhetorical history in family business. *Family Business Review, 36*(1), 119–142. https://doi.org/10.1177/08944865231152283

Lyle, M. C. B., Walsh, I. J., & Coraiola, D. M. (2022). What is NORML? Sedimented meanings in ambiguous organizational identities. *Organization Studies, 43*(12), 1991–2012. https://doi.org/10.1177/01708406211057725

Maclean, M., Harvey, C., Golant, B. D., & Sillince, J. A. A. (2020). The role of innovation narratives in accomplishing organizational ambidexterity. *Strategic Organization, 19*(4), 693–721. https://doi.org/10.1177/1476127019897234

Maclean, M., Harvey, C., Sillince, J. A. A., & Golant, B. D. (2014). Living up to the past? Ideological sensemaking in organizational transition. *Organization, 21*(4), 543–567. https://doi.org/10.1177/1350508414527247

Maclean, M., Harvey, C., Sillince, J. A. A., & Golant, B. D. (2018). Intertextuality, rhetorical history and the uses of the past in organizational transition. *Organization Studies, 39*(12), 1733–1755. https://doi.org/10.1177/0170840618789206

Makortoff, K. (2020, February 13). Barclays boss Jes Staley's links to Jeffrey Epstein investigated. *The Guardian*. https://amp.theguardian.com/us-news/2020/feb/13/barclays-boss-jes-staley-links-to-jeffrey-epstein-investigated

Makortoff, K. (2021, November 1). Barclays chief Jes Staley steps down after Epstein investigation. *The Guardian*. https://www.theguardian.com/business/2021/nov/01/barclays-jes-staley-steps-down-fca-investigation

Manelli, L., Magrelli, V., Kotlar, J., Messeni Petruzzelli, A., & Frattini, F. (2023). Building an outward-oriented social family legacy: Rhetorical history in family business foundations. *Family Business Review, 36*(1), 143–168. https://doi.org/10.1177/08944865231157195

Megaw, N. (2019, August 30). After PPI, what could be the next banking mis-selling scandal? *Financial Times*. https://www.ft.com/content/2abb8482-c9b3-11e9-a1f4-3669401ba76f

Mena, S., Rintamäki, J., Fleming, P., & Spicer, A. (2016). On the forgetting of corporate irresponsibility. *Academy of Management Review, 41*(4), 720–738. https://doi.org/10.5465/amr.2014.0208

Morris, S. (2021, November 1). Jes Staley's Barclays legacy shattered by Epstein links. *Financial Times*. https://www.ft.com/content/b96a25c2-a5e1-4d06-8278-ed1f703f2dfd

Nissley, N., & Casey, A. (2002). The politics of the exhibition: Viewing corporate museums through the paradigmatic lens of organizational memory. *British Journal of Management, 13*, 35–45. https://doi.org/10.1111/1467-8551.13.s2.4

Oertel, S., & Thommes, K. (2018). History as a source of organizational identity creation. *Organization Studies, 39*(12), 1709–1731. https://doi.org/10.1177/0170840618800112

Parker, M. (2002). Contesting histories: Unity and division in a building society. *Journal of Organizational Change Management, 15*(6), 589–605. https://doi.org/10.1108/09534810210449550

Parris, M. (2016, May 3). We're mad to turn our backs on vibrant Africa; Whitehall and the British political elite don't think the continent matters any more, which is a colossal misjudgment. *The Times*. https://advance.lexis.com/api/document?collection=news&id=urn:contentItem:5J7B-TFM1-JBVM-Y0MX-00000-00&context=1519360

Poor, S., Novicevic, M. M., Humphreys, J. H., & Popoola, I. T. (2016). Making history happen: A genealogical analysis of Colt's rhetorical history. *Management & Organizational History, 11*(2), 147–165. https://doi.org/10.1080/17449359.2016.1151361

Rowlinson, M., & Hassard, J. (1993). The invention of corporate culture: A history of the histories of Cadbury. *Human Relations, 46*(3), 299–326.

Rubin, H., & Rubin, I. (2005). *Qualitative interviewing: The art of hearing data* (2nd ed.). Sage. https://doi.org/10.4135/9781452226651

Ryan-Collins, J. (2015, October 7). Antony Jenkins' sacking from Barclays may be the death knell for banking reform; The ousting of Barclays' chief executive appears to send a clear message: Banks are back to business as usual and genuine reform is as far away as ever. *The Guardian*. https://advance.lexis.com/api/document?collection=news&id=urn:contentItem:5GD7-F4P1-F021-60FD-00000-00&context=1519360

Salz, A., & Collins, R. (2013). *Salz review: An independent review of Barclays' business practices*. Barclays Bank.

Seifried, C. S., Novicevic, M. M., & Poor, S. (2023). Forms of nostalgia in the rhetorical history of Jack Daniel's. *Journal of Management History*, *30*(3), 409–432. https://doi.org/10.1108/JMH-04-2023-0029

Shubber, K. (2017, April 10). Jes Staley, Barclays' rogue CEO. *Financial Times*. https://www.ft.com/content/6fc1c914-b684-31c9-98ac-9ea9807cabde

Smith, A., & Russell, J. (2016). Toward polyphonic constitutive historicism: A new research agenda for management historians. *Management & Organizational History*, *11*(2), 236–251. https://doi.org/10.1080/17449359.2015.1115742

Smith, A., & Simeone, D. (2017). Learning to use the past: The development of a rhetorical history strategy by the London headquarters of the Hudson's Bay Company. *Management & Organizational History*, *12*(4), 334–356. https://doi.org/10.1080/17449359.2017.1394199

Staley email to Barclays staff. (2017, April 10). *Financial Times*. https://www.ft.com/content/182c7d6c-1de9-11e7-a454-ab04428977f9

Suddaby, R., Foster, W. M., & Trank, C. Q. (2010). Rhetorical history as a source of competitive advantage. In B. J. A. C. & L. Joseph (Eds.), *The globalization of strategy research* (Vol. 27, pp. 147–173). Emerald. https://doi.org/10.1108/S0742-3322(2010)0000027009

Sydow, J., Schreyögg, G., & Koch, J. (2009). Organizational path dependence: Opening the black box. *AMRO*, *34*(4), 689–709.

Tooze, A. (2018). *Crashed: How a decade of financial crises changed the world*. Penguin.

U.S. Commodity Futures Trading Commission. (2012, June 27). CFTC orders Barclays to pay $200 million penalty for attempted manipulation of and false reporting concerning LIBOR and Euribor benchmark interest rates. https://www.cftc.gov/PressRoom/PressReleases/6289-12

Wadhwani, R. D., Suddaby, R., Mordhorst, M., & Popp, A. (2018). History as organizing: Uses of the past in organization studies. *Organization Studies*, *39*(12), 1663–1683. https://doi.org/10.1177/0170840618814867

Walvin, J. (1997). *The Quakers: Money and morals*. John Murray.

Walvin, J. (2014). The slave trade, Quakers, and the early days of British abolition. In B. Carey & G. G. Plank (Eds.), *Quakers and abolition* (pp. 166–179). University of Illinois Press.

Wilson, H. (2017, November 4). Curse of the super (and not so super) Barclays men. *The Times*. https://advance.lexis.com/api/document?collection=news&id=urn:contentItem:5NDN-NKJ1-DY9P-N41J-00000-00&context=1519360

Ybema, S. (2014). The invention of transitions: History as a symbolic site for discursive struggles over organizational change. *Organization*, *21*(4), 495–513. https://doi.org/10.1177/1350508414527255

Zundel, M., Holt, R., & Popp, A. (2016). Using history in the creation of organizational identity. *Management & Organizational History*, *11*(2), 211–235. https://doi.org/10.1080/17449359.2015.1124042

Pamela A. Popielarz
Chapter 10
Obstacles to change in racialized organizations: Imprinting, memory, and legacy

Recently in the United States, calls for change in police agencies have been particularly urgent.[1] The deaths of George Floyd, Breonna Taylor, and many other Black people during encounters with police have fed an ongoing "national movement against police brutality and daily police killings of unarmed African Americans" (Taylor, 2016, p. 2). Calls for action range from reforming police agencies to defunding or abolishing them.

One conventional approach to reform is to push for more racially diverse police agencies. This assumes that agencies whose officers reflect the demographics of the local community enjoy more legitimacy (Theobald & Haider-Markel, 2009). Instead, many agencies are significantly more White (and male, high-income, and Republican) than the communities they serve (Ba et al., 2024). Compared to these communities, police officers' attitudes are also "more racist, a pattern especially apparent among white male officers" (Roscigno & Prieto-Hodge, 2021, p. 1). Yet officer behavior, including use of deadly force, does not differ strongly by race (Prieto-Hodge & Tomaskovic-Devey, 2021). This calls into question whether increasing racial diversity in police agencies would in fact reduce violence. In other words, *who* the police are, in terms of racial identity, may not be as important as *how* they operate.

Other responses to police violence, including more radical calls for defunding or abolishing the police, cite how policing developed throughout American history and its underlying assumptions and practices (Akbar, 2020; Clarno et al., 2024). Indeed, the very name of the police abolition movement recalls a history of policing that included antebellum patrols to enforce slave codes. In the decades after the Civil War, police enforced laws that "criminalized every form of African American freedom and mobility, political power, economic power, except . . . the right to work for a white man on a white man's terms" (Abdelfatah & Arablouei, 2020). The abolition movement's objection is to the police as an institution, and thus *what* policing is and *how* it is practiced, not just *who* carries it out.

---

[1] Policing in the United States operates through layers of agencies, from local police departments in towns and cities to state and national law enforcement agencies. It also includes specialized police agencies associated with, for example, public universities, public transportation, and public housing. The author gratefully acknowledges funding from the University of Illinois Chicago Institute for Research on Race & Public Policy.

Studying *how* policing is done, not just *who* does it, necessitates a combination of two approaches: (1) taking an organizational point of view on race and policing, and (2) considering the organizational legacies of the past for the present. In this chapter, I review and apply new theory about *how* race operates in organizations. I also extend this theory by putting it in conversation with literature on organizational imprinting, identity, and memory. I illustrate these contributions with a study of policing in the United States, focusing on the Fraternal Order of Police (FOP).

Racialized organizations

In the past, organization studies generally assumed that race was relevant only with respect to *who* belonged to an organization, rather than being encoded into *how* it operated. But recently American sociologists answered a decades-old call to theorize race and organizations in a meaningful way (Nkomo, 1992). The concept of racialized organizations (Ray, 2019; Wooten & Couloute, 2017) paves the way for a parallel to the long-established literature on gendered organizations (Acker, 1990). Racialized organizations foster an unequal distribution of resources across racial groups, constrain the agency of people of color, treat Whiteness as a credential, and decouple formal and informal structures in ways that reinforce racial inequality (Ray, 2019).

Racialized organizations are an important component of the racialized social system (Bonilla-Silva, 2021). Under this approach, racism is not just a result of individual attitudes or behaviors, it is not a static remnant of the past, and it can be colorblind rather than overt. Colorblind racism leans heavily on abstract liberal reasoning that stresses individual choices in a context of meritocratic equal opportunity. It naturalizes segregation and is usually embedded in processes that lack explicitly racial terminology, making it invisible to most White people.

One conceptualization of racialized organizations argues that race is a property operating at the organizational level as a racialized identity (Wooten, 2006, 2019). Obvious examples include organizations with race as part of their strategic orientation, such as those pursuing blatantly White supremacist agendas, or Black-identified organizations such as historically Black colleges and universities (Wooten & Couloute, 2017). Less obvious yet more plentiful examples include organizations that are colorblind, in the sense described above, yet operate on a fundamentally White logic (Couloute, 2019; Popielarz, 2025; Ray & Purifoy, 2019).

Another prominent conceptualization of racialized organizations describes them as having racialized schemas built into their structures and practices (Ray, 2019). Schemas are "generalizable, often unconscious, cognitive 'default assumptions' (DiMaggio 1997:269) acting as situationally applicable templates for social action" (Ray, 2019, p. 31). In other words, racialized schemas are basic cognitive rules about *who* can legitimately operate *how*. In the United States, they generally privilege Whiteness and/or operationalize anti-Blackness (Jung & Costa Vargas, 2021). For instance, racialized schemas induce many White people to fail to recognize, or even to deny, the professional status of Black doctors, lawyers, professors, and engineers (Wingfield, 2023).

Racialized organizations theory conceives of all organizations as being racialized. What varies across organizations is how racialized identities and schemas are built into their structures and practices. In the next two sections, I frame my contributions to racialized organizations theory, based on considering how imprinting and memory shape racialized identities and schemas in organizations. Each leaves a legacy that can be an obstacle to change.

Legacies of imprinting in racialized organizations

An important but undertheorized aspect of racialized organizations is their history and its legacy for the present (Ray et al., 2023). I use the concept of imprinting to flesh out this connection (Stinchcombe, 1965). Imprinting is the process by which "organizations in any historical conjuncture take on elements of their founding contexts, elements that may be an important consequence for their later trajectories" (Johnson, 2008, pp. 113–114). I am concerned with two aspects of imprinting.

First, imprinting can shape the identity of an organization, which contains shared constructions of its traits (Casey, 2019; Hatch & Schultz, 2002). In many organizations, a White organizational identity is normalized or taken for granted (Macalpine & Marsh, 2005). This often occurs because organizations are imprinted with "non-explicit White-racialized values, norms and traditions" (Ray & Purifoy, 2019, p. 132). These render the organization's identity White, but colorblind.

Second, structures and practices that are taken for granted during an organization's founding period are imprinted onto it (Johnson, 2008; Stinchcombe, 1965). These carry racialized schemas, meaning that the organization is imprinted with the conceptions of racial hierarchy that prevailed during its founding period (Popielarz, 2025).

Identities and schemas imprinted onto organizations leave legacies (Lamertz et al., 2016). Invoking legacy "nudges both management scholars and historians to understanding how elements of history—individual, organizational, or local geographical history—can be used to explain stability in a world that tends toward entropy and change" (Suddaby, 2016, p. 57). Specifically, racialized identities and schemas imprinted onto organizations reproduce over time, leaving legacies of past racial inequality within today's organizations (Garbes, 2022). Legacies pose a serious, but often hidden, hindrance to organizational change. They also explain how racial inequality is systemic and seems intractable or invisible, especially to White people.

Legacies of memory practices in racialized organizations

Another fruitful addition to racialized organizations theory is to put it into conversation with the literature on collective memory in organizations. Linking memory to racial inequality makes sense because in many organizations, collective memory and forgetting are exercises in "the reproduction of extant power relations" (Foroughi et al., 2020, p. 1735; Casey & Olivera, 2011). Collective memory can also silence the memories of less powerful groups of people (Foroughi & Al-Amoudi, 2020). I am particularly interested in two memory practices: *remembering*, which refers to "practices used to preserve the integrity of the past against the inexorable force of forgetting," and *historicizing*, which is "strategically used to advance the goals of the organization in the present by providing an authoritative version of the past" (Coraiola et al., 2023, pp. 379, 381). I highlight two impacts of collective memory practices in racialized organizations.

First, memory practices reinforce an organization's identity through identity stewardship (Ravasi et al., 2019), thus preserving a racialized identity even if it is a legacy from the past. Specifically, I argue that memory practices can effectively naturalize or rationalize colorblind Whiteness in racialized organizations, even those that became more racially diverse in the post–Civil Rights era in the United States.

Second, memory processes reinforce the racialized schemas operating within an organization, including those that are legacies from the past, by valorizing practices that support those schemas. In other words, memory practices perpetuate basic, taken-for-granted cognitive rules about *who*, in terms of race, should be treated *how*. This is one mechanism by which racial power hierarchies of the past are reproduced in the present.

Note that this application of theory about memory in organizations helps to explain the difficulty of change in many organizations and again illustrates the systemic nature of racial inequality.

Race and policing in the United States

Racialized organizations theory has been used to study several types of organizations, from universities to churches to strip clubs (Diefendorf & Pascoe, 2023; Hamilton & Nielsen, 2021; Lerma et al., 2020; Silva et al., 2022). Government agencies have also received scrutiny, including police agencies (Prieto-Hodge & Tomaskovic-Devey, 2021; Ray et al., 2023). In the words of Victor Ray and his coauthors (2018):

> We have argued that police departments should be thought of as "racialized organizations" whose operation both reflect and reinforce widely held schemas about the proper place of people of color within organizations. . . . We hope to reframe studies of policing away from the notion

that racial inequality is the result of a few bad actors, towards an understanding of race as being inextricably intertwined with the act, and organization, of policing itself. (p. 27)

This point of view is helpful in the context of understanding continued police violence against community members, particularly Black people, and the resulting calls to change U.S. police agencies, whether their aim is cosmetic or existential change.

In this chapter, I apply racialized organizations theory at one remove from police agencies themselves. I argue that many employing organizations, such as police agencies, overlap in membership with voluntary associations that are less in the public eye. These include professional associations, labor unions, and private clubs. The racialization of such a voluntary association may continually replenish the racialization of an overlapping employing organization. Thus, efforts to change an employing organization face not only *its* racialized identity and schemas, but also those of any overlapping voluntary associations. Note that voluntary associations are often seen as carriers of positive legacies. I counter this by allowing for negative legacies, specifically in terms of perpetuating the racialized social system.

To recap my argument thus far: One reason why organizations find it difficult to change is their racialized nature. All organizations are racialized, but in varying ways. Elements of racialization include schemas and identity. They are imprinted onto organizations during their early history and sustained through memory practices, leaving legacies for the future. Furthermore, when an employing organization overlaps significantly in membership with a voluntary association, the racialization of the latter may bolster that of the former.

One difficulty of reforming U.S. police agencies is their racialized nature and that of their overlapping professional associations and labor unions. American police departments were first created in Northeastern cities several decades before the Civil War. The first police associations came later in the century, including the New York City Patrolmen's Benevolent Association in 1892 (Hardaway, 2022). But true labor unions were slow to develop among police officers. Although, like other workers, police officers were intensely interested in improving their labor conditions, unions were not a popular solution. Police unions were also not popular with the public, and less so after the Boston police strike of 1919. In addition, police have always had an extremely troubled relationship with the labor movement because they are frequently deployed against striking workers (Rad et al., 2023). After decades of legal barriers and deep unpopularity, police unionism took off in the 1960s and 1970s.

The Fraternal Order of Police

I specifically focus on the FOP, an association founded by two patrol officers in 1915 in Pittsburgh, Pennsylvania. The FOP grew to a nationwide stature and is today the largest police association in the United States. As the name suggests, it was organized as a ritual brotherhood for police officers, a fraternal order with local lodges federated under a national organization (Schmidt, 1980). Fraternal orders were fantastically popular in the United States between the Civil War and World War I. As I argue below, the FOP was imprinted with many characteristics of this organizational form, including its close association with Whiteness (Popielarz, 2018, 2025).

Today, the FOP is a hybrid voluntary association. It retains some traits of a fraternal order, but primarily functions as a professional association for sworn officers from a multitude of police agencies. Although it serves as a labor union in some parts of the United States, there are also lodges in states where police have no collective bargaining rights. Police officers are also represented by non-FOP police unions in a few jurisdictions (Rad et al., 2023). The FOP is thus "both a public-sector union and a conservative, mass-membership fraternal association" (Zoorob, 2019, p. 243). The FOP currently has over 350,000 members in 2,000 active local lodges. Its impact is wide-reaching, including in politics, where it has been linked to Donald Trump's 2016 election and the White supremacist beliefs of many of his supporters (Zoorob & Skocpol, 2020).

Sources on the FOP

I critically analyzed sources published by and for the FOP to understand how this voluntary association is racialized and thus how it might shore up the racialization of the police agencies with which it overlaps. Because I added considerations of imprinting and memory to racialized organizations theory, I engaged with sources from different points in time during the lifespan of the FOP. Studying imprinting necessitated social documents that were as unfiltered and contemporaneous with the FOP's founding as possible. These allowed me to construct a story going forward in time about the imprinting of racialized identity and schemas onto it. On the other hand, the ideal sources for studying collective organizational memory were explicitly retrospective narratives from multiple points in time after the FOP's founding.

I relied on three sources. The first was an original copy of the ritual used to initiate new members into the order (FOP, 1918). The second was a history of the order published privately in 1977 and reprinted in 2001 (Walsh, 1977).[2] This book was researched and written by a historian employed by the publisher, who was a friend of the president of the FOP Grand Lodge. I focused on the book's first six chapters, which covered the FOP's founding and early years. In these chapters, the author included some quotes from founding-era FOP records, with the rest being his own summary of the organization's history from his vantage point in the 1970s. I also focused on the book's front matter. The original 1977 publication included a foreword by the Grand Lodge president, a

---

2 I bought these two rare books from a used book website.

publisher's foreword, a preface by the FOP's national counsel, and an introduction by the Grand Lodge president. The 2001 reprint also included a foreword by that era's Grand Lodge president. The third source was the *FOP Journal*, which I accessed through the FOP's online archive (https://www.fopconnect.com/fop-journal/past-issues/). The archive included quarterly issues from Winter 2011 through Winter 2020, and monthly issues from January 2021 through March 2024. I focused on the FOP's portrayals of its history, particularly in the following columns: President's Message, Vice President's Message, Sergeant-at-Arms' Message, and History Committee.

My basic analytic strategy was to assess founding-era passages in the ritual and the history for evidence of imprinting and to search for memory practices in the history and the journal. I combined modes of inquiry, specifically historical organization studies and historical organizational memory (Decker et al., 2021). In doing so, I attempted to achieve dual integrity in organization studies and history (Decker et al., 2018).

Below, I show how imprinting and memory molded first the racialized identity of the FOP and then one of its prominent racialized schemas.

The racialized identity of the FOP

The racialized identity of the FOP can be characterized as colorblind, but normatively White. That is to say, the organization does not explicitly identify as White, but initially its normal operations maintained a White membership and even now its default point of view is European and White. I should note that this is true of a multitude of organizations in the United States. To explain how this identity was imprinted onto the FOP and maintained through its habits of memory, the discussion below also briefly covers some of the important historical factors that framed both processes.

Imprinting in the 1910s

Key historical factors operating when the FOP was founded in 1915 included the Great Migration of Black Americans, industrial labor strife, scientific racism, World War I, immigration to the United States, and its nativist backlash. The Great Migration began during the 1910s, as Black Americans started leaving Southern states for the North after the failure of Reconstruction. Although they still faced Jim Crow racism, the North promised jobs. The growing steel industry in Pittsburgh helped to boost the Black population from 4.8% in 1910 to 6.4% a decade later (Trotter, 2020, p. 3). Black workers' entry into industrial work was contentious because mill owners frequently used them as replacements for striking White workers. The Homestead Strike of 1892, a pivotal event in U.S. labor history that occurred just outside of Pittsburgh, was still a fresh memory for many workers. This labor dynamic, combined with scientific racism's pernicious claim that Black people were innately predisposed to criminality, justified anti-Black racial violence, including lynching, throughout the period (Muhammad, 2019). Although the United States did not enter World War I until 3 years after it started in 1914, the decade of the 1910s was rife with patriotic rally 'round the flag rhetoric in the United States. This was a cultural and political boundary–defending exercise by White nativists incensed by high levels of immigration from Europe and other parts of the world. Entering the war did nothing to dampen the sense of a stark boundary separating patriotic (White) Americans from their dangerous enemies.

One more historical factor was crucial: the huge popularity of clubs and voluntary organizations between the Civil War and World War I, including fraternal orders that catered to men. Fraternal orders are characterized by invitation-only membership, exclusion of women, and an emphasis on moral improvement, esoteric ritual, and constitutional rule. The fraternal form long predated the FOP's founding. It drew from the rationalism of the Enlightenment and arguably echoed the social organization of medieval European guilds and Christian monastic and military orders (Kieser, 1998). Thus, the historical roots of the fraternal form lie among men of European origin—whom today we would generally call White. In the late 19th and early 20th centuries, American men adapted the fraternal form to a great variety of purposes, including organizing within occupations (Schmidt, 1980). The FOP is one example.

The original 1915 Constitution of the FOP stated that it was formed "for the purpose of bettering existing condition of Policemen" [sic] and "for advancing Social, Benevolent and Educational undertakings among Policemen" (Walsh, 1977, p. 27). Regarding membership in the FOP, the Constitution stipulated that "all Policemen are eligible for membership" and "Race, Creed or Color shall be no bar" (Walsh, 1977, p. 27). The 1915 articles of incorporation granted in Pennsylvania further provided, "The membership of said corporation shall be limited to males, of the full age of 21 years, of good moral character and repute" (Walsh, 1977, p. 37).[3] The 1918 Ritual of the FOP revealed that after passing scrutiny for moral character, a new member's candidacy was voted on by all members using a blackball procedure, where a single 'no' vote meant rejection (FOP, 1918, pp. 4–5).

From this evidence, it appears that at its founding in 1915, the FOP was formally open to membership by any male police officer, regardless of race. But several factors temper this apparent liberality: it was decades before Pittsburgh's police force included any Black officers, and the FOP was founded by White (mostly Irish) men. In addition, like most fraternal orders, the FOP's traditional membership procedures (nomination by current members, the blackball vote) effectively limited membership to men like the founders, in a way that seemed quite natural (Popielarz, 2025). These two factors are hallmarks of colorblindness: the abstract liberalism of "Race, Creed or Color shall be no bar" (Walsh, 1977, p. 27) and the seemingly natural racial segregation

---

3 Later revisions lowered the age of membership to 18 and did away with the male requirement.

that followed from relying on current members' networks to supply new members. Both were imprinted onto the FOP when its founders chose the fraternal form that was so exceedingly popular at the time. The early FOP was also normatively White because the normal practice of its various traditions made deviations from Whiteness extremely unlikely.

Memory in the 1970s

By the time the FOP's history was published in 1977, the historical context was very different, and the FOP membership was no longer all White. The 1970s was a reactionary period for police and the FOP. Just as the police had been used in an earlier era to curb the efforts of striking workers, by the mid 20th century they were also often called on to stymie even legal, peaceful efforts to change the racial status quo. They had faced decades of opposition from the civil rights movement and, more recently, from the Black power movement (Rad et al., 2023). The violence that often resulted led to widespread protests about police brutality and calls for civilian oversight of the police. Work conditions for police officers had changed in other ways, too, because of the *Miranda* and other Supreme Court decisions, which clarified the rights of accused persons and further standardized police procedure.

Within this context, how did the FOP remember its origins and the origins of policing, and what did these memory practices convey about the organization's identity? The answer involves the memory practice called historicizing (Coraiola et al., 2023), or strategically constructing a narrative. The author of the FOP history confirmed the colorblind White identity of American policing without using explicitly racial terminology, but by invoking popular conceptions of the ancient European roots of civilization and the 19th century British origin of policing. Thus, "a policeman in the tradition of Western Civilization is a citizen who guards the city and thereby makes possible the process of civilized life" (Walsh, 1977, p. 4). America's first police departments were remembered as originating in the mid 19th century because of hindrances to civilized life, including "older Americans' fear of newly arrived immigrants" and "increasing racial tensions growing out of the agitation over slavery" (Walsh, 1977, p. 8). From this, "the result was clear—American cities were becoming ungovernable without disciplined local police power" (Walsh, 1977, p. 8). The author cemented the White racialized identity of the FOP by invoking Sir Robert Peele—founder of the London Police, sometimes described as the father of modern policing—concluding that "quite clearly, the Fraternal Order of Police, [is] an American organization of policemen developing out of the Anglo-American tradition of limited power and individual liberty" (Walsh, 1977, p. 6). Thus, the 1977 history of the FOP stewarded its colorblind and normative White identity, despite the fact that it was no longer an all-White organization.

Memory in the 21st century

Recent issues of the *FOP Journal* contended with a historical context of disagreement and distrust, including deep political polarization around the presidential elections of 2016 and 2020, the beginning of the coronavirus pandemic in 2020, and the January 6, 2021, attack on the U.S. Capitol. That attack resulted in law enforcement deaths, yet the FOP's reaction was uncharacteristically muted (Serwer, 2021). But the FOP has been far from silent about the Black Lives Matter (BLM) movement, which arose in 2013 to protest lethal police violence against unarmed Black people. BLM continued to garner police opposition after subsequent deaths, protests, and calls for civilian oversight of police or outright abolition. Social media mobilized and inflamed public discourse by spreading (dis)information, images, and videos.

Again, within this context, what did the FOP remember about its past and how did its memory practices portray the organization's identity? Through cursory recognition of Black achievements in policing and the FOP, the *Journal* avoided discussing why they occurred so late in the organization's history. In contrast, the *Journal*'s relatively lavish depictions of its own history remembered the lives and accomplishments of White men.

On the eve of its centennial in 2015, the *FOP Journal*'s pictorial timeline of the organization's history included the following item: "September 2004: Frank Gale is the first African-American to be elected to the National Executive Board" (*FOP Journal*, November 2014, p. 16). Several years later, the *FOP Journal* first mentioned Black History Month in its February 2022 issue. A half-page of text noted "the accomplishments and sacrifices that Black officers have made through the years" (*FOP Journal*, February 2022, p. 26). The article's bullet-point list began by highlighting the first Black police officers in the late 1860s, without explaining that this was during the short-lived period of Reconstruction. The list ended by noting that the first Black police commissioner was appointed in 1988—thereby seeming to imply that nothing of note occurred since 1988. In 2023, the *FOP Journal* did not mention Black History Month, but the February 2024 issue included a two-paragraph article (not listed in the table of contents) under the headline "FOP Celebrates Black History Month." It announced that recently, "the FOP proudly welcomed the first Black woman National trustee" (*FOP Journal*, February 2024, p. 19). In each case, the *FOP Journal* signaled the organization's colorblind White identity. Specifically, focusing on 'firsts' without problematizing the systemic barriers they faced left the impression that organizational leadership was a meritocracy in which Black people had previously failed to measure up.

In contrast, a semi-regular column by the History Committee provided a glimpse of what the FOP regarded as important in its own history. These articles also conveyed a normative White identity. Generally, they commemorated the deaths of high-ranking members, celebrated milestones by long-serving members, or featured visits to well-known lodges, such as Philadelphia #5 and Chicago #7. The January 2024 column was a five-page pictorial spread remembering the National Police Softball Tournament, held annually between 1974 and 2012 (*FOP Journal*, January 2024, pp. 33–37). Given these articles' emphasis on older members and events, they focused on White men. But, juxtaposing them with the list of 'firsts' mentioned above reveals that the accomplishments of those Black pioneers figured very little in the FOP's sense of its own history. Although the FOP congratulated itself for no longer being all White, its memory practices of commemorating, preserving, and reminiscing telegraphed a White identity (Coraiola et al., 2023).

Racialized schema in the FOP

Scholars and observers of American policing recognize a prominent schema among American police, which might be summarized as 'it's us versus them and they are a danger to us.' One version poses a sharp distinction between police/civilization and criminals/barbarism. Another version draws a tighter circle around the police and those who empathize with, understand, and actively support them, in contrast to everyone else (Fox, 2023; Sierra-Arévalo, 2021). In both cases, police face a dangerous opponent whose threat is not just symbolic or economic but physical and existential (Prieto-Hodge & Tomaskovic-Devey, 2021). Put succinctly, in police academy training, recruits learn that "'everybody wants to murder you' and 'if you do not heed your training and plan for violence, you're gonna die'" (Sierra-Arévalo, 2019, p. 82). These messages are transmitted through training, 'war stories' from senior officers, and symbols and artifacts like memorial walls and tattoos (Sierra-Arévalo, 2019). Under this schema, police must be hyperaware of threats and ready to react immediately with violence if necessary. In this section, I show how this schema was imprinted onto the FOP at its founding, trace its legacy through the FOP's memory practices, and argue that although colorblind, this schema is racialized and became more pointedly so over time.

Imprinting in the 1910s

The 1918 Ritual of the FOP welcomed newly sworn-in members with instructions that echoed the 'us versus them' schema by using the racially loaded language of civilization and barbarism. One part of the initiation ritual explained the FOP's emblem. Among other symbols, it contained "the eye of vigilance, the ever watchful eye, which notes the danger, and offers protection to the public, asleep or awake" (FOP, 1918, p. 9). The all-seeing eye is a very popular symbol, but this is an odd reversal of its usual meaning. Normally, the eye is meant to remind a person that *they are being watched* by a higher power and thus should behave in a moral way. In the FOP's interpretation, the eye reminds its members that *they are the eye*, watching godlike for a menacing enemy.

Moreover, in explaining the FOP's Latin motto 'Jus, Fidus, Libertatum,'[4] members were told:

> Justice, my friends, is one of the greatest necessities of our Country, for without Justice our Country would no doubt be over-ridden with lawless men and eventually become barbarous. It is therefore the defenders of Justice we must thank for the state of civilization existing today. (FOP, 1918, p. 9)

I argue that among other messages, this speech bears an imprint of anti-Blackness in the coded language of the time. The equation of Blackness with barbarism had long been employed to justify slavery (Kendi, 2016). After slavery ended, scientific racism stepped up to claim a statistical link between Blackness and criminality (Muhammad, 2019).

Memory in the 1970s

The schema of 'it's us versus them' also appeared in the 1977 history of the FOP. Like the ritual, the Preface to this book mentioned the opposition between civilization and barbarism. But the author also remembered recent history with alarm and disgust. He cited grievances under a thin veil of racially neutral language that nonetheless conveyed White resentment in the face of Black civil rights advancements and fear over the advent of the Black power movement.

The Preface proclaimed that despite being "the first line of defense in the preservation of civilization," the police were "under assault from every quarter" and subject to both a "civil rights assault" and "false charges of brutality and violations of civil rights" (Walsh, 1977, p. ix). The federal government was also cited as an opponent. The author leveled criticism at the Civil Rights Division of the U.S. Justice Department because it seemed "determined to destroy law enforcement while giving free reign to criminals" and made police "the prime target of groups who operate through poverty and welfare programs" (Walsh, 1977, p. x). The author concluded that "the individual officer's only defense is through the collective defense available through a Brotherhood such as the Fraternal Order of Police" (Walsh, 1977, p. x). Thus, the FOP was posed as protecting police from their potent—and violent—enemies. These enemies included criminals but also the civil rights movement and poverty and welfare programs, all empowered by a co-opted federal government. In the context of the 1970s, even without explicitly mentioning race, this schema pointed to Black people and Black-identified social movements.

---

4 FOP founder Delbert Nagle coined this motto, thinking it meant "Fairness, Justice, Equality." In fact, it is nearly untranslatable, but was later rendered as "Law is a Safeguard of Freedom" (Walsh, 1977, pp. 18, 20).

Memory in the 21st century

A January 2021 column in the *FOP Journal* by the national sergeant-at-arms conveyed more 'it's us versus them' sentiment about the police standing alone against a dangerous existential threat. The column bid "good riddance to 2020!" (*FOP Journal*, January 2021, p. 16). Indeed, many Americans were grateful for 2020 to end, with its contentious pandemic lockdown and presidential election, but the columnist's overriding memory pointed instead to the protests that erupted in the wake of George Floyd's murder by police in Minneapolis. As the columnist observed to the *Journal*'s readers, "We all feel rather betrayed by some of the communities we serve who need us the most" (*FOP Journal*, January 2021, p. 16). The latter phrase appeared frequently in the *FOP Journal* and referred to Black communities, which accounted for some but not all the protests. He went on to explain, "I am not trying to diminish the violence that we are currently experiencing, but rather to understand it better so that we all may deal with it better and be better prepared to face the dangers that lurk" (*FOP Journal*, January 2021, p. 16). Here, events of 2020 were remembered as violence and danger emanating from Black communities and threatening police officers, not vice versa.

Two and a half years later, an August 2023 column by the national vice president did away with the FOP's usual colorblind rhetoric and specifically named BLM as the opposing force in the 'us vs. them' schema. The column remembered and celebrated FOP leaders' actions against BLM, which "call[ed] them out for their harmful, hateful and threatening rhetoric. We called them out for the damage they have done to our profession, our communities and our country" (*FOP Journal*, August 2023, p. 12). Thus, across the three periods I studied, the FOP maintained a pugnacious stance against its perceived enemies. In this racialized schema, the FOP consistently remembered itself as defending against barbarous threats to civilization and as the victim of Black-identified social movements, from civil rights to Black power to BLM.

Conclusion

Organizations are not racially neutral structures; they are all racialized in some way. Here I have demonstrated how FOP carried a racialized identity, which can generally be characterized as colorblind but normatively White, and a racialized schema, which I labeled 'it's us vs. them and they are a danger to us.' As I showed, these were imprinted onto the FOP at its founding. The popular fraternal form shaped the FOP's identity by endowing it with a colorblind approach to membership—formally open, but informally preserving a White membership. Early 20th century thinking about race imbued the FOP with a schema that posed Blackness as an innately criminal threat to the civilized society that police alone could protect. I further showed that collective memories in the FOP kept both this identity and this schema alive through the 1970s and to the present day. This legacy from over a century ago is not unique, but it is consequential.

Like any organization, racialization in the FOP is not just a matter of *who* belongs to it, but also *how* it operates. Both would be difficult to change. In the words of one observer,

> Even as law enforcement has become more racially diverse, the FOP seems committed to putting white men in charge. Those leaders consistently take stances against the safety and rights of black Americans. As a result, the organization serves as a union cum fraternity for white cops and has a retrograde effect on policing, especially related to civil rights. (Butler, 2017)

As I argued here, racialization in the FOP can replenish the racialized nature of the police agencies its members work in. This hampers police reform and prolongs the negative consequences of police violence (Sewell, 2017).

This study raises several possible topics for future research on police organizations and race. One possibility is police associations that might be racialized differently. Researchers could study Black police associations, such as the National Association of Black Law Enforcement Officers (NABLEO) and others, to see whether they reproduce Whiteness in policing or possibly offer avenues for change in police agencies. Another focus of study could be other more radical organizations that overlap with police agencies, such as the Oath Keepers (Mihalopoulos & Schuba, 2024).

Overall, this chapter applied and extended the theory of racialized organizations by joining it with established organizational research on imprinting, memory, and legacy. The result is an illustration of systemic racism, in which White supremacy escapes the bounds of ideology or individual attitudes to become durably installed in organizations that are racialized not just in terms of *who* belongs to them, but in *how* they operate. These legacies make change difficult, not just by restricting imagined alternatives, but by enabling subtle, taken-for-granted exercises of hegemonic power.

References

Abdelfatah, R., & Arablouei, R. (2020, June 4). American police. *NPR Throughline*. https://www.npr.org/transcripts/869046127

Acker, J. (1990). Hierarchies, jobs, bodies: A theory of gendered organizations. *Gender & Society*, 4(2), 139–158. https://doi.org/10.1177/089124390004002002

Akbar, A. A. (2020). An abolitionist horizon for (police) reform. *California Law Journal*, 108(6), 1781–1846. https://ssrn.com/abstract=3670952

Ba, B., Ge, H., Kaplan, J., Knox, D., Komisarchik, M., Lanzalotto, G., Mariman, R., Mummolo, J., Rivera, R., & Torres, M. (2024). *Political diversity in U.S. police agencies*. Working Paper, Princeton University.

Bonilla-Silva, E. (2021). What makes racism systemic? *Sociological Inquiry*, 91(3), 513–533. https://doi.org/10.1111/soin.12420

Butler, P. (2017, October 11). Why the Fraternal Order of Police must go. *The Marshall Project*. https://www.themarshallproject.org/2017/10/11/why-the-fraternal-order-of-police-must-go

Casey, A. J. (2019). *Organizational identity and memory: A multidisciplinary approach*. Routledge. https://doi.org/10.4324/9781315669786

Casey, A. J., & Olivera, F. (2011). Reflections on organizational memory and forgetting. *Journal of Management Inquiry*, 20(3), 305–310. https://doi.org/10.1177/1056492611408264

Clarno, A., Alvear Moreno, E., Bonsu-Love, J., Dana, L., De Anda Muñiz, M., Ravichandran, I., & Volpintesta, H. (2024). *Imperial policing: Weaponized data in carceral Chicago*. University of Minnesota Press.

Coraiola, D. M., Foster, W. M., Mena, S., Foroughi, H., & Rintamäki, J. (2023). Ecologies of memories: Memory work within and between organizations and communities. *The Academy of Management Annals*, 17(1), 373–404. https://doi.org/10.5465/annals.2021.0088

Couloute, L. (2019). Organizing reentry: How race structures the post-imprisonment terrain. In M. E. Wooten (Ed.), *Race, organizations, and the organizing process* (Research in the Sociology of Organizations Vol. 60, pp. 89–109). Emerald. https://doi.org/10.1108/S0733-558X20190000060006

Decker, S., Hassard, J., & Rowlinson, M. (2021). Rethinking history and memory in organization studies: The case for historiographical reflexivity. *Human Relations*, 74(8), 1123–1155. https://doi.org/10.1177/0018726720927443

Decker, S., Üsdiken, B., Engwall, L., & Rowlinson, M. (2018). Special issue introduction: Historical research on institutional change. *Business History*, 60(5), 613–627. https://doi.org/10.1080/00076791.2018.1427736

Diefendorf, S., & Pascoe, C. J. (2023). In the name of love: White organizations and racialized emotions. *Social Problems*, 20, 1–17. https://doi.org/10.1093/socpro/spad019

FOP Journal. Winter 2011 through March 2024. Archive available at https://www.fopconnect.com/fop-journal/past-issues/

Foroughi, H., & Al-Amoudi, I. (2020). Collective forgetting in a changing organization: When memories become unusable and uprooted. *Organization Studies*, 41(4), 449–470. https://doi.org/10.1177/0170840619830130

Foroughi, H., Coraiola, D. M., Rintamäki, J., Mena, S., & Foster, W. M. (2020). Organizational memory studies. *Organization Studies*, 41(12), 1725–1748. https://doi.org/10.1177/0170840620974338

Fox, A. (2025). Anti-Black and blue: Neighborhood identity and local racial ideologies in Chicago's police neighborhoods. *Social Problems*, 20, 1–19. https://doi.org/10.1093/socpro/spae076

Fraternal Order of Police. (1918). *Ritual of the Fraternal Order of Police*. Herald Printing Company.

Garbes, L. (2022). When the 'blank slate' is a White one: White institutional isomorphism in the birth of National Public Radio. *Sociology of Race and Ethnicity*, 8(1), 79–94. https://doi.org/10.1177/2332649221994619

Hamilton, L. T., & Nielsen, K. (2021). *Broke: The racial consequences of underfunding public universities*. University of Chicago Press. https://doi.org/10.7208/chicago/9780226747590.001.0001

Hardaway, A. B. (2022). Rise of police unions on the back of the Black Liberation Movement. *Connecticut Law Review*, 55(1), 179–238. https://digitalcommons.lib.uconn.edu/law_review/552

Hatch, M. J., & Schultz, M. (2002). The dynamics of organizational identity. *Human Relations*, 55(8), 989–1018. https://doi.org/10.1177/0018726702055008181

Johnson, V. (2008). *Backstage at the revolution: How the Royal Paris Opera survived the end of the Old Regime*. University of Chicago Press.

Jung, M., & Costa Vargas, J. H. (2021). *Antiblackness*. Duke University Press.

Kendi, I. X. (2016). *Stamped from the beginning: The definitive history of racist ideas in America*. Bold Type Books.

Kieser, A. (1998). From Freemasons to industrious patriots: Organizing and disciplining in 18th century Germany. *Organization Studies*, 19(1), 47–71. https://doi.org/10.1177/017084069801900103

Lamertz, K., Foster, W. M., Coraiola, D. M., & Kroezen, J. (2016). New identities from remnants of the past: An examination of the history of beer brewing in Ontario and the recent emergence of craft breweries. *Business History*, 58(5), 796–828. https://doi.org/10.1080/00076791.2015.1065819

Lerma, V., Hamilton, L. T., & Nielsen, K. (2020). Racialized equity labor, university appropriation and student resistance. *Social Problems*, *67*(2), 286–303. https://doi.org/10.1093/socpro/spz011

Macalpine, M., & Marsh, S. (2005). 'On being White: There's nothing I can say'—Exploring Whiteness and power in organizations. *Management Learning*, *36*(4), 429–450. https://doi.org/10.1177/1350507605058138

Mihalopoulos, D., & Schuba, T. (2024, January 11). UIC campus cop with extremist ties is banned from testifying in Cook County court cases. *Chicago Sun-Times*. https://chicago.suntimes.com/2024/1/11/24034535/oath-keepers-uic-police-banned-kim-foxx

Muhammad, K. G. (2019). *The condemnation of Blackness: Race, crime, and the making of modern urban America, with a new preface*. Harvard University Press. https://doi.org/10.4159/9780674240919

Nkomo, S. M. (1992). The emperor has no clothes: Rewriting 'race in organizations.' *Academy of Management Review*, *17*(3), 487–513. https://doi.org/10.2307/258720

Popielarz, P. A. (2018). Moral dividends: Freemasonry and finance capitalism in early-nineteenth-century America. *Business History*, *60*(5), 655–676. https://doi.org/10.1080/00076791.2016.1248946

Popielarz, P. A. (2025). *Order of business: The Golden Age of Fraternity and its legacy of inequality*. [Book manuscript under contract with University of North Carolina Press].

Prieto-Hodge, K., & Tomaskovic-Devey, D. (2021). A tale of force: Examining policy proposals to address police violence. *Social Currents*, *8*(5), 403–423. https://doi.org/10.1177/23294965211017903

Rad, A. N., Kirk, D. S., & Jones, W. P. (2023). Police unionism, accountability, and misconduct. *Annual Review of Criminology*, *6*, 181–203. https://doi.org/10.1146/annurev-criminol-030421-034244

Ravasi, D., Rindova, V., & Stigliani, I. (2019). The stuff of legend: History, memory, and the temporality of organizational identity construction. *Academy of Management Journal*, *62*(5), 1523–1555. https://doi.org/10.5465/amj.2016.0505

Ray, V. (2019). A theory of racialized organizations. *American Sociological Review*, *84*(1), 26–53. https://doi.org/10.1177/0003122418822335

Ray, V., Herd, P., & Moynihan, D. (2023). Racialized burdens: Applying racialized organization theory to the administrative state. *Journal of Public Administration: Research and Theory*, *33*(1), 139–152. https://doi.org/10.1093/jopart/muac001

Ray, V., Ortiz, K., & Nash, J. (2018). Who is policing the community? A comprehensive review of discrimination in police departments. *Sociology Compass*, *12*(1), e12539. https://doi.org/10.1111/soc4.12539

Ray, V., & Purifoy, D. (2019). The colorblind organization. In M. E. Wooten (Ed.), *Race, organizations, and the organizing process* (Research in the Sociology of Organizations Vol. 60, pp. 131–150). Emerald. https://doi.org/10.1108/S0733-558X20190000060008

Roscigno, V. J., & Prieto-Hodge, K. (2021). Racist cops, vested 'blue' interests, or both? Evidence from four decades of the General Social Survey. *Socius: Sociological Research for a Dynamic World*, *7*, 1–13. https://doi.org/10.1177/2378023120980913

Schmidt, A. J. (Ed.). (1980). *The Greenwood encyclopedia of American institutions: Fraternal organizations*. Greenwood Press.

Serwer, A. (2021, August 5). The Capitol rioters attacked police. Why isn't the FOP outraged? *The Atlantic*. https://www.theatlantic.com/ideas/archive/2021/08/blue-wall-silence/619612/

Sewell, A. A. (2017). The illness associations of police violence: Differential relationships by ethnoracial composition. *Sociological Forum*, *32*(Suppl 1), 975–997. https://doi.org/10.1111/socf.12361

Sierra-Arévalo, M. (2019). The commemoration of death, organizational memory, and police culture. *Criminology*, *57*(4), 632–658. https://doi.org/10.1111/1745-9125.12224

Sierra-Arévalo, M. (2021). American policing and the danger imperative. *Law & Society Review*, *55*(1), 70–103. https://doi.org/10.1111/lasr.12526

Silva, C., Newton-Francis, M., & Vidal-Ortiz, S. (2022). Negotiating racialized organizational spaces and intimacies: An ethnography of Playpen strip club. *Gender, Work and Organization*, *29*(6), 1831–1848. https://doi.org/10.1111/gwao.12882

Stinchcombe, A. L. (1965). Social structure and organizations. In J. G. March (Ed.), *Handbook of organizations* (pp. 142–193). Rand McNally.

Suddaby, R. (2016). Toward a historical consciousness: Following the historic turn in management thought. *M@n@gement*, *19*(1), 46–60. https://management-aims.com/index.php/mgmt/article/view/3897

Taylor, K.-Y. (2016). *From #BlackLivesMatter to Black liberation*. Haymarket Books.

Theobald, N. A., & Haider-Markel, D. P. (2009). Race, bureaucracy, and symbolic representation: Interactions between citizens and police. *Journal of Public Administration: Research and Theory*, *19*(2), 409–426. https://doi.org/10.1093/jopart/mun006

Trotter, J. W. (2020). *Pittsburgh and the Urban League movement: A century of social service and activism*. University of Kentucky Press.

Walsh, J. E. (1977). *The Fraternal Order of Police, 1915–1976: A history*. Joseph Munson Co.

Wingfield, A. H. (2023). *Gray areas: How the way we work perpetuates racism and what we can do to fix it*. HarperCollins Publishers.

Wooten, M. E. (2006). Soapbox: Editorial essays: Race and strategic organization. *Strategic Organization*, *4*(2), 191–199. https://doi.org/10.1177/1476127006064068

Wooten, M. E. (2019). Race, organizations and the organizing process. In M. E. Wooten (Ed.), *Race, organizations, and the organizing process* (Research in the Sociology of Organizations Vol. 60, pp. 1–14). Emerald. https://doi.org/10.1108/S0733-558X20190000060001

Wooten, M. E., & Couloute, L. (2017). The production of racial inequality within and among organizations. *Sociology Compass*, *11*(1), 1–17. https://doi.org/10.1111/soc4.12446

Zoorob, M. (2019). Blue endorsements matter: How the Fraternal Order of Police contributed to Donald Trump's victory. *PS, Political Science & Politics*, *52*(2), 243–250. https://doi.org/10.1017/S1049096518001841

Zoorob, M., & Skocpol, T. (2020). The overlooked organizational basis of Trump's 2016 victory. In T. Skocpol & C. Tervo (Eds.), *Upending American politics* (pp. 79–100). Oxford University Press. https://doi.org/10.1093/oso/9780190083526.003.0004

Hamid Foroughi, Andrea Casey, and Sonia Coman

Chapter 11
Conclusion: Legacy—New frontier in research and practice

The chapters in this book explore how legacies and imagined futures impact organizational identity and change. Legacies, both enabling and restricting, play a crucial role in organizational renewal, social change, and new forms of organizing. Tangible and intangible legacies provide authentication and legitimation yet often restrict imagined futures by enforcing path dependency. This book brings together varied perspectives on legacy—geographical, methodological, and contextual—to contribute to a deeper understanding of the intricate dynamics of legacy, organizational identity, and change.

In this chapter, the key contributions from this text are integrated into four sections that address the complex relationships between legacy, organizational identity, and change. The first section explores the theoretical perspectives, underlying assumptions, and related definitions employed to understand legacy. The second section describes the internal and external factors that influence legacy as well as its relationship with organizational identity and change. The third section articulates contributions and opportunities for theory and research. The chapter closes with implications for practice.

Legacy: Toward a multidisciplinary perspective

The chapters in this text highlight legacy as a multifaceted construct that can be defined and understood by drawing upon multidisciplinary perspectives. Broadly, legacy is a process of bringing forward an event or a person from the past to influence the present or future. Despite this shared understanding, scholars still use various definitions, which are not always consistent, and we do not yet have a universally accepted clear and discrete construct to explain the transmission and construction of legacy over time.

For instance, while some definitions of legacy focus on both actors and events from the past (Eisenman & Casey, 2025), others define legacy primarily in terms of key actors from the past (Israelsen & Suddaby, 2025; Lyle, 2025) and how aspects of their lives and actions are transmitted across generations in organizations or, at times, across organizations and communities. In contrast, some perspectives on legacy underscore critical events from the past and how their legacies are constructed over time and become attached to other events from a more distant or recent past or to a proposed future event (Eisenman & Casey, 2025). Other perspectives focus on actors such as founders and their actions in the context of the more mundane aspects of their everyday life (Sergi et al., 2025). Finally, legacy is also theorized as the process of the transmission of knowledge and culture through generations in and across organizations, as well as social networks, communities, and geographies (Spink et al., 2025; Truemmel et al., 2025). The interactions across actors and levels of analysis are critical in the transmission process. Similar to Sergi et al. (2025), many of these perspectives highlight the psychological, relational, and historical aspects of legacy as theorized by Radu-Lefebvre et al. (2024) in the context of family businesses.

Another factor affecting construct clarity is the differing perspectives through which legacy has been researched (see Foroughi et al., 2025, in this volume; Radu-Lefebvre et al., 2024). Scholars working from these diverse perspectives (e.g., imprinting, collective memory, and heritage) rarely embrace other perspectives. For instance, imprinting research often does not engage with different perspectives on memory and vice versa. This results in limited theoretical conversations across different perspectives.

Several of the chapters in this volume represent bold attempts to bring these diverse perspectives together to shed light on the complexity of legacy and change. The idea is that these perspectives, rather than serving as competing explanations, can be integrated. For example, Popielarz (2025) draws on several theoretical perspectives to explore legacy, history, and identity in racialized organizations. In her account, imprinting is interwoven with other theories such as collective memory and schema to explore the process of legacy in relationship to change and organizational identity. Aschhoff and Waldkirch (2025) also reference legacy in their research on acquisitions and how aspects of the history of the acquired organization, i.e., "foreign imprints," are transformed and integrated into the history of the acquiring organization. Aschhoff and Waldkirch acknowledge that theories of collective memory and history assist in understanding how legacies from the past are chosen and commemorated in the present, yet they chose imprinting theories to serve as a robust foundation for their research. Imprinting offers a platform for understanding how organizational characteristics that are created and embedded during the organization's founding might persist or decay over time.

In so doing, these authors acknowledge that the theoretical foundations for legacy and the definitions of legacy as a process are grounded in a range of disciplines from organizational studies to sociology, organizational communication, psychology, and history. Sociological theories include institutional theories, imprinting, sociology of events (Eisenman & Casey, 2025), racialized organizations (Popielarz, 2025; Ray, 2019), and collective memory (Halbwachs, 1992; Schwartz, 2000). Theoretical perspectives from psychology include mental models and schemas (Popielarz, 2025), among others.

Together, the chapters in the book show that taking a multidisciplinary approach, combining theories across disciplines, to investigate legacy is a promising avenue that can lead to the generation of novel insights. For example, Sergi et al. (2025) explore ideas about legacy and small stories by drawing upon the Montreal school of communicative constitution of organization (CCO), which takes a performative standpoint on communication and perspectives on family stories as narratives from the family business literature. These family stories as "legacy artifacts" are critical factors in the transmission process across generations in family businesses. In other studies, researchers intertwine theories such as rhetorical history (Jones, 2025) and strategic change to explore how memories of past organizational change initiatives continue to influence the present and how these memories can be used and managed by organizations as a resource to create the present and the future.

In summary, all chapters in the book advance the conceptualization of legacy as a dynamic process of bringing the past forward in time to influence the present and the future. This process is relevant across levels of analysis as it crosses generations, organizations, communities, and geographies. Legacy can both constrain and enable present and future actions and, as highlighted in this text, relates to organizational change and organizational identity. The next section discusses the contributions of the book to organizational identity and organizational change as two areas of significant interest to management research and practice.

Factors influencing legacy and its relationship to organizational identity and change

In this text, legacy as a process is most frequently studied in relationship to organizational identity and change. Legacy is characterized as a dynamic process as opposed to a static representation of history and, as a process, it evolves over time. Equally dynamic is its sometimes paradoxical nature, in that it supports both continuity and change (Sergi et al., 2025) and can be positive, negative, or ambivalent depending on what is at stake in the organization or community. Aspects of the process itself and the factors that influence it also vary depending on the theoretical lens(es), the context, and the methodologies employed in the research.

Legacy and organizational identity

The researchers in this book have chosen a social constructionist perspective of organizational identity, which assumes that organizational identity is constructed and reconstructed over time (Ybema, 2020). This perspective departs from the seminal work on organizational identity by Albert and Whetten (1985), which is grounded in institutional theory. Although both perspectives frame organizational identity as characteristics of the organization that are most core or central to it and that distinguish it from other organizations in a given sector, they differ in how they characterize organizational identity over time. For example, Albert and Whetten (1985) assert that organizational identity is temporally continuous; the social constructionist perspective assumes that organizational identity is constructed over time. Both perspectives link organizational identity to the past (Casey, 2019). Whetten (2006) asserts that identity comes into focus at fork-in-the-road decisions that test or bring to the present binding commitments from the past.

Lyle (2025) acknowledges the critical relationship between organizational identity and memory in referencing legacy organizational identities (Patvardhan et al., 2015). He further questions if organizational identity is conceptually different from memory or the past and advocates for framing organizational identity as a distillation of memories as part of the process of assigning meaning and labels to the past. Drawing from organizational memory studies, he describes how memories can be curated through individual and collective actions to shape the past. He proposes this area for future research, noting that "our field lacks knowledge surrounding how ecologies of memory (Coraiola et al., 2023) become distilled into organizational identity claims and, once constructed, how identity, image, and strategy act as connective tissue between organizational realities."

Israelsen and Suddaby (2025) offer potential insights into how memory becomes "distilled" into organizational identity and is transmitted and interconnected with present and future strategies. They theorize how residuals such as values, assets, and power are transmitted over time as the core purpose of inheritance organizations. They suggest that transmission occurs through the process of inheritance and historical conflation. Similar to Lyle (2025), they also define legacy as primarily focused on individual actors from the past. They define inheritance as a process of transmitting and managing residuals across generations, indicating that legacy plays a key role in this process. They further propose that historical conflation has the potential to explain the inheritance process as organizations "manage to bring together and compress entities across time and space into a narrativized tapestry that blends lives and values together back across generations." Key aspects of this process include language and narratives. Conflation also minimizes or collapses "distinctions between values and their carriers" through narratives as they conflate or link events from the past with other events from the past, present, or future.

Eisenman and Casey (2025) also address the dynamic transmission of legacy and its relationship with organizational identity. In defining legacy, they include actors and events from the past and theorize how a collective understanding of the past through legacy is used to influence present and future decisions. They draw in part from the sociology of event theories (Wagner-Pacifici, 2017) to understand the transmission process. Similar to historical conflation, event theories suggest that narratives of significant events become linked with other events from the past or present. The meanings of these events are often constructed and transmitted through narratives and rely on material artifacts (see also Lubinski & Gartner, 2023; Maclean et al., 2018; Wagner-Pacifici, 2017). The relationship between legacy, as a form of collective memory, and organizational identity is also highlighted in that organizational identity plays a role in what events are chosen and how their legacies evolve (Casey, 2019; Ravasi et al., 2019). Their theorization highlights how legacy can be managed to balance continuity and change and the importance of interpretive flexibility, as well as the limitations of malleability in this process.

Sergi et al. (2025) also theorize the importance of narratives, i.e., small stories as carriers of legacy. They explore the transmission process through stories of the more mundane or everyday events in a founder's life that, while ambivalent, can be used to sustain organizational identity. Drawing from the CCO theories, they explore how the narratives are constituted through interactions and communication and are transmitted. They too acknowledge the paradoxical nature of these small stories as potential to support both continuity and change.

Overall, these studies found a robust relationship between legacy and organizational identity. Legacies are transmitted over time to sustain organizational identity. Narratives and material artifacts are key factors, along with values, individual agency, and power. The transmission process primarily focuses on internal factors that influence the robust relationship between legacy and organizational identity. Multiple stakeholders across generations, in addition to managers, are critical in this relationship.

Legacy and organizational change

To understand more broadly the relationship between legacy and organizational change, the studies in this book involve multilevel contexts and diverse forms of organizing. They explore both internal and external factors that influence the interconnections between legacy and change in the contexts of acquisitions (Aschhoff & Waldkirch, 2025), business ecosystems (Trümmel et al., 2025), tightly intertwined organizations (Popielarz, 2025; Spink et al., 2025), and during strategic change initiatives (Jones, 2025). The research questions addressed at these unique sites and the studies' findings offer significant insights into the relationship between legacy and change. In addition to articulating legacy through actors and events from the past, these studies also expand on how knowledge and culture are integrated into the legacies that are transmitted across generations and geographies in embedded networks (Trümmel et al., 2025) and in everyday organizations as they interact with their communities (Spink et al., 2025). In these cases, legacies serve as a platform for both sustaining traditions and well-established knowledge as well as creating new knowledge across entrepreneurial families and communities (Trümmel et al., 2025). New knowledge has also been created about an organization after acquisition, as foreign imprints from the acquired organization become legitimized and integrated into the acquiring organization's history and culture (Aschhoff & Waldkirch, 2025). In other settings, legacy hinders strategic change initiatives (Jones,

2025) or prevails as racialized identities and schemas as part of legacies sustained in intertwined organizations (Popielarz, 2025).

Trümmel et al. (2025) address the intertwined nature of entrepreneurial family legacies across families, organizations, communities, and geographies in a business ecosystem. They chose relational agency theory (Burkitt, 2016) to explore how legacies are created and sustained. Relational agency focuses on "agency that unfolds across time and space, within the social relations between interacting parties that are dialogically, polyphonically, and emotionally interconnected" (Trümmel et al., 2016). In this case study, the embedded legacies help to improve the effectiveness of organizations in the ecosystem as well as create new efficiencies through exchange of knowledge and aspects of their organizational cultures. The study focuses on interactions across levels (organizations, families, communities, and geographies) versus internal interactions in organizations. Spink et al. (2025) also offer an analysis of how everyday organizations described as local and embedded in places with flexible organizing and hierarchies share their legacies of knowledge and skills to learn, grow, and create new knowledge.

The importance of exploring interactions across and within organizations in the transmission of legacies also emerges in Aschhoff and Waldkirch's (2025) case study of an organization after acquisition, where foreign imprints from another organization's history are present. Processes such as integration and legitimation are key to sustaining knowledge of the past as well as creating new knowledge as foreign imprints become part of the acquiring organization's present and past.

Sustaining knowledge from the past through legacies can become problematic if it constrains new perspectives or knowledge creation in organizations, particularly in changing external environments. External factors in the broader ecology of organizational legacy are addressed in Popielarz's study of police agencies in the United States and their interconnected professional associations and labor unions. Popielarz's multitheoretical approach includes imprinting, schema, and identity theories to explore how racialized identities and schemas are embedded and reproduced through memory practices, creating overlapping legacies of inequality in historically intertwined organizations such as labor unions and professional organizational fraternities. Legacy constraints change in that it facilitates hegemonic power embedded in the schemas.

In summary, in these studies of legacy and organizational change, definitions of legacy are broadened to include a focus on the knowledge transmitted in legacies and how it facilitates the creation of new knowledge in organizations to create change. These studies are multilevel, and across organizations, economies, communities, geographies, and ecological interactions are key to how legacy is transmitted. Legacy constrains or hinders change in organizations rooted in broader contexts such as societies where historically schemas of inequality and racism exist. These cross-level studies broaden our understanding of legacy and the importance of addressing networks of internal and external relationships beyond a single focus on internal leaders and organizational members.

Implications and opportunities for theory and research

Legacy, as defined and theorized in this text, is a complex, dynamic process of bringing forward the past to the present and its implications for the present and the future. It is not a static entity or interpretation of the past but instead is an understanding that is constructed and reconstructed over time. The extent of its malleability is constrained or limited by authenticity and history. The multidisciplinary approach advocated in the book offers promising new avenues to cross-fertilize well-established theories in organizational studies such as organizational memory, collective memory, rhetorical history, organizational identity, and schemas, as well as new theoretical perspectives from other disciplines.

Going beyond these established theories of legacy, the book provides promising new approaches, including theories from the sociology of events (Wagner-Pacifici, 2017), CCO (Basque et al., 2022), and relational agency (Burkitt, 2016), among others.

For example, in the sociology of events literature, an event is defined as a discrete situation from the past that is captured or retold as a story. Events are ongoing, yet they are selected from a stream of situations because they are significant to a group or individual. They often become attached to other events as they are told and retold in different contexts. The theoretical focus is on the nature of the event and how it is selected, takes shape, creates meaning, and is transformed. Events feature individuals, groups, places, and time and are often the substance of legacy. The theories can be challenging, particularly in relation to creating guidance for organizations on how to link their past to the present and future. Theories of events take research beyond organizational studies theories that emphasize power and individual actors as the primary factors in transmitting legacy and unlimited malleability.

Theories from organizational communication, such as the Montreal school, offer new perspectives that can inform a process-based view of legacy. Sergi et al. (2025) employ the lens of the Montreal school that is embedded in the CCO theoretical framework, along with narrative theories, to explore the transmission of legacy. The ontological foundations of these theories are aligned with the processual approaches to legacy. In CCO, communication is more than interorganizational or intraorganizational; it is the process of how organizations are constituted over time (Cooren et al., 2011). It focuses on the coordinated activities of actors and emphasizes other-than-human actors such as texts as important participants in constituting organizations. Additionally, Cooren's (2012) metaphor of ventriloquism reflects how various forms of actors speak and how the interactions between human and other-than-human actors constitute organizing. In addition to offering a useful theoretical perspective for understanding legacy, it also offers a methodological approach.

Relational agency theory, as employed by Trümmel et al. (2025) to understand how legacies emerge in business ecosystems, is a theoretical tradition in relational sociology. This lens assumes that agents are embedded in diverse and interconnected social relations. This perspective theorizes agents as interconnected actors "who are interdependent, vulnerable, intermittently reflexive, possessors of capacities that can only be practised in joint actions, and capable of sensitive responses to others and to the situations of interaction" (Burkitt, 2016, p. 322). Agency then develops through "emotional relatedness to others as social relations unfold across time and space" (Burkitt, 2016, p. 322). Theories that highlight the interconnectedness of humans and materials, such as the ventriloquism approach in CCO, offer more nuanced perspectives to understand the processes at work in creating and transmitting evolving interconnected legacies across space, time, and populations, as found by Trümmel et al. (2025). In addition, these theoretical perspectives offer opportunities to further understand and explore the relationships between organizational identity and change and legacies.

Many of these theoretical perspectives emerge from different ontologies and assumptions than those found in organizational studies. Often, theoretical approaches to organizational memory studies are grounded in assumptions that memory can be managed or controlled, and that managers or leaders are the most influential actors in memory transmission. Taking a relational agency approach, with its focus on interactions over time or an event-focused approach, has the potential to move beyond the emphasis on individual actors or leaders to understand legacy processes. Different ontologies from critical perspectives such as feminist standpoint theory, combined with microhistory approaches (Lantela, 2024), help to further our work to surface, understand, and integrate marginalized voices from the past and present into conceptualizations of legacy and history and how it is transmitted. These theoretical perspectives also offer the possibilities of new research designs and methods from other disciplines to incorporate into our work on legacy and its implications for organizations.

Implications and opportunities for practice

Legacy cannot be switched off or on. It permeates organizational structures, routines, and practices. It manifests in how we act, how we are perceived, and what is expected of us as an organization. As a salient presence in organizational life, legacy seeps into an organization's identity and requires consideration and even action, especially in times of organizational change.

Legacy can present both a challenge and an opportunity for organizations, as managers need to decide which aspects of legacy are going to be an asset in the future and which aspects might be a burden. Yet, this is not an easy task, as intangible assets, such as organizational legacy, can become a liability due to changes in the business or sociocultural environment.

Many managers mistakenly assume that legacy assets should be preserved at all costs. Consider the case of a family business portfolio owner who decided to prioritize protecting the firm's legacy business, even if it is underperforming, over pursuing potential future opportunities in satellite businesses, including successful ones. This paradoxical approach can ultimately place the overall business at risk (see Ireland et al, 2025). As such, understanding and managing organizational legacy are vital for leaders and managers, entrepreneurs and investors, and consultants.

Across this volume, managing legacy is presented as a dynamic process of balancing the organizational history with present realities and future demands. This means that leaders and managers are to take an active interest in understanding their organizations' legacies, not as a reference point fixed in the past but as a dynamic aspect of organizational identity affecting the organization's present and future. This perspective is explored in detail in the volume's introductory chapter, in which legacy is defined as a semi-fluid concept that is not "stuck" in the past but active in the present and consequential in the future. Several chapters in the book outline a perspective that suggests that an active approach to managing legacy is advantageous for organizations. Managers can benefit from perusing the volume's case studies as real-life examples of how active approaches to legacy provide insight and tools for change.

The introduction and Chapters 1 to 3 present a broad discussion about the function of legacy in organizations. The ideas presented in these chapters can broadly apply across industries and business sectors. The remaining six chapters present empirical evidence and provide lessons learned about managing legacy in different geographies (North and South America, Europe, and the UK), different business sectors, and different types of firms, from family businesses to the food industry to purpose-driven community organizations.

Below we present three key practical applications of our learning on legacy: first, creating and monitoring legacy assets retrospectively; second, examining the broader ecology (i.e., interrelationships with other organizations, the larger field, and society) in understanding the dynamics of legacy in the context of organizational knowledge and responsibility; and third, knowing the merits and limits of storytelling in creating and modifying legacy narratives.

One of the key lessons presented in several of the chapters is that organizational heritage and history should be seen as assets that can be harvested by organizations. In their chapter, Eisenman and Casey (2025) argue that managers can benefit from familiarization with, and analysis of, the textual and material carriers of legacy within the organization (histories, origin stories, archival documents, transmitted artifacts). They also point out that legacy is intrinsically tied to key internal and external stakeholders who inherit and carry forth the institutionalized narratives and myths that effectively activate the material traces and define the organization's legacy at any given moment. Similarly, Lyle suggests that organizational identity results from the distillation of organizational memory to shape its desired future image. Therefore, organizations that have more knowledge and familiarity with their past are better equipped to leverage a shift in their organizational identity when faced with critical decisions.

Brooks Brothers, an American heritage brand known for its classic menswear and especially its suits, provides an interesting example. Founded in 1818, it has a long history of outfitting U.S. presidents and business professionals. Yet the same strong legacy that built its reputation on traditional American menswear proved to be a hurdle for Claudio Del Vecchio, who acquired Brooks Brothers in 2001 and sought to balance the Brooks Brothers heritage with a more contemporary image. Bruce Weindruch, History Factory founder, showed that the element of innovation from the history of Brooks Brothers was essential in authenticating the evolution of this brand, in that while it is mostly known for its traditional attire, the company has indeed in the past also served alternative and trend-breaking clientele. Awareness of this history and the ability to find such records from the past equipped the company to successfully manage its rebranding and identity shift in the early 2000s.

The second key lesson drawn from the volume is that organizational legacy does not affect organizations in an isolated manner; instead, legacy is inexorably defined in relation to the organization's larger field and relevant business ecosystems, as well as the field's fluctuations of identity over time. Eisenman and Casey (2025) introduce a useful barometer for this dynamic relationship that managers may otherwise find difficult to parse out, namely the "cognitive legitimacy" of a field. In summary, they argue that within fields with high cognitive legitimacy (i.e., industries that are large, expanding rapidly, and/or have a long history, such as the automobile industry), organizations that are well established should emphasize clearly defined and widely recognized ideas about their legacies and identities. Conversely, organizations that are marginal to fields with high cognitive legitimacy or that operate in fields with lower cognitive legitimacy (i.e., smaller, younger, and/or stagnant industries, such as biotechnology) are better served by leaving more room for ambiguity and adopting more flexible definitions of their legacies and identities.

This insight can have diverse applications in practice. For example, we propose that managers could use it as a brand health assessment entailing a Cartesian graph where the field is plotted on one axis and the organization (and its competitors) can be plotted on the other axis, thus zeroing in on the organization's brand recognition, field embeddedness, and legitimacy vis-à-vis competitors (Figure 11.1). Insights from this type of exercise can benefit recommendations for managing (or changing) identities, brands and sub brands, or other organizational aspects.

Similarly, Trümmel et al. (2025) emphasize the importance of interconnections in business ecosystems, arguing in their chapter that an actionable understanding of organizational legacy takes into account not only the histories that live within the organization but also the histories of the organization's interrelationships with other organizations within its business sectors and even within the broader societal and

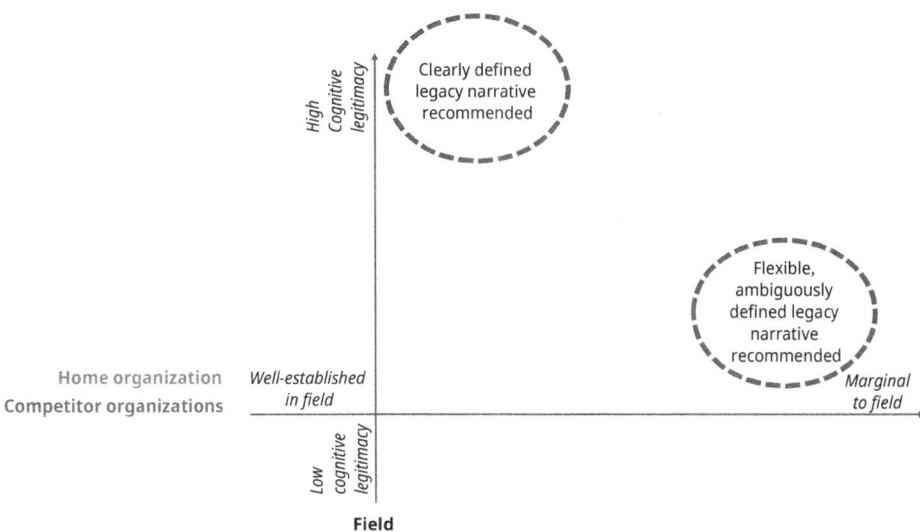

Figure 11.1: Visualization for Organizational Positioning Exercise: Graphing a Field's Cognitive Legitimacy and the Organization's Place in the Field as Compared with Competitors, for Decisions About Organizational Legacy and Identity.

geocultural spheres. Leaders and managers are well served by assessing their organizations' identities in relation to their fields and the broader society in the present; however, activating a longitudinal understanding of that relationship by analyzing their organizations' legacies as embedded in these larger contexts will provide, we argue, a richer and more nuanced definition of identities, narratives, and tools for growth and transformation.

This insight is important because it helps us locate legacy assets not only within organizations but also within their broader ecology, such as in the organizations' business ecosystems. Understanding the embeddedness of organizations' legacies can also help leaders cultivate authenticity and reflexivity, as both Popielarz (2025) and Eisenman and Casey (2025) argue in their respective chapters. Utilizing a dynamic and embedded understanding of organizational legacy can be very useful, we would propose, in articulating more transparent and thoughtful leadership positions that increase credibility, trustworthiness, and thereby greater organizational legitimacy within the sector or the larger societal circles in which the organization operates. Organizations can use their legacies to demonstrate how current choices are related to a clear strategic past when these legacies echo cultural tropes and well-known myths.

In relation to an organization's rapport with the larger society, chapters in this volume also highlight that with legacy comes responsibility. Whether positive or negative, legacy is what an organization has inherited from the past (see Israelsen & Suddaby, 2025, in this volume). This inheritance is not simply a matter of tradition or reputation—

it also includes the consequences of historical actions, structures, and decisions. Organizations must recognize that legacy is not always neutral; it often carries ethical weight, particularly when it intersects with histories of exploitation (Burton et al., 2025; Clinton et al., 2025; Eury et al., 2018). For instance, for some long-established U.S. brands such as Brooks Brothers, this responsibility extends to confronting the legacy of slavery. Historical records show that Brooks Brothers, like many companies with deep roots in the 19th century, profited from the institution of slavery. As Popielarz (2025, in this volume) shows, organizations could also inherit certain dysfunctions from the past such as sexism or economic exclusion. Many longstanding institutions have reinforced systems that marginalize entire groups through workplace segregation or other exclusionary practices. Organizations can benefit from learning about their legacy and course-correcting in relation to any inherited dysfunctional structures.

In terms of legacy vis-à-vis the interrelationships of organizations, especially in mergers and acquisitions, organizational legacy can become an invaluable tool for organizational learning, both internally and in terms of the acquired organization's external relationships. In their chapter, Trümmel et al. (2025) argue that legacy, as an organizational learning tool, can also lay the foundation for new knowledge creation within the organization and especially across the organization's broader ecosystems. In this volume, Israelsen and Suddaby (2025) shed light on the intergenerational transmission of legacy within an organization, connecting this type of inheritance (epistemological and organizational) not only with organizational knowledge but also with how such transmission of legacy affects (deliberately or residually) an organization's stated purpose. Similarly, Aschhoff and Waldkirch (2025) argue in their chapter that the history that an acquired organization brings to the newly created entity can be integrated as a legitimizing foundation for innovation, sensemaking, and new narratives for nascent postmerger identities. Leaders and consultants in mergers and acquisitions can leverage the premerger/preacquisition legacy—as defined in this volume—not as an intangible burden, but as an invaluable tool for organizational learning, for strategic positioning, and for a legitimizing platform from which to fuel innovation or build a solid postmerger/postacquisition origin story and, ultimately, longer-term organizational brand. Acknowledging and leveraging legacies in mergers and acquisitions contexts can also contribute to effective internal organizational change management, by addressing and utilizing inherited stakeholder knowledge. Aschhoff and Waldkirch (2025) detail the case of the acquisition of Italian-based wine producer Vinox by the German-owned international conglomerate Oechsle, explaining how the acquiring firm actively learned about the legacy of the acquired firm and strategically utilized that knowledge to orchestrate key transformations in the narrative of the postmerger firm's history.

The third issue highlighted in the volume is knowing the merits and limits of storytelling. Several chapters show the importance of storytelling as a tool for strategic positioning in managing legacy. In their chapter, Sergi, Basque, Langley, and Meziani (2025) emphasize the importance of what they call "small stories" related to key figures in an organization's legacy, such as the founder. They recommend that leaders assess how these anecdotes or vignettes from the organization's history or origin story relate to the organization's current identity and envisioned future strategic changes. Thinking of scenarios where such "small stories" can benefit the organization's present and future orientations, these authors recommend that leaders look for ways to leverage these stories and weave them more prominently into the organization's narrative, for example by bringing more mundane details to life, activating archival artifacts, and marking anniversaries with celebrations or commemorations. Whether ambiguously complex or clearly positive or negative, the anecdotes and narratives that make up an organization's legacy are powerful rhetorical tools for shaping the organization's positioning and messaging in the present.

Organizations might be able to pick and choose these 'small stories' to serve a certain purpose. Nonetheless, as Jones (2025) clearly demonstrates, storytelling can become problematic if it is perceived as story-selling. His chapter speaks to a key challenge in corporate heritage branding—how organizations curate historical narratives to serve strategic goals while maintaining authenticity. Analyzing Barclay's successful managerial use of rhetorical history strategies to change organizational culture, he shows that such efforts can appear manipulative if the audience senses selective history—excluding inconvenient truths and/or overpromising a legacy to which the brand can no longer live up. He also shows that organizations cannot too frequently change their narrative of their legacy, as the rhetorical narration of the past will have a legacy of its own —which can be boosting or damaging—in the organization's strategies for the future.

In conclusion, we hope that leaders, managers, and consultants can benefit from the ideas and tools presented above and others discussed in the volume. The key is to actively seek to understand organizations' legacies not as static inheritances from the past but as dynamic assets that can increase knowledge of their organizations' positioning within their fields and larger cultural contexts as well as offer opportunities to leverage this knowledge for strategic change and messaging.

References

Albert, S., & Whetten, D. A. (1985). Organizational identity. In L. L. Cummings & B. M. Staw (Eds.), *Research in organizational behavior* (pp. 263–295). JAI Press.
Aschhoff, H., & Waldkirch, M. (2025). Acquiring history? Foreign imprint management during postmerger integration. In H. Foroughi, A. Casey, & S. Coman (Eds.), *Managing legacy and change: New frontiers for theory and practice* (Chapter 5). DeGruyter.
Basque, J., Bencherki, N., & Kuhn, T. (2022). *Routledge handbook of the communicative constitution of organization*. Routledge.
Burkitt, I. (2016). Relational agency: Relational sociology, agency and interaction. *European Journal of Social Theory, 19*(3), 322–339. https://doi.org/10.1177/1368431015591426

Burton, N., Sinnicks, M., Hedley, C., Discua Cruz, A., Wong, N.D. & Smith, A. (2025). Firms as Quasi-Traditions: The Moral Backbone of Social Legacy. *Academy of Management Perspectives*, online, forthcoming https://doi.org/10.5465/amp.2023.0296

Casey, A. (2019). *Organizational identity and memory: A multidisciplinary approach*. Routledge. https://doi.org/10.4324/9781315669786

Clinton, E., Faherty, C. M., O'Gorman, C., & Kammerlander, N. (2025). Managing the Liability of Legacy in Family Firms. *Academy of Management Perspectives*, online, forthcoming.https://doi.org/10.5465/amp.2023.0319

Cooren, F. (2012). Communication theory at the center: Ventriloquism and the communicative constitution of reality. *Journal of Communication*, 62, 1–20.

Cooren, F., Kuhn, T., Cornelissen, J. P., & Clark, T. (2011). Communication, organizing and organization: An overview and introduction to the special issue. *Organization Studies*, 32(9), 1149–1170.

Coraiola, D. M., Foster, W. M., Mena, S., Foroughi, H., & Rintamäki, J. (2023). Ecologies of memories: Memory work within and between organizations and communities. *The Academy of Management Annals*, 17(1), 373–404. https://doi.org/10.1007/s10551-019-04323-8

Eisenman, M., & Casey, A. (2025). Constructing legacy: Managing legacy in discursive and embodied ways. In H. Foroughi, A. Casey, & S. Coman (Eds.), *Managing legacy and change: New frontiers for theory and practice* (Chapter 3). DeGruyter.

Eury, J. L., Kreiner, G. E., Treviño, L. K., & Gioia, D. A. (2018). The past is not dead: Legacy identification and alumni ambivalence in the wake of the Sandusky scandal at Penn State. *Academy of Management journal*, 61(3), 826–856.

Foroughi, H., Casey, A., & Coman, S. (2025). Perspectives on organizational legacy and change. In H. Foroughi, A. Casey, & S. Coman (Eds.), *Managing legacy and change: New frontiers for theory and practice* (Chapter 1). DeGruyter.

Halbwachs, M. (1992). *On collective memory*. University of Chicago Press.

Ireland, R. D., Chirico, F., Akhter, N., Rondi, E., & Ijaz, R. (2025). The Show Must Go On: Preserving the Legacy Business through Exit in Family Business Portfolio Firms. Academy of Management Perspectives, online, https://doi.org/10.5465/amp.2023.0293

Israelsen, T., & Suddaby, R. (2025). Inheritance as an organizational purpose. In H. Foroughi, A. Casey, & S. Coman (Eds.), *Managing legacy and change: New frontiers for theory and practice* (Chapter 3). DeGruyter.

Jones, I. G. (2025). Rhetorical history as history: Legacies of a rhetorical history strategy. In H. Foroughi, A. Casey, & S. Coman (Eds.), *Managing legacy and change: New frontiers for theory and practice* (Chapter 9). DeGruyter.

Lantela, P. (2024). Knowledge from the margins—the epistemological promise of microhistorical theorizing in organization studies. *Organizational Theory*, 5, 1–17.

Lubinski, C., & Gartner, W. B. (2023). Talking about (my) generation: The use of generation as rhetorical history in family business. *Family Business Review*, 36(1), 119–142. https://doi.org/10.1177/08944865231152283

Lyle, M. C. B. (2025). Distilling memories—a redefinition of organizational identity. In H. Foroughi, A. Casey, & S. Coman (Eds.), *Managing legacy and change: New frontiers for theory and practice* (Chapter 2). DeGruyter.

Maclean, M., Harvey, C., Sillince, J. A. A., & Golant, B. D. (2018). Intertextuality, rhetorical history and the uses of the past in organizational transition. *Organization Studies*, 39(12), 1733–1755. https://doi.org/10.1177/0170840618789206

Patvardhan, S. D., Gioia, D. A., & Hamilton, A. L. (2015). Weathering a meta-level identity crisis: Forging a coherent collective identity for an emerging field. *Academy of Management Journal*, 58(2), 405–435. https://doi.org/10.5465/amj.2012.1049

Popielarz, P. A. (2025). Obstacles to change in racialized organizations: Imprinting, memory, and legacy. In H. Foroughi, A. Casey, & S. Coman (Eds.), *Managing legacy and change: New frontiers for theory and practice* (Chapter 10). DeGruyter.

Radu-Lefebvre, M., Davis, J. H., & Gartner, W. B. (2024). Legacy in family business: A systematic literature review and future research agenda. *Family Business Review, 37*, 08944865231224506. https://doi.org/10.1177/08944865231224506

Ravasi, D., Rindova, V., & Stigliani, I. (2019). The stuff of legend: History, memory, and the temporality of organizational identity construction. *Academy of Management Journal, 62*(5), 1523–1555. https://doi.org/10.5465/amj.2016.0505

Ray, V. (2019). A theory of racialized organizations. *American Sociological Review, 84*(1), 26–53. https://doi.org/10.1177/0003122418822335

Schwartz, B. (2000). *Abraham Lincoln and the forge of national memory*. University of Chicago Press.

Sergi, V., Basque, J., Langley, A., & Meziani, N. (2025). The power of the mundane: Small stories as ambivalent carriers of legacy. In H. Foroughi, A. Casey, & S. Coman (Eds.), *Managing legacy and change: New frontiers for theory and practice* (Chapter 8). DeGruyter.

Spink, P. K., Spink, M. J. P., Hercílio P. de Oliveira, J., & Tavanti, R. M. (2025). Legacy and collective action: Learning from faith-based communities and parishes. In H. Foroughi, A. Casey, & S. Coman (Eds.), *Managing legacy and change: New frontiers for theory and practice* (Chapter 7). DeGruyter.

Trümmel, P., Magrelli, V., Rovelli, P., De Massis, A., & Rissbacher, C. (2025). Embedded legacy and the role of entrepreneurial family firms in business ecosystems:The Aspiag case. In H. Foroughi, A. Casey, & S. Coman (Eds.), *Managing legacy and change: New frontiers for theory and practice* (Chapter 4). DeGruyter.

Wagner-Pacifici, R. (2017). *What is an event?* University of Chicago Press.

Whetten, D. A. (2006). Albert and Whetten revisited: Strengthening the concept of organizational identity. *Journal of Management Inquiry, 15*(3), 219–234. https://doi.org/10.1177/1056492606291200.

Ybema, S. (2020). Bridging self and sociality: Identity construction and social context. In A. Brown (Ed.), *Oxford handbook of identities in organizations* (pp. 52–68). Oxford University Press. https://doi.org/10.1093/oxfordhb/9780198827115.013.50.

List of figures

Figure 2.1 Theoretical Relationships Among Organizational Memory, Identity, and Strategy —— 26
Figure 6.1 Foreign Imprint Mechanisms —— 113
Figure 6.2 Foreign Imprint Management Process During Postmerger Integration —— 123
Figure 8.1 Paying homage to Bill Hewlett —— 149
Figure 8.2 Materializing an open-door policy —— 150
Figure 11.1 Visualization for Organizational Positioning Exercise: Graphing a Field's Cognitive Legitimacy and the Organization's Place in the Field as Compared with Competitors, for Decisions About Organizational Legacy and Identity —— 217

List of tables

Table 1.1 Four Perspectives on Legacy and Change in Organizations —— 16
Table 2.1 Key Construct Definitions —— 29
Table 2.2 Examples of Organizational Identity/Memory Overlap in Extant Scholarship —— 31
Table 5.1 Data and Its Analytical Purposes —— 92
Table 5.2 Data Structure —— 94
Table 5.3 Relationships Within a Business Ecosystem —— 97

Index

Albert, S. 209–210
Albu, N. 11
Anteby, M. 14, 27, 33, 167
anti-trust laws 56
Apple Company 13, 15, 153, 165, 167
artifacts 10, 12, 13, 23–24, 68, 69, 75–78, 96, 149, 153, 168, 199, 209–211
Aschhoff, H. 4, 11, 107–124, 208, 212, 218
Aspiag Service srl 4, 89–90
- affiliation with 98, 100
- *Aspiag–Families* relationships 101
- case study approach 90
- methodological approach 91–93
- relationships 100
- research setting 90–91
- resources or services 99
- territory 93, 94, 96–97
assets 9, 10, 47, 51, 54–57, 87, 123, 130, 163, 210, 215

Barbera, F. 151–152
Barclays Bank PLC 5, 173–177, 183
- corporate culture 178–181
- employees 176
- "Made by Barclays" narrative 179
- Payment Protection Insurance 177–178
- transform programme 180–182
Barclays Group Archives (BGA) 177, 179
Basque, J. 5, 16, 73, 132–133, 149–169, 218
Bastian, E. 158–160
Bell, E. 13, 15
Benevolent Association 193
Bernhard, F. 151
Bible 50, 59, 141
Black Lives Matter (BLM) movement 198, 201
Black power movement 197, 200
Brooks Brothers 216–218
The Buddy Holly Center 47
Burkitt, I. 89
business ecosystems 87–90, 100–103, 211
- affiliated EFs 90
- Aspiag (See Aspiag)
- efficiency 99–100
- entrepreneurial family firms 4
- exchange among legacies 98–99
- geographic locality 89
- legacies roles 87–91, 96–100
- leverage of legacies 97–98

- relationship dynamics 97, 100
- retail network 89–90
- structure 90

Cailluet, L. 151
The Cambridge Dictionary 53
Cappelen, S. M. 76
Carlsberg Group 14, 27, 71, 76, 176
Casey, A. 1–6, 9–17, 67–81, 131, 142, 207–219
Catechism of the Catholic Church (1997) 47
cathedral imprints 115–119
Catholicism 130, 135–136, 141, 164
Chianti wine brand 115, 117
civil rights movement 132, 197, 200
Civil War 161, 189, 193, 194, 196
cognitive legitimacy 72, 80–81, 216, 217
Coleman, J. S. 51–52
collective memory 2–3, 157, 160, 210–211
- carriers 164
- collective interpretation 72
- construction 27, 28
- empirical setting 137–138
- everyday organizations 133–137
- grassroots lobby 30
- humanity and attention 160
- legacy 14–16
- materiality and rhetoric 27
- organizational culture 167
- organizational identity 69, 208
- organizational scholarship 27
- power relations 192
- small stories as carriers (see 'small stories')
- spatial framework 134
colorblind racism 190–192, 195–199, 201
Colquitt, J. 74
Colt Company 174
Coman, S. 1–6, 9–17, 207–219
communication 38, 121–122, 152, 155, 179, 208–213
communicative constitution of organization (CCO) 152–156, 160, 164, 209, 211, 213, 214
conscious articulation 13
conservation imprints 108, 112–114, 116, 119–123
Cooren, F. 156, 157, 165, 213
Coraiola, D. M. 27, 37, 88
Corley, K. G. 30, 31
coupling imprints 11, 16, 110, 114–117
Crawford, B. 27

Crayola Factory 74
cultural alignment 79–81
cultural myths 69, 72, 75, 76, 79–81
custodianship 13, 16
Cutcher, L. 33, 34

Dacin, M. T. 12–13
data collection 91, 110, 111
De Certeau, M. 133
decision-making 9, 10, 23, 25, 35–37, 39, 40, 71, 183
Decker, S. 78
de Cuyper, L. 109, 124
Delta Airlines 153, 158–159, 166
De Massis, A. 87–103
de Oliveira, J. 129–143
Derry, R. 27
Desjardins, A. 132–133, 153, 162–164
Desjardins Group 132–133, 153, 162–164, 167
Deutsche Bank 178
De Vaujany, F.-X. 77
DeWitt, R.-L. 151–152
discursive transmission 73, 75–77
Do, B. 74
Dukerich, J. M. 31–34, 38
Dutton, J. E. 31–34, 38

ecclesiastical base communities (CEBs) 140–141
Economy and Society (Weber) 60
Eisenman, M. 3–4, 67–81, 131, 142, 210, 215–217
embodied transmission 77–79
emotional resonance 73, 75, 76, 79
enactment imprints 108, 112, 113, 119–123
entrepreneurial families (EFs) 87–89. *See also*
    Aspiag; business ecosystem
– data and analytical purposes 92
– data structure 93–95
– embeddedness 88–89, 98, 101, 102, 217
– exchanged knowledge 100
– *Families–Territory* relationships 101
– legacy and connection 90–91
– and relationships 93
– territory legacies 93, 96
– values and norms 93
European Group for Organization Studies (EGOS) 2
evocative power 157–158, 162

Fairhurst, G. 156
family business 9, 54, 87, 89, 103, 118, 153, 209, 215
family dynasties 54, 57, 60

family lineage 50, 54–56
FamilySearch 48
Far from the Tree: Parents, Children and the Search for Identity (Solomon) 55
Ferriani, S. 109
Financial Services Authority (FSA) 178, 181
The Financial Times 177
first-order codes 111–112
Floyd, G. 189, 201
FOP Journal 195, 198–199, 201
foreign imprints 4, 11, 107, 108, 111, 113, 116, 208. *See also* imprinting theory
– appropriation 10, 108, 123
– cathedral 115–119
– conservation 108, 112–114, 116, 119–123
– coupling 114–115
– enactment 108, 112, 113, 119–123
– logo, "X" 116–117
– *our firm, our family* imprint 119–121, 124
– quality and innovation excellence 112, 114
– reformation 108, 112, 113, 115, 117, 121, 123
– restoration 108, 112, 113, 119–123
– substitution 108, 112, 113, 117, 123
Foroughi, H. 1–6, 9–17, 133, 207–219
Foster, W. M. 14, 70, 174
founder figure, legacy 5, 14, 27, 56, 70–75, 78, 149–162, 167–169
Fraternal Order of Police (FOP) 190, 193–194
– patrol officers 193–194
– racialized identity 195–199
– racialized schema 199–201
– sources 194–195
Frenkel, M. 77–78

Gartner, W. B. 70, 79, 80
Ge, B. 88
Geertz, C. 133
Gioia, D. A. 24, 28, 30–33
Global Financial Crisis, 2018 180
Goldman Sachs Bank 178
Grand Lodge, FOP 194–195
grassroots lobby 28–30, 57, 129
The Guardian 177

Halbwachs, M. 133–134
Hamilton, A. L. 24, 32, 33
Hammond, N. L. 151
Hatch, E. 135–136
Hatch, M. J. 14, 27, 71, 73, 76, 176

Index — **229**

Haug, C. 137
Haveman, H. A. 142
Hercílio P. 129–143
heritage/traditions 12–13, 16, 49, 60–61, 76, 96–99, 119, 130, 140, 164, 168, 191, 208
Hernes, T. 33, 71, 154, 166
Hershey Trust Company 47, 56, 58
Hewlett, B. 149, 157
Hewlett-Packard (HP) Company 149, 153, 166
Hindu Dharmashastras 51
historical conflation 48, 50, 210. *See also* inheritance
– of assets 54–57
– figurative language 53
– of power 60–61
– sociocognitive structure 54
– of values 57–60
historical narratives 13, 33, 58, 59, 108, 173–178, 180–183, 219
Holt, D. B. 174, 183
Holt, D. T. 151
Howard-Grenville, J. 78
Hudson's Bay Company 14
Huët, R. 156
Hunter, E. G. 151, 154

imprinting theory 2–5, 11–12, 16, 107–108, 152
– attraction and sharing 110
– foreignness 122–123
– historicizing 108–109
– methodology 110–112
– organizational legacy 109
– racialized identity 195–197
– racialized organizations 191
– racialized schemas 199–200
– reforming and coupling 110
– rhetorical history 108
influential articles 1
Ingold, T. 50
inheritance
– historical conflation 48, 53–61
– historical origins 50–52
– intergenerational transmission 47
– intrinsic value 48
– legacy/tradition form 52
– organizational purpose 47, 50–52
– organizational theory 48–49
– tradition and legacy 49–50
– vocabulary of motive 47–48
integrated imprints 4, 33, 103, 122–123, 207–208, 218

intergenerational transmission 3, 47–48, 50, 56, 57, 59–62, 218
intrafamilial relationships 95, 98
Israelsen, T. 47–62, 72, 210, 217, 218

Jack Daniels Company 174
Jenkins, P. 178, 179, 180, 182
Jim Crow racism 195
Jobs, S. 13–15, 68, 72, 152, 165, 167
Jones, I. G. 173–184, 219

King, M. D. 142
Kotlar, J. 71
Kuhn, T. 165

Labaki, R. 151
Langley, A. 5, 16, 73, 132–133, 149–169, 218
Latour, B. 131
Law, J. 131
legacy conceptualization 3, 67–71, 129–130, 151
– affordances 10
– collective memory 14–16
– as expression 130–131
– historical organization studies 1
– imprinting theory 11–12
– intergenerational transmission 3–4
– management 74–81
– memory and identity 3
– mnemonic communities 71–73
– multidisciplinary perspective 207–209
– multiple facets 10
– and organizational change 211–213
– and organizational identity 209–211
– organizations 1
– path dependency 2–3
– for practice 214–219
– public square 1–2
– as rhetorical history 13–14
– theory and research 213–214
– as traditions/heritage 12–13
– trust and credibility 9
legacy senders 10, 49
legatees 10, 49, 54
legators 10, 49, 54, 62
legitimization 110, 123
Lehman Brothers 177–178
Lim, D. S. 72
lineage 49–52, 54–56, 60, 71, 75
Lloveras, J. 129

London Interbank Offered Rate (LIBOR) 177-178
Lubinski, C. 70, 75, 79, 80
Lyle, M. C. B. 3, 23-41, 74, 210, 215

Maclean, M. 183
Magrelli, V. 87-103
Marcus, G. E. 57
MAXQDA 111
M'Boi Mirim 138-141
McFarlane, J. 180, 181
McIlhenny, E. 161-162
McIlhenny Company 153, 161-162
memory 24, 25, 32-37
- construct definitions 29
- filtration of 37-38
- identity, image, and strategy 35-36, 39-40
- and identity work 30, 36-37
- mnemonic theory 40
- racialized identity 197
- racialized organizations 192
- racialized schemas 200, 201
- redefinition 28-35
Mena, S. 24, 27
mergers and acquisitions (M&As) 107-110, 123
Meziani, N. 5, 16, 149-169, 218
migrants 130, 136, 138-141, 197
Mitchell, J. R. 72
mnemonic communities 15, 16, 23, 27, 30, 32, 34-38
- cognitive legitimacy 72
- conceptualization 72
- organizing skills 130
- rhetorical history 72
- social groups 71
- strategic sense 72
- vitality 76
Mol, A. 131
Molnar, V. 14, 27, 33, 167
monolithic legacy 57, 68, 74
Montreal school. *See* communicative constitution of organization (CCO)
mothers' club movement 140-141
Mutch, A. 131-132

National Association of Black Law Enforcement Officers (NABLEO) 202
National Conference of Brazilian Bishops (CNBB) 136
Nelson, T. 152
New Anatolian cuisine 79
New York Times 15

Oechsle's imprint 110, 112, 114-122, 218
Oertel, S. 174
open-door policy 122, 150, 166
Operation Periphery 140-142
organizational ghosts 10, 49
organizational history 2, 14, 24, 123, 129-132, 142
- legacy and narrative 151-152
organizational identity 1-4, 88
- collective memory 69
- fixer doers 23
- and legacy conceptualization 209-211
- and long-term strategy 9
- M&A processes 110
- memory and 25-40
- redefinition 24
- rhetorical history 174-175
- rhetorical power 123
- self-definitions 23-25, 28, 38
- territory 88
organizational legacy 4, 6, 109, 215-218
organizational memory studies (OMS) 1, 24-30, 34-41, 195, 213. *See also* organizational identity
- collective memory 27
- labeled memory work 25-27
- myths and ideas 69
organizational past 10-11, 25-36, 49, 53, 57-60, 89, 96, 131, 178-180
organization's mission (*raison d'être*) 3, 5, 164-165, 167
our firm, our family imprint 112, 118, 119-121, 124

Packard, D. 149, 157
parishes 4-5, 129-135, 139-140, 163
- and Catholicism 135-137
- priests and 142
Patvardhan, S. D. 24, 32, 33
Payment Protection Insurance (PPI) 178
Pearson, A. W. 151
philanthropic foundation 48, 54, 56, 60
Poor, S. 174
Popielarz, P. A. 11, 189-202
power, political 49, 52, 54, 60-61, 72, 78, 123
Power and the Structure of Society (Coleman) 51
Presbyterianism Church 132

Quakers 174, 179-183
Quran 51

racialized identity 190–195, 201
- imprinting (1910s) 195–197
- memory (21st century) 198–199
- memory (1970s) 197
racialized organizations 5, 7, 189–190
- abolition movement's objection 189–190
- conceptualization 190–191
- conventional approach 189
- Fraternal Order of Police (FOP) 193–195
- imprinting, legacies of 191
- memory practices 192
- policing 189–190
- race and policing 192–193
- social system 190
racialized schemas 190–192, 194, 195
- imprinting (1910s) 199–200
- memory (21st century) 201
- memory (1970s) 200
- police academy training 199
- symbols and artifacts 199
Radu-Lefebvre, M. 93, 151, 168
Rantakari, A. 155
Ravasi, D. 24, 27, 28, 32, 71, 73
Ray, V. 192–193
reformation imprints 108, 112, 113, 115, 117, 121, 123
Reisch, H. F. 91
religious organization 10, 51, 57, 59, 129–133
restoration imprints 108, 112, 113, 119–123
rhetorical history 1, 5, 16, 27, 70, 108, 173–176
- Barclays 177–182
- frictions 75
- interviews 176–177
- legacies 182–184
- legacy as 13–14
- methodology 176–177
Rhodes Must Fall movement 80
Rindova, V. 24, 27, 28, 32
Rissbacher, C. 87–103
Robinson, N. 130
Rothschild Bank 178
Rovelli, P. 87–103
Rowles, G. D. 151, 154

Salz, A. 178
Sasaki, I. 71
Schultz, M. 14, 27, 33, 71, 73, 76, 154, 166, 176
second-order codes 111–112
selective forgetting 16, 27, 34
Sergi, V. 5, 16, 149–169, 208–209, 211, 213, 218

Simeone, D. 14
Simsek, Z. 11
skepticism 174, 179
Sky Magazine 159
'small stories' 1, 5, 16, 149–150, 218–219
- ambivalence 167
- artifacts 153
- carriers of legacy 159–164
- and characteristics 156–158
- founders 154
- fragility 168–169
- narratives 151–152, 155–157, 173–183
- power of 164–166
- vignettes 5, 158–164, 167, 168, 218
- visual representations 154
Smith, A. 14
Solomon, A. 55
Southern Christian Leadership Conference 132
SPAR Austria 90–92
Spink, M. J. P. 129–143
Spink, P. K. 129–143
Stake, R. E. 134–135, 138
stakeholders 4, 9, 13–14, 35, 58, 72, 75, 87–88, 108, 173, 178, 215
Staley, J. E. 173, 180–182
Stamm, I. 151–152
Stigliani, I. 24, 27, 28, 32
Stonemason's Guild 47–48
St. Patrick's Missionary Society 137–138
Strandgaard-Pedersen, J. 76
strategic legacy 70–71
Studebaker Factory 34, 74
substitution imprints 108, 112, 113, 117, 123
Suddaby, R. 27, 28, 35, 39, 47–62, 72, 210, 217, 218
synecdoche 53, 54, 60

Tabasco® 161–162
Taraday, H. 10
Tavanti, R. M. 129–143
Taylor, B. 189
Taylor, S. 13, 15
text-conversation dynamic 152–153
Thatcher, M. 15
Thommes, K. 174
The Times 177
Tim Horton Company 14, 70, 174
Transform Programme 173–174, 176–183
transmission of legacy 73–74
Trümmel, P. 87–103, 214, 216, 218

trustworthiness 53–56, 120, 181
– and corporations 51
– and credibility 9
– and testamentary trusts 55

Vaara, E. 71, 155
Vaast, E. 77
values, historical conflation 57–60, 180
– business ecosystem 89
– cognitive legitimacy 72, 80
– and practices 71
– psychological components 96
– value-based threats 59
Vandenventer, J. S. 129
Vinox's imprint 110, 111–122, 218
vis-à-vis civic 1, 216, 218

Waldkirch, M. 4, 11, 107–124, 208, 212, 218
Walsh, I. J. 74

Warnaby, G. 129
Weber, M. 60
Weindruch, B. 14, 216
Wertsch, J. W. 134
Whetten, D. A. 209–210
whistle-blowing 181
White organizational identity 191, 197–198
Wittenberg, J. 131
Woolman, C. E. 158–160, 166, 167
World of Coke in Atlanta (Museum) 74
World War I 14, 194–196

Ybema, S. 35

Zona Sul Mothers' Clubs 141